Palestinia
and Pc
that Shaped the
Old Testament

*

Morton Smith

SCM PRESS LTD

First published 1971 by Columbia University Press,
New York and London.

British Library Cataloguing in Publication Data

Smith, Morton
Palestinian parties and politics that
shaped the Old Testament.—2nd corr. ed.
1. Bible. O.T.—History of contemporary
events, etc.   2. Israel—History—
To 70 A.D.
I. Title
221.9'5   BS1197

ISBN 0–334–02238–X

Second, corrected edition published 1987
by SCM Press Ltd,
26–30 Tottenham Road, London N1 4BZ

Phototypeset by Input Typesetting Ltd
and printed in Great Britain by
Richard Clay Ltd, Bungay, Suffolk

Palestinian Parties and Politics
that Shaped the Old Testament

CONTENTS

PREFACE TO THE SECOND EDITION

This reissue has been improved by a considerable number of small changes made for the Italian translation (*Gli Uomini del Ritorno*, Verona, Essedue 1984), by the translator, Dr Paolo Xella, and by myself. Also I have corrected a few details that have come to my attention since 1984. No major changes have been made – 'what I have written I have written' – nor have I tried to bring the bibliography up to date, a great labour of small use. However, I must call the readers' attention to one important book, J. Tigay's *You Shall Have No Other Gods*, (Atlanta, Scholars Press 1986). By collection of epigraphic and other data Tigay has shown that from monarchic times on Yahweh was by far the most often mentioned god of the Israelites. Worship of other gods has left comparatively little evidence. How Tigay's facts relate to those set out in this book is a problem for further research.

London 1987 MORTON SMITH

PREFACE TO THE FIRST EDITION

The first draft of the following text was delivered as a course of lectures at the Graduate School of Drew University in 1956–57 and was accepted as a thesis for the degree of Doctor of Theology at the Harvard Divinity School in 1957. Then it was remade into a new series of lectures delivered in 1961–62 under the auspices of the Committee on the History of Religions of the American Council of Learned Societies. These lectures were revised in 1964; the present book is the product of that revision, with the minor additions and corrections that have accumulated through the years as new discoveries and new arguments appeared in the literature while circumstances beyond my control delayed the present publication.

It is hoped that the book will be of interest to the layman as well as to the professional student of the Old Testament. For this reason an introductory chapter on the problems and methods of Old Testament criticism has been added, footnotes have been cut down as far as possible, and (except in one appendix) extended discussions of conflicting theories have been excluded. The layman should not be misled by this fact to believe that conflicting theories do not exist. On the contrary, there is hardly any text of the Old Testament which has not been interpreted in several different ways in the interests of as many different theories. The professional will often realize that in the following pages one or another theory is defended or attacked by implication. He will also understand the reasons which have thus limited both attack and defence.

Of the many persons who have discussed the book with me in the course of its making, I am indebted for particularly important criticisms and suggestions to Professors Elias Bickerman, Gerson Cohen, William Farmer, H. L. Ginsberg, Moshe Greenberg, Walter Harrelson, and Krister Stendahl, and to the late Isaac

Mendelsohn, A. D. Nock, and Robert Pfeiffer. In preparing the present text I had valuable help from my former research assistant, Mr Stanley Isser, my present assistant, Mr Levon Avdoyan, and Mrs Reginald Coleman, who typed most of the manuscript. For whatever errors or oversights remain, I have only myself to thank.

Much of the research was done during a year when I held a Guggenheim Fellowship for a quite different purpose. I am grateful to the authorities of the Guggenheim Foundation (and particularly to the former director, Mr Henry Allen Moe) not only for their support, but also for their tolerance in permitting me to follow unexpected leads. The opportunities to teach the subject at Drew and to lecture about it for the American Council of Learned Societies enabled me to profit from many discussions; accordingly, my thanks are due to the authorities of those institutions and particularly to Professor Stanley Hopper, then dean of Drew University Graduate School, and to Mr D. H. Daugherty, then of the ACLS. Much of the revision was done at Chicago House in Luxor, where Professor Charles Nims, then director of the Epigraphical Survey of the Oriental Institute of the University of Chicago, kindly permitted me to use the facilities of the Institute. Finally, I must thank the Columbia University Council for Research in the Social Sciences for grants which assisted me in preparation of the manuscript, and Mr. William F. Bernhardt and the other members of the staff of the Columbia University Press for their patience and their care.

Columbia University, 1971   MORTON SMITH

1

The Old Testament and its Interpretation

The term 'the Old Testament' is used, chiefly by Christians, to refer to a number of different collections of ancient books, collections preserved primarily by different religious groups. The collection which here mainly concerns us is the one preserved principally by the Jews and taken over by most Protestant denominations; it is commonly referred to as 'the Hebrew Bible'. It was originally the collection approved by the rabbinic successors of the Pharisees who, about the end of the first century AD, accepted as holy the books it contains.[1] Other Jewish parties in the first century had recognized other collections – for instance the Sadducean high priests of the Jerusalem temple who until AD 70 were the official heads of Judaism, recognized only the five books of the Mosaic law[2] – but after the destruction of Jerusalem in 70 the heirs of the Pharisaic party gradually won out and its collection came to be generally accepted. This Pharisaic collection is itself composed of four smaller collections of which the latest, called 'the Writings', was formed by the Pharisees and their predecessors, while the earliest, 'the Laws', had been accepted by the priests of the temples at Jerusalem and Mt Gerizim long before the Pharisaic party came into existence.

All the books in these collections date, in their present forms, from the years between 500 and 100 BC. 'In their present forms', however, is an ambiguous expression which requires explanation. It is extremely difficult to copy a manuscript with absolute accuracy. Therefore, so long as the books of the Old Testament were handed down as manuscripts, each successive copy differed slightly from its predecessors by reason of the copyist's mistakes. Moreover, besides accidental mistakes, copyists made deliberate corrections, or what they believed to be corrections, and these might be anything from slight changes in spelling or word order to omission, rearrangement, or addition of words or phrases or even large sections of the text. How far these changes can go is shown by the Septuagint, an Old Testament which contains Greek texts of all the books in the Pharisaic collection and about a dozen others. These Greek texts date from the third to the first century BC and therefore reflect a Hebrew text far earlier than most of the present Hebrew manuscripts, which, except for the Dead Sea finds, are of the sixth century AD and later. Not only does the Septuagint arrange most of its books in groupings different from those of the Pharisaic collection, but also the texts of the individual books show innumerable minor differences from the present Hebrew texts, and major differences of arrangement or content appear in the books of Jeremiah, Psalms, Proverbs, Esther, Daniel, and I Esdras. Some of these differences are due to the translators who produced the Greek texts, or to later interpolations in either the Greek or the Hebrew, but many must have existed in the Hebrew manuscripts which the translators used. Some of the Hebrew texts from the first centuries BC and AD, found in the caves near Qumran, by the Dead Sea, seem to be representatives of the textual tradition which lay behind the Septuagint,[3] while the major differences between the Septuagint and the Hebrew texts are recalled by the fact that a Qumran text of Habakkuk does not have the last of the three chapters found in the later Hebrew book, but a Qumran text of Psalms does have psalms hitherto found only in the Septuagint and other early translations. Again, some Qumran texts show many agreements with the Samaritan text of the Pentateuch, another manuscript tradition which, in the five books of the Law, differs from the present ('Massoretic') text of the Pharisaic collection in some 6,000 instances, in about 2,000 of which it agrees with the Septuagint.[4]

This fluidity inherent in manuscript tradition must be kept in mind when it is stated that the books of the Hebrew Bible date 'in their present forms' from the years between 500 and 100 BC. The statement means that after this period the copyists of these books no longer made deliberate, major alterations of that systematic sort which run through the whole text and produce what can be called 'a new edition', or which combine two or more texts or 'improve' a single text by so many deletions and/or additions as to produce what can be called 'a new book'. Such major alterations seem to have been inflicted on almost all the books of the Hebrew

Bible and the date of the last major alteration is conventionally spoken of as the date when the book reached 'its present form'.

What form a book had before its present form we can only guess. The most reliable guide for such guesswork is a careful study of the actual procedures of the copyists, editors, or authors – which-ever one call them – of the Old Testament tradition. In the differences between the Hebrew and the Septuagint texts of Jeremiah, Psalms, Proverbs, Esther, Daniel, and I Esdras we have objective evidence to show the extent and nature of possible changes.[5] The revision of Genesis by the editor of Jubilees affords further evidence of the same sort. But in all these instances evaluation of the evidence is complicated; allowance must be made for the changes produced by translation. More important, therefore, is the revision of Kings preserved in II Chronicles, for here we have in the original both the editor's work and – with only minor textual variations – the major source he used. Comparison of the two makes clear what he did. His work is dominated by the political and theological interests of the Judaean levitical party to which he belonged.[6] He freely suppresses what is unfavourable to those interests and adds, either from other sources or from his own invention,[7] what he deems desirable. When he preserves material he is apt to copy it verbatim, but even in the course of copying he will often make small additions or omissions in the interests of his favourite theories. If Kings were lost it would be impossible to construct a reliable account of it from Chronicles, and hardly possible to decide with confidence just what parts of Chronicles came from Kings.

Ideally, the critical study of the Old Testament should have begun with the relationships between these books, for in the study of transmitted material a knowledge of the character of the transmission is prerequisite for an evaluation of the data trans-mitted.[8] As things happened, however, the critical study began with observations of discrepancies in wording and content between various parts of single books, and was carried forward, especially in the nineteenth century, by the methods of literary source analysis then in vogue. These methods were based largely, though not entirely, on subjective criteria – especially on the critic's notion of the consistency and historical reliability which might be expected of an ancient author – and the results they yielded were accepted (at least, by the critics) with the uncritical optimism characteristic of much nineteenth-century 'scientific' thought. Consequently their results were sharply attacked in the pessimistic reaction which accompanied the world wars in the first half of the present century. It was pointed out that there is no need to refer inconsistency or nonsense to an editor – if an editor could write such stuff, so could the original author; attempts were made to explain differences of terminology by differences of subject matter;[9] and the applicability of the techniques of literary source criticism to most Old Testament material was challenged on the supposition that the tradition behind the present Old Testament documents had been mostly oral.[10] The objections, while not wholly without justification, went far beyond the limits of plausibility. Archaeological discoveries have shown that writing was in use among the Israelites from the beginning of the first millennium BC;[11] the differences of Old Testament terminology (especially between the law codes, where the subject matter is identical) are scarcely assignable to a single author; and while it is true that authors of the early iron age should not be expected to have the intellectual standards of the present, nevertheless some concern for consistency is characteristic of all rational thought, and inconsistencies are often more plausibly explained by the supposition that an editor has combined inconsistent documents than by the supposition that the original author was not rational.

In sum, therefore, the major results of nineteenth-century Old Testament criticism remain generally accepted.[12] To be specific: it is recognized by all competent scholars that in the Pentateuch and Joshua four major strands of literary material are to be distinguished (though there is considerable dispute as to whether or not all four strands run through all six books). Of these strands, the narrative ones referred to as J and E are commonly assigned to the early periods of the kingdoms of Judah and Israel respectively; the present form of the legal material symbolized by D and exemplified especially in Deuteronomy is assigned to the age of Jeremiah, to whose style it is particularly close; finally, the legal and narrative material symbolized as P (because of its priestly concerns) is so close in style to the Book of Ezekiel as to be dated, at least as far as its language goes, by this relationship. It is generally believed that some part of the D material was in the book 'found' in the Jerusalem temple in 621 BC and implemented by King Josiah in the reforms described in II Kings 23. There is no serious doubt that the books of Judges, Samuel, and Kings were produced by one or more redactors of the D school, who put together sections of material from earlier sources; the redaction must date, at least in part, from the exilic period or later. As to the prophets, there is general agreement that Isaiah 1 to 39 has been heavily interpolated and that chapters 40 to 55 are the work of an author contemporary with Cyrus the Great (who took Babylon in 539 BC). Everyone would agree that numerous interpolations are to be found in the other prophetic books, but there is much disagreement as to specific passages; perhaps the most important item of agreement is that the genuine prophecies of Zechariah stop with chapter 8. That Psalms and Proverbs are composed, each, of several collections is undisputed, and there is general agreement that the material in these collections ranges in date from the monarchic to the postexilic periods, inclusive. Few would assign the speeches of Elihu in Job to the author who produced chapters 3 to 27. That the close stylistic connection of Chronicles, Ezra and Nehemiah requires their assignment to a single author or school is not seriously disputed, and the special interest which these works have in the levites is clear to everyone. There is little doubt that at least Nehemiah 1–7.5 and 13.4–31 come mainly from the hand of Nehemiah himself and are incorporated, as excerpts from an earlier document, in the later levitical work. Finally, this list covers only the major items of general agreement; it could be vastly increased by reference to individual passages. To this extent the nineteenth-century literary criticism of the Old Testament has yielded valid results.

On the other hand, one of its more valuable results has been the demonstration – by reduction to absurdity – of its own limitations. The attempt to produce *exact* analyses of the present books, to indicate precisely the content of the original sources and the contribution of each glossator or redactor, has resulted in a cats' concert of conflicting accounts which discredit each other and may therefore be neglected.[13] This is not to say that all of them are necessarily false, but that even if one of them should happen to be correct, its correctness could not be demonstrated. There are always alternative possibilities. Literary analysis has determined clearly the stylistic traits and structural outlines of most of the major sources. By so doing it has also shown clearly that a great many minor passages are either stylistically or structurally incompatible with these sources and are therefore secondary. But between these clear extremes there remains a vast area of uncertainty, an enormous number of passages which may or may not, with more or less probability, be assigned or denied to this document or to that redactor. Repeated experiments have shown that the traditional methods are not likely to diminish this area much further.

Accordingly, during the past half century, minute source analyses of Old Testament books have commanded less and less attention, as scholars have turned to more promising approaches, notably to the general study of the more ancient Near East, to Near Eastern archaeology, and to form criticism. All of these disciplines have made important incidental contributions to the understanding of the Old Testament, but only one of them, form criticism, has been primarily and directly concerned with the history – or prehistory – of the biblical texts.

Form criticism has two objectives: first, the description and classification of the literary forms – folk tales, sermons, hymns, love songs, or whatever – which occur in a given body of texts; second, the discovery of their *Sitz im Leben* – the roles these forms had in the societies which produced the texts. Under what circumstances, for instance, were the folk tales told; on what occasions and to what audiences were the sermons delivered? And so on. In pursuing the first of these objectives – description and classification – the form criticism of the Old Testament has been notably successful (the extent and importance of its achievements are admirably outlined by the survey in the first section of Eissfeldt's *Introduction*).[14] As regards the second objective, however – reconstruction of the social background – the record has been surprisingly bad. On the one hand, historical reports of the background have been carefully studied for their references to social groups – but some of the groups thus discovered do not fit the preserved material. Thus, for instance, it has been established that the Israelite holy places had official prophets on their staffs, and that these prophets had some role in the cult;[15] but it has also become clear that the bulk of the prophetic material in the Old Testament cannot be accounted for as pronouncements of cult prophets.[16] On the other hand, students of the Old Testament literary forms have repeatedly been led to hypothecate social backgrounds for which there is no specific testimony. The Israelite religious amphictyony of which the sacred ark was the movable, central shrine,[17] the annual ceremony of the renewal of the covenant, the annual enthronement festival,[18] are examples of such hypothecated social entities for which there is, in the preserved literature, no reliable evidence.[19] Whether or not they ever did exist is here beside the point. The point is that form criticism has revealed an important gap between the documents in the Old Testament and the society from which they are supposed to derive. The prophecies in the Old Testament do not come from the official prophets of the great Israelite shrines, and the utterances of those official prophets have not been preserved. (Why?) If amphictyony, annual covenant renewal, and enthronement festivals existed, then the Old Testament has preserved no direct mention of some of the most important elements of Israelite political structure and religious ceremony. (Why?) If they did not exist, then the fact that eminent scholars have been forced to hypothecate such nonexistent entities to explain the preserved texts shows that the relationship of those texts to their true historical background is something strange. (Why?)

Once it is recognized that we are dealing with a body of texts which do not directly or fully represent their original environment, then the importance of the history of selection, copying, and edition, sketched earlier in this chapter, becomes clear. The partial preservation of the evidence may be explained by the partiality of those who preserved it. Except for archaeological finds, ancient texts have never simply 'survived'. Those which survive have always been preserved by copying, and copying a text is a long, tedious job which is not done without some strong motive. Therefore, of the texts produced by any one generation, only a few were copied by the next, and the motives for copying those few were also the motives for editing or 'correcting' them. The primary *Sitz im Leben* of the books of the Old Testament therefore is their role in the life of those who wrote, copied, and corrected them; like the books of the New Testament, they testify primarily and reliably about the life of the church or the synagogue, only secondarily and unreliably about the events they purport to narrate.

Accordingly the Hebrew Bible, as we have it, is primarily evidence of the interests of the Pharisees and their successors, who not only selected and interpreted the books but also carefully determined and corrected their texts.[20] Behind the Pharisees, the previous critical period of selection was probably the Maccabean revolt, when the hellenizing party of the Jerusalem priesthood[21] tried to destroy the books of the Mosaic Law and presumably other books defending or representing the Mosaic tradition, but Judas Maccabaeus collected and preserved those of which his party approved.[22] Such collection, if it involved copying, must necessarily have involved revision of the texts, and evidence of drastic revision is probably to be found in Daniel (where a somewhat earlier text seems to have been expanded by occasional interpolations and terminal addition of a series of prophecies from Maccabaean times) and in the addition of several Maccabaean compositions to the book of Psalms.[23] Members of the Maccabaean party not only revised old texts but also wrote new ones, imitating the style of earlier books so successfully that some of their new compositions – notably I Maccabees and perhaps Esther – have been preserved in one or more Old Testament collections. From the time before the Maccabees we have the report that Nehemiah 'founded a library and collected the books about the kings and prophets and the writings of David and letters of kings about votive offerings'.[24] Nehemiah, as appears from his memoirs, was no less a party man than was Judas Maccabaeus. His selection of documents to be preserved will have represented no less surely the interests and opinions of his party, and the documents will have been thoroughly edited – if we can judge from the work of the editors of Chronicles, Ezra, and Nehemiah, whose circle preserved and edited Nehemiah's account of his own work. Before Nehemiah's time a similar party programme of collection and edition had evidently been carried out by the Deuteronomic school which produced the earlier historical books, and party interests are obviously represented by the work of the editors responsible for the priestly (P) material in the Pentateuch and Joshua.[25]

Thus the Hebrew Bible is the product not merely of partisan collection and revision but of a long series of partisan collections and revisions. Moreover, the relation between the parties concerned has not been one of simple succession and pious preservation, as represented in the Mishnah.[26] On the contrary, the Pharisees kept Daniel in their canon and Hanukah in their calendar, but dropped the Books of the Maccabees, although these were accepted in other (certainly Jewish) Bibles. The 'letters of kings about votive offerings' collected by Nehemiah were evidently preserved by the Maccabees (since a Maccabaean author reports them) but have been dropped from all later collections. On the other hand, although II Chronicles may have been intended to replace Kings (which it repeatedly contradicts) both have been preserved. The editors of the Pentateuch not only preserved, but combined in a single corpus, legal codes of which the details were obviously contradictory;[27] in addition, the legislation of Ezekiel was independently preserved, although its contradictions of the Pentateuch continued to give trouble until Pharisaic times.[28]

Thus what we have in the various Old Testaments is not the literature of a single party but the literature of a large number and long succession of parties which sometimes have come together by compromise in more or less enduring alliances, sometimes have been separated by quarrels, and finally, because of their separation, have preserved different collections of the literature – Pharisaic and Samaritan, Greek and Syriac. Evidence of their earlier differences appears in the contradictions between and within the various Old Testament books; evidence of their alliances appears in the common preservation of such contradictory material.

This common preservation was facilitated by the fact that the written material which we have was never the whole of the tradition. This is particularly true of the legal material, in which contradictions were most serious. The ancient Israelites were not much concerned for historical accuracy (and even among the Greeks Herodotus is often willing to give several contradictory reports of the same event). But contradictions in legal codes would have had serious consequences had they not been reconciled in the oral tradition of which the codes were never more than selections and developments. This dependence of the codes on the oral tradition is immediately clear from the content of the codes themselves. None is complete in its coverage of unavoidable legal problems (e.g., none contains the rules of procedure necessary for its own enforcement). Israelite law is generally recognized to have developed from a multitude of sources – the tribal traditions of the nomads, the laws of the Canaanite cities, the rules of the various shrines, and the rulings of the kings. From the earliest history of Israel, therefore, 'problems in conflicts of laws' must have been frequent, and the traditions of harmonistic oral exegesis must go back far beyond the oldest of the preserved codes.[29]

If we wish to understand the Old Testament, therefore, we must attempt to discover the traditions its documents presuppose. But traditions, like documents, never merely exist; they must always be perpetuated and their perpetuation, like the preservation of documents, is usually the work of one or another party ('party' is here used loosely to mean 'a body of like-minded individuals'; it does not imply formal organization). Therefore, as the study of the documents should begin with the history of the tradition, so the history of the tradition should begin with the history of the parties[30] – the attempt to distinguish and describe them, to trace their developments, conflicts, and alliances, and to follow, as far as possible, the convolutions of each 'party line', convolutions which explain the traditions that the party preserved and invented, and indicate those which it suppressed or denied.[31]

Unfortunately, almost all the important evidence for the early history of Israelite parties is that preserved in the documents which the parties produced – that is to say, in the Old Testament. Hence, while the analysis of the documents depends to some extent on knowledge of the parties, yet knowledge of the parties depends largely on the analysis of the documents. Fortunately, the analysis which earlier studies based on the common criteria of literary criticism is, in its major results, reliable. We can therefore presuppose such generally accepted results as were listed above (pp. 4ff.) and we shall often use as hypotheses, for the sake of the argument, other, less widely accepted, analyses which have been proposed by various scholars. Moreover, we shall not think it necessary (especially since it would be practically impossible) to discuss, or even to specify, the alternative interpretations of every passage cited. The following history, like every historical study of the Old Testament, must stand or fall by its accord with the clear passages of those documents about which there is no serious dispute. If it stand by this criterion, then its interpretations of obscure passages and of disputed documents must be considered primarily in the context of the structure, not of the innumerable conjectures with which almost every verse of such material has been encumbered. Accordingly, presentation of evidence in the notes has generally been limited to citation of Old Testament texts and other primary material; secondary works are not usually cited, except in support of disputed positions or acknowledgment of indebtedness.

2

Religious Parties among the Israelites before 587

The Old Testament is primarily concerned with the cult of the god Yahweh, cult being understood in its widest sense to include all ways of securing/retaining the god's favour.[1] The Old Testament undertakes to show how this cult was established, to outline the rules for its practice (including the laws which must be observed by its adherents), and to show that, throughout history, its proper practice led to prosperity, its neglect to disaster. This argument from history the Hebrew Bible reinforces by a collection of prophetic pronouncements to the same point, by two collections of hymns, testifying to the same belief, by two collections of proverbs which identify wisdom with the fear of Yahweh,[2] by four stories telling how Yahweh saved his worshipers, and by a collection of love songs which the Pharisees interpreted as describing the relations between Yahweh and Israel. In sum, the purposes of the Bible are to tell the worshipers of Yahweh what they should do and to persuade them that they had better do it.

Since the Hebrew Bible is thus a cult collection, the party differences which shaped the collection will have been primarily those which concerned the cult. Accordingly our investigation should begin with the cult of Yahweh. Here, as in the history of any cult, the first problem is to determine the adherents. To this problem the Bible affords a brief answer. The bulk of it is concerned with Yahweh as the god of 'Israel' and with 'Israel' as the principal worshippers of Yahweh. We have therefore to ask, What is 'Israel'?[3]

Fortunately, we need not engage in the dispute as to origins. Whether 'Israel' came into being as a religious amphictyony of originally unrelated Palestinian tribes, or whether there was in the desert some tribal group, the *Benē Yisra'el* ('Children of Israel'),[4] from which all these tribes ultimately derived, are questions scarcely to be settled from the heavily edited legends of the heroic past which the Old Testament preserves. Even if we accept its story that all Isreal came out of Egypt, that story knows of the mixed multitude which accompanied the Israelites, of the peoples – Midianites and Moabites – who became associated with them in the desert, and of the others – Gibeonites and Jebusites, Jerahmeëlites and Kenites and Hebrews – who joined them after their entrance into the promised land.[5] It knows that many Canaanite cities were left unconquered and that the Israelites soon began to marry the women and worship the gods of Canaan.[6] Relationships thus formed seem to have resulted in the assimilation of Israelite to Canaanite groups and the incorporation of Canaanite towns into Israelite tribes.[7]

Marriage with aliens seems to have been common and generally accepted in the early period, since it is reported of such heroes as Judah, Simeon, Joseph, Moses, Gideon, Samson, David and Solomon – to mention only the most eminent – and foreign women became national heroines – Jaël and Rahab, for example. These stories must have been established in revered legends or they would not have survived the editors, who have expressed their disapproval of the actions they felt compelled to report.[8] It is presumable that many reports of intermarriage were suppressed. We hear almost nothing of the assimilation to Israel of the Canaanite cities which became parts of the kingdom of David,[9] although this must have been one of the major social phenomena of the following century. Nor do we hear of the relationships which must have followed David's establishment of his court in a Jebusite city (for Jerusalem remained Jebusite)[10] and the settlement in Jerusalem of considerable foreign groups – David's mercenaries (who must have numbered in the thousands), the trains of the foreign queens and the staffs of the 'high places' built for them, the colony of Phoenician artisans required by the building programme of Solomon, and the settlement of foreign merchants whom the court may be supposed to have attracted.[11] Yet the presence of these foreigners doubtless resulted in numerous mixed marriages. One case we happen to hear of is that of the mother of Solomon; she was married first to a Hittite, then to David.[12] One of David's sisters had a son by an Ishmaelite.[13]

Significantly, marriage with aliens is not attacked by the pre-exilic prophets.[14] (Had any attacked it, the post-exilic reformers would have preserved those prophecies.) Few criticisms of the practice can securely be dated before the Deuteronomic school of the late seventh and sixth centuries.[15] The Deuteronomists are violently opposed to it, but their opposition seems to derive chiefly from their concern to prevent the worship of gods other than Yahweh.[16] When there is no danger of such worship (for instance, in the case of a female captive) Deuteronomy permits the practice.[17] And even when there is danger of alien influence, Deuteronomy is not consistent: 23.8f. expects intermarriage with Edomites and Egyptians and, at least, does not wholly disapprove it. Presumably, therefore, the Israelites in general had no greater resistance to exogamy than that normal among rural groups in hill countries.

Accordingly 'Israel', before the Assyrian and Babylonian conquests, seems to have been about as distinct an entity as 'Austria' is today. That is to say, there was a nucleus of persons united by common interest, common language,[18] common traditions, common religious feeling (loyalty to local shrines and to the national god), and such ethnic uniformity as can be produced by the amalgamation of many elements, but on every side this nucleus blended into the surrounding populations.

One would expect that this various and amorphous nature of Israel would be reflected in a corresponding variety of religious practices and in assimilation to the religion of the neighbouring peoples. This expectation is confirmed by the Old Testament, but with an important reservation. The Old Testament contains a great many stories of agreements made between Yahweh and the Israelites or their alleged ancestors, in most of which Yahweh stipulated that they were to do something he wanted, and himself undertook to help them in return.[19] Many of these agreements – and particularly the most famous of them, that reported in Exodus 24[20] – stipulate that the Israelites shall worship no god besides Yahweh. In accordance with these agreements, the editors of the historical books have represented the course of Israelite history as a function of the Israelites' exclusive worship of Yahweh. When exclusive worship was maintained all went well; when other gods were worshipped all went badly; repeated breaches of contract led to the destruction of Samaria in 722 and of Jerusalem in 587.[21] This interpretation of history supposes – and the Old Testament often declares[22] – that Israelite worship of gods other than Yahweh was frequent and important. But it also supposes that already before the conquest of Palestine there was one proper 'religion of Israel' – the cult of Yahweh – and all other Israelite worship was deviation from this.

In accord with this latter supposition, both the Old Testament and most modern historians of 'the religion of Israel' have concerned themselves chiefly with the relations of Yahweh to the Israelites and have referred to Israelite worship of other gods only by the way.[23] This is what we should expect of the Old Testament, given its character as a cult collection. It is concerned to heroize the patrons, priests, and prophets of the cult and to magnify the cult deity. Of course the collectors did not include material in praise of competing deities and their patrons and personnel. For that material – psalms celebrating the tender mercies of Asherah, stories of the miracles worked by the prophets of Baal or of the zeal of the priests of Anath, histories of the piety and devotion of Manasseh and Jezebel and of the reformations they effected in the national religion – for all this we can argue only from analogy. Only from analogy, too, can we guess at the polemics produced by the opposition – the denunciations of Jehu's murders (by the prophets of Baal) and of Josiah's sacrileges (by the priests of the rural shrines). Unfortunately, analogy cannot recover the lost material, but it can enable us to realize that the impression produced by the outspoken theory and tacit bias of the Old Testament may be misleading: although the cult of Yahweh is the principal concern of the Old Testament, it may not have been the principal religious concern of the Israelites.

As to the period prior to the settlement of the Israelites in Palestine – roughly, before 1250 BC – we shall attempt no decision. That the *Benē Yisra'el* (if any) in the desert worshipped only Yahweh is reported and possible, but it is also reported that they also worshipped a calf, and both reports may derive from theological theory rather than historical tradition.[24] It is more significant that the accounts of the conquest of the land, in Joshua and Judges, say nothing of wars against alien gods or cults.[25]

For the two and a half centuries between the settlement and the establishment of the monarchy (about 1000 BC) we have the reports in Judges that the Israelites frequently worshipped the gods of the neighbouring peoples. Again these reports may be true, but they are part of the editorial framework of the book, they reflect the Deuteronomic editor's theological theory and serve his homiletic purpose; therefore they may be editorial invention. That a story is possible is no proof that it is true; late inventions may resemble early facts.[26]

More reliable indications of what happened in the time of the judges are to be found in the divine names, holy places, ceremonies, laws, and traditions of the cult of Yahweh as these gradually come to light in the monarchic period.[27] From them it appears that the Canaanite gods 'El 'Elyon, Shaddai, and Tsur have been identified with Yahweh.[28] The great Canaanite shrine of Bethel ('the Temple of El') has become without change of its name one of the principal sanctuaries of Yahweh.[29] Shechem, where the local Baal was known as 'the Baal of the contract', has become the site of a contract between Yahweh and the Israelites.[30] The worship of Yahweh has been established in many other Canaanite cities and holy places throughout the land, but in most cases there is no evidence that the cults of the other gods have been extirpated from these sites.[31] The major festivals of Yahweh's worship have become those of the Canaanite agricultural year – the feasts of unleavened bread, of weeks, and of booths[32] – and along with them the Canaanite use of copulation as a religious ceremony, an understandably popular fertility rite, has been established in the major shrines of Yahweh, including the temple of Jerusalem.[33] This temple itself has been built on Canaanite lines.[34] Yahweh has become the sponsor of Canaanite agricultural law.[35] The Israelites have acquired a body of traditions which evidently had little original relation to Yahweh,[36] since neither Adam nor Noah nor any of the patriarchs down to Abraham, nor Abraham himself, nor Ishmael nor Isaac nor Esau nor Jacob nor any of Jacob's sons (the legendary ancestors of the Israelite tribes) nor Ephraim nor Manasseh nor Moses nor Aaron nor Eleazar nor Phineas, nor any of the judges, nor Samuel nor Saul nor David nor Solomon nor any kind of Israel or Judah prior to Jehoshaphat (c. 875–850 BC) had a name compounded with Yahweh.[37] Yahwist names are not entirely absent from the early stories[38] – witness Jonathan and possibly Joshua – but names originally compounded with those of other deities – El, Baal, Gad, Anath, Am Yam, Zedek, Shalem, Asher and Tsur – are also common in the preserved records of the early period[39] and were probably more common in the records which have now been lost by censorship.[40] The state of affairs at the beginning of the monarchy is indicated by the facts that Saul, the first king, named one of his sons for Yahweh, another for Baal, and that the son he named for Yahweh – Jonathan, the friend of David – named his son for Baal.[41] Starting with this state of affairs, we have to explain by what steps the cult of Yahweh acquired or regained that exclusive preeminence which it eventually enjoyed in Judaism.

One step was undoubtedly royal patronage. David was a worshipper of Yahweh – as well as of other gods[42] – and after he took Jerusalem he brought up to the city a mysterious 'divine box which was . . . called by the name of "Yahweh of armies (? Tseba'ot) who sits on[43] the Kerubim"'.[44] This box (the subject of much ancient and modern fiction) David established in a tent in Jerusalem, 'and offered burnt offerings and peace offerings before Yahweh',[45] that is, before the box. Later on there was an altar in or before 'the tent of Yahweh'[46] – presumably the tent which contained the box. Prophets reputedly inspired by Yahweh were listened to at David's court. On the occasion of a plague one of them ordered David to build an altar to Yahweh on the property of a Jebusite.[47] But Solomon, at the beginning of his reign, went to Gibeon to sacrifice, 'because it was the great high place',[48] and the chief temple of Jerusalem, throughout David's time, must have been that of the old city god ('El 'Elyon?).[49] With Solomon's building of his temple of Yahweh, the pre-eminence of the deity patronized by the ruling family was given expression.[50] Probably the city god was soon identified with him. We find in the circles of David and Solomon a high percentage of names compounded with Yahweh.[51] Accordingly, foremost among the parties responsible for the growth of the cult of Yahweh we must suppose a circle at the Judaean court.

On the other hand, Solomon's worship of Yahweh was not exclusive; he built high places to Moabite, Sidonian, and Ammonite gods and worshipped others, too.[52] And there is no evidence that his subjects were more Yahwist than the king. When the northern tribes broke away from Solomon's son, Rehoboam, about 925 BC and set up the separate kingdom of 'Israel' in central and northern Palestine, as opposed to 'Judah' in the south, the first king, of Israel, Jeroboam, showed his devotion to Yahweh by endowing the shrines of Bethel and Dan with golden images of the deity in the form of a bull calf.[53] The form probably reflects Yahweh's identification with 'El, who in Ugaritic texts is regularly referred to as a bull. For Judah in the same period, the Deuteronomic editor of Kings reports that the people built high places and sacred posts and pillars to Asherah and maintained temple 'prostitutes' and followed 'all' the Canaanite ritual practices ('abominations').[54]

The first signs of a change appear two generations later in the reign of the Judaean king Asa. Here again personal names afford valuable evidence. Asa (who died about 875) is said to have put down ritual copulation, destroyed the idols his ancestors made, and deposed his mother from her position as dowager queen because of her devotion to Asherah.[55] Asa's son, Jehoshaphat – the name means 'Yahweh judged' – was the first king of either Israel or Judah to have a Yahwist name. He was a contemporary of the prophet Elijah – the name means 'Yahweh is my God' – who reportedly was driven out of the kingdom of Israel because he incited a mob to murder some prophets of Baal.[56] In the generation after Elijah, a revolution in Israel led to a massacre of worshippers of Baal.[57] Shortly after this, the priest of the temple of Yahweh in Jerusalem organized a revolution in the kingdom of Judah and when it succeeded the rival temple of Baal was destroyed.[58] From this period on, names compounded with Yahweh are customary in both kingdoms. Evidently, from this period on there was a newly important element in the situation: the demand that all Israel worship Yahweh *and Yahweh alone*.

This was a demand all Israel was not willing to satisfy. In spite of the Yahwist revolutions of the ninth century, the cult of the various Baals continued.[59] It was evidently popular in the eighth century, when Hosea denounced it, and still popular at the end of the seventh century, when denounced by Zephaniah[60] and Jeremiah. The prophets, Jeremiah said, prophesied by Baal[61] and the people swore by him.[62] Jerusalem had as many altars to him as it had street corners – perhaps an exaggeration.[63] Sacrifices and incense were commonly offered to him.[64] Nor were the Baals Yahweh's only competitors. Judea had as many gods as it had cities.[65] When another Yahwist reformation was put through in the time of King Josiah (621 BC) the priests throughout Judaea had to be stopped from burning incense on the high places, not only to Baal, but also to the sun, the moon, the planets, and all the host of heaven;[66] around Jerusalem the high places of 'the satyrs'(?)[67] and of the gods Ashtoreth,[68] Kemosh, and Milkom had to be destroyed;[69] and the temple of Yahweh itself had to be purged of the vessels of Baal, Asherah, and the host of heaven, the chariots of the sun, and the houses of the sacred 'prostitutes'[70] where the women wove coverings for the pillar which symbolized the goddess Asherah.[71] Josiah's reforms seem to have had little success with the masses and to have died with him in 609,[72] for the later prophecies of Jeremiah and Ezekiel are full of denunciations of Judaean worship of other gods than Yahweh.[73]

Such complaints are not to be dismissed as mere exaggeration; the evidence of archaeology supports them. Among the commonest objects found in excavations of Israelite cities are figurines of naked women, most of them representations of some divine power conceived as a goddess.[74] This significance is particularly clear for those found in shrines together with other cult objects, as in the shrines of the Israelite period at Deir 'Alla and Ta-anek.[75] Names compounded with Baal are common on the ostraca from eighth-century Samaria.[76] Common also are seals on which Hebrew, and sometimes Yahwist, names are combined with figures of deities.[77] Some of these deities may be representations of Yahweh,[78] but others represent the sun or moon god, or the Queen of Heaven. A man named Saul had a seal which showed the sun disc being worshipped.[79] One 'Elishama' ('My God heard') had on his seal the picture of the god who heard – a four-winged serpent wearing the crowns of Upper and Lower Egypt; this 'Elishama' was of the royal house and may have been the grandfather of the Ishmael who murdered Gedaliah.[80] The Israelite shrine at Hazor in the eleventh century contained a seated image of a war god and incense burners like those found in contemporary strata at Megiddo.[81] Kenyon thinks that two of the Beth Shan temples were in use throughout the Israelite and down to the Persian period; here again are found incense stands like those at Megiddo, and snake- and dove-houses of a fertility cult, probably of Ashtoreth.[82] Some of the high places that flourished around Jerusalem have been excavated. The ninth to eighth century shrine (?) at Kuntillet Ajrud has yielded inscriptions invoking Yahweh, Baal and Ashera, and a pithos with pictures of several figures, one of whom seems to be the Egyptian god Bes.[84] Such evidence from archaeology is supplemented by the evidence of place names like 'Temple of Shemesh' (Beth Shemesh), scarcely to be separated from the cult of Shemesh reported by the Book of Kings,[85] 'Temple of Anath' (Beth Anath) and Anathoth, recalling the association of Anath with the cult of Yahweh in

Elephantine,[86] and Beth Baal Berith, Beth Baal Meōn, Baal Tamar, Baal Perizim,[87] and so on, which are evidence for the cult of Baal.[88]

Syncretism was dominant in the cult of Yahweh at Jerusalem to the very last days of the first temple. Ezekiel has described Yahweh's departure from that temple, before its destruction by the Babylonians.[89] Yahweh excuses his departure by showing the prophet the abominations practised there: north of the altar gate is an image which provokes his jealousy. Inside the wall of the court, by the gate, is a secret room, its walls decorated with reliefs of creeping things, animals, and 'all' the idols of Israel; here seventy elders are burning incense to these images (and Yahweh's comments indicate that such worship, though secret, is common – many private individuals have such rooms).[90] In the north gate 'of the house' there are women weeping for Tammuz, and in the inner court, at the door of the sanctuary itself, there are twenty-five men prostrating themselves toward the east, to the sun, 'their behinds towards the temple'.

The temple was the temple of Yahweh; such things could not have happened in it without the consent and co-operation of the priests of Yahweh. This proves that the cult of Yahweh was not conceived as exclusive by the priests of his principal temple.[91] Those who did conceive of it as exclusive were not at this time the official representatives of the country's legally established religion.

It cannot be supposed, however, that the worship of other gods was limited to the priests and principal temples and was solely a matter of official syncretism, imposed by the royal court for reasons of foreign policy. The prophetic complaints summarized above indicate that many Israelites worshipped other gods in small shrines and in their homes. Nor can it be maintained that those who worshipped other gods abandoned completely the worship of Yahweh,[92] so that the population was divided between Yahweh-worshippers and their opponents. We have seen that the worship of other gods was carried on in the temples of Yahweh, with the co-operation of his priests. It is true that the prophets and their disciples sometimes denounce the people for 'abandoning' Yahweh in order to worship other gods, but the 'abandonment' must be understood as comparative neglect or as prophetic interpretation, probably the latter. For the people did not actually abandon Yahweh; a string of prophetic sarcasms testifies to the assiduity with which they maintained his cult.[93] Therefore the charges of abandonment are to be explained by the fact that those prophets whose prophecies have been preserved thought the cult of Yahweh exclusive and considered the worship of Yahweh together with any other god as tantamount to abandonment, whereas the people and the priests and probably most of the prophets – those whose prophecies have been destroyed – saw no objection to worshiping both Yahweh and other deities too.[94] Accordingly, in reckoning the parties which advanced the worship of Yahweh, we must include a widespread popular devotion to him which found its expression in syncretistic worship. This seems to have been rather the general attitude of the population than a party position. However, since it formed the background from which the minor parties distinguished themselves, we may for convenience list those who shared this common attitude as 'the syncretistic party'.

From this account it follows that in pre-exilic times we cannot draw a clear boundary between the religion of the Israelites and the religion of the surrounding peoples. The cult of Yahweh played a larger part in Judaea than elsewhere, true, as the cult of Kemosh was predominant in Moab. But early legend can represent Yahweh as a god of other people besides Israelites,[95] and as there were high places of Kemosh, Milkom, and Ashtoreth in the suburbs of Jerusalem,[96] so there were presumably high places of Yahweh adjacent to Dibon, to Rabbath Ammon, and to Tyre. As for Damascus, we have in II Kings 5 the story of how the cult of Yahweh came to be established there: A general of the king of Syria was afflicted with 'leprosy'. His wife heard from a Hebrew slave girl of the powers of a prophet of Yahweh. The general was persuaded to go to the prophet and was cured. In gratitude he undertook to build an altar to Yahweh in Damascus and to worship in the future only Yahweh – except when, because of his governmental position, he had to worship the god of Damascus, Rimmon. A consequence of the general's cure may be seen in the story that the King of Syria sent to consult Yahweh as to his own health[97] (as a king of Israel sent to consult Baal Zebub of Ekron).[98] On a lower social level, we have a story of a Sidonian woman rewarded for her charity to a wandering prophet of Yahweh, although she herself was not formerly a worshipper of Yahweh.[99] Such stories show the cult of Yahweh being adopted by Gentiles outside Palestine,[100] as the cults of Kemosh and Ashtoreth may have been adopted by Palestinians. (Of course, Gentiles living in Palestine often become worshippers of Yahweh; already in David's time Uriah the Hittite had a Yahwist name.[101] And Israelites who went to live in alien territories were expected to worship alien gods.)[102]

All this indicates that to consider 'the religion of Israel' as a unique entity may be misleading. We shall better understand the state of affairs during the monarchies if we think of the religion of the Israelites as one form of the common religion of the ancient Near East.[103] This common religion was diversified at different places and times by the predominance of the cults of different gods, of whom one or another may be loosely described as 'the god' of the politico-ethnic group in which his cult was predominant. Thus Ashur may be called 'the god' of the Assyrians, as Dagon was called 'the god' of the Philistines, Kemosh of Moab,[104] and so on. But since other gods were regularly worshipped in these countries no one would describe the cult of Ashur as 'the religion of Assyria', or the like. In the hill country of Palestine, by the tenth century BC, the predominant cult was that of Yahweh and he was recognized to be 'the god' of Israel, as opposed to the gods of the neighbouring peoples.[105] But the cults of the other gods of the common religion of the Near East were not neglected. These other gods were worshipped not only at altars and high places dedicated to them but also, together with Yahweh, in the temples of the major cities. Therefore to describe the cult of Yahweh as 'the religion of Israel' in the period of the monarchies has little more *de facto* justification than to describe the cult of Kemosh as 'the religion of Moab'.

To say that it has 'little more' implies that it has some. In Israel we know that there was considerable demand for Israelites to worship only Yahweh and that this demand found expression in Yahwist reformations. Whether similar demands were made by adherents of the 'national' gods in Moab and in other neighbouring states, we do not know. It is not unlikely that they were. We happen to know of analogous developments in Egypt,[106] Persia,[107] Caunia,[108] and Rome in 428 BC if Liby IV,30.11 can be trusted; and since we are almost totally ignorant of the history of religion among the Israelites' neighbours, our ignorance of such developments there is no proof that they did not occur. But it remains ignorance, whereas we do have knowledge of the reformations in the Israelite kingdoms and of the belief, there, that Israelites should worship *only* Yahweh. This belief seems to have been held by a number of groups who sometimes co-operated, but who differed in social make-up and motivation. For convenience' sake, however, we may speak of them together as 'the Yahweh-alone party' (or 'movement', if 'party' suggest too strongly an organization). With the court patronage and the popular, syncretistic piety discussed above, this Yahweh-alone movement constitutes the third of the major factors shaping the history of the cult of Yahweh in the Israelite kingdoms. During the time of the kingdoms it was probably the least important of the three, but its importance for the subsequent history of the world is enormous beyond reckoning. Its triumph resulted in that cult of Yahweh alone of which the greatest centre was the second temple of Jerusalem and from which came not only the Old Testament, but Christianity, rabbinic Judaism and Islam.

At the root of this importance lay the fact that in the ancient world religious observances were attached to most acts of everyday life; any festivity or misfortune was an occasion of sacrifice and the meat of most sacrifices was used for food. Therefore if a man refused to worship the gods commonly worshipped in his city, his refusal would normally make it impossible for him to participate in any municipal ceremony, hold any civil or military office,[109] or eat at his neighbour's table. Any group which insisted on worshipping only one god thereby made themselves a peculiar people – with the consequences, for better, for worse, which this entailed – and made the joining of their group a matter of conversion, not mere adherence.[110] Here, consequently – in the belief that the Israelites should worship *only* Yahweh – is the essential of the exclusive religions of the Western world. Appropriately, the Deuteronomic formulation of this belief is the centre of Jewish devotion: 'Hear, O Israel, Yahweh is our God, Yahweh alone'.[111]

As to the sources of this belief – the Old Testament explains it as the result of Yahweh's orders, given by him *viva voce* (Ex. 20.1ff., etc.). This legend needs no refutation, but one may remark that while the practice of worshipping no god save Yahweh may go back to the desert, the prohibition of worshipping any other god can only have arisen when the Israelites came into contact with other gods. None of the texts in which this requirement appears can securely be dated before the ninth century,[112] but the requirement itself is probably earlier and various conjectures may be advanced as to its origin. The priests and prophets of Yahweh would not have wished the Israelites to resort to his (and their) competitors; Israelites attached to desert life would have opposed the worship of the gods of Canaan as part of an alien culture; military leaders would have tried to keep their followers distinct from the subjugated population and united by the cult of their peculiar deity; Israelites who wished to preserve their own segregation, as members of a ruling people, from the conquered Canaanites, would have demanded that Israelites worship only the Israelite god. But none of these conjectures can pretend to more than probability.[113]

Turning from legends and conjectures to the reliable evidence for the Yahweh-alone movement in the Israelite kingdoms,[114] we find it chiefly of four sorts: 1. the general statements about kings and their policies, by the editors of Kings and Chronicles; 2. the specific stories in these books, especially those about religious persecutions (or 'reformations', depending on one's viewpoint);[115] 3. the stories and pronouncements in the books of the prophets; and 4. the laws and hortatory developments in the pre-exilic law codes. Full treatment of this material and of the questions it raises is impossible in this volume; the following account is limited to the principal points.

1. *The general statements in Kings and Chronicles.* The editor of Kings declares, about most kings of Judah, that they 'did what was right in the eyes of Yahweh. . . . only, the high places were not suppressed'.[116] About almost all kings of Israel he declares that they 'did what was evil in the eyes of Yahweh' and continued in 'the sins of Jeroboam the son of Nebat which he made Israel sin'.[117] Both judgments are of limited value as evidence. The approval of the Judaean kings derives from the editor's devotion to the memory of the Davidic dynasty[118] and indicates only that he did not have (or did not credit) traditions hostile to those of the kings whom he approved. Since the 'high places' were centres of the syncretistic worship of Yahweh, Asherah and other deities (e.g., Kemosh and Milkom),[119] a king who did not suppress them did not push the Yahweh-alone policy beyond the limits of Jerusalem, at most. On the other hand, the editor was convinced that worship at the shrines of Bethel and Dan, patronized by Jeroboam, was idolatrous, and that worship of idols was worship of gods other than Yahweh.[120] Idolatry and worship of alien gods were to him the worst sins.

Therefore, since all the kings of Israel supported the shrines of Bethel and Dan, he dismissed them all with his cliché about the sins of Jeroboam, and did not give minor details, even when he happened to mention that a king was worse than his predecessors.[121] (He disposed of the reigns of most kings of Israel in four or five verses each.) Accordingly this cliché should not be taken to imply that there was no idolatrous worship nor worship of alien gods in the kingdom of Israel *save* at Bethel and Dan. Also, the editor uses the cliché to refer only to royal policy, not to popular practise; but he concludes his history of the kingdom of Israel with a survey of Israelite religion which indicates far more various and widespread syncretism: II Kings 17.7–23. Accordingly his approval of most Judaean kings and his disapproval of all kings of Israel tell us little of the religious practices of the people. The editor of Chronicles omits the kings of Israel completely, and his judgments on the kings of Judah reflect theological theory rather than historical information.

2. *The specific statements in Kings and Chronicles.* The reports of religious persecutions/reformations in Chronicles are unreliable. The Chronicler freely invented pseudo-historical material to support his theological convictions.[122] He also used historical material for this purpose, and although he got most of it from Kings, he is now recognized to have had other sources as well.[123] Accordingly when he reports something not in Kings but not absurd, one can rarely determine whether it comes from one of his sources or from one of his fantasies. Consequently little of his peculiar material can be used for the history of the reigns it purports to describe.[124]

The stories in Kings about specific religious reforms are more reliable. The first of them, concerning the reforms of Asa in the early ninth century, has already been mentioned. It reports suppression of the sacred 'prostitutes', destruction of the idols his ancestors made, and deposition of the queen mother because she made for Asherah some object which the king cut down and burned.[125] It is uncertain to what extent these reforms were motivated by the concern that Yahweh alone should be worshipped, to what extent they reflect attachment to the desert way of life and hostility to the traits of peasant culture (especially fertility rites and iconic worship).[126] The latter theme is not necessarily connected with Yahweh-alone theology,[127] but the connection is easily made (hostility to the traits of peasant culture being completed by hostility to its gods), and Asa probably made it. His devotion to Yahweh is suggested by the name of his son, Jehoshaphat ('Yahweh judged').

Jehoshaphat is credited by Kings with having carried on the policy of Asa and put down the remnants of sacred 'prostitution' which survived Asa's time.[128] (Asa's inability to stamp out the practice during his forty-year reign in the tiny territory of Judah indicates its popularity.) On the other hand, Jehoshaphat left the high places undisturbed and married his son to Athalia, a daughter (or sister?) of King Ahab of Israel and Queen Jezebel.[129] Given Jezebel's devotion to Baal,[130] the marriage contract must have contained provisions for Athalia's worship of Baal in Jerusalem.[131] That Kings says nothing of this and classes Jehoshaphat as a 'good king' shows the limited significance of its editorial praise.

Jezebel not only patronized Baal but also reformed the religion of Israel by executing a number of devotees of Yahweh.[132] This persecution is indirect evidence of the existence of the Yahweh-alone movement, for Jezebel herself presumably worshipped Yahweh. Her daughter and sons had Yahwist names.[133] Her husband, Ahab, repeatedly relied on prophets of Yahweh, and most of them were friendly to him.[134] His chief minister, Obadiah ('the slave of Yahweh'), was a devoted Yahwist.[135] Therefore the persecution was probably directed against those Yahwists who held that Israelites should worship Yahweh alone and who opposed the queen because of her patronage of Baal.

In the stories of Elijah and Elisha we see two prophets who led the Yahweh-alone movement, as they lived on in popular legend.[136] In the Elisha stories, too, we glimpse communities of 'sons of the prophets' who supported such leaders.[137] Here, so far as our records go, the movement comes closest to a party organization, an organization which may even have attempted to purify the religion of Israel by terrorist activities. An unexplained saying equates Elisha with King Jehu, who wiped out the followers of Ahab, and King Hazael of Syria, who devastated northern Trans-Jordan: those who escape Hazael, it is said, shall be killed by Jehu, and those who escape Jehu, by Elisha.[138] These terrorist tactics may have been rewarded by some concessions under Ahab's second successor, Jehoram (II Kings 3.2).

At the same time it appears that more prophets sided with the syncretists. Elijah sets himself as the sole prophet of Yahweh against four hundred and fifty prophets of Baal.[139] A story from a different cycle represents Ahab as having four hundred prophets of Yahweh on whom he could rely for favourable predictions, against one who always threatened him with disaster.[140] These kindred exaggerations in unrelated traditions suggest that the Yahweh-alone groups, which preserved both stories, were conscious that their prophets had been a small minority. And although the stories about Elisha represent him as respected, yet II Kings 9.11 indicates the officers of the army of Israel took for granted that a member of the 'sons of the prophets' was a crank, not to say a lunatic.

The revolution of Jehu, who overthrew the house of Ahab about 842, is represented by II Kings 9.1ff. as a triumph of Elisha and the Yahweh-alone movement. The editor wanted to connect Elisha closely with the last great dynasty of Israel. His sources did not do so. A story now lost attributed the anointing of Jehu to Elijah;[141] Elisha disappears from the present story of the revolt after giving the initial command[142] and the remaining text emphasizes the fulfilment of Elijah's prophecies.[143] Jehu's murder of 'all' the worshippers of 'the Baal', his destruction of 'the' temple of 'the Baal', and his successful 'obliteration' of 'the Baal' from Israel[144] are best explicable by the supposition that this Baal was a Phoenician one patronized by Jezebel, and the adherents of the cult were mostly supporters of the house of Ahab.[145] He continued to patronize the idolatrous cults of Bethel and Dan.[147] He even left in Samaria 'the Asherah' made by Ahab[148] – evidently its popularity outweighed its origin. Significantly, the prophet Hosea, a fanatical representative of the Yahweh-alone movement, thought Jehu not a hero but a murderer.[149] Whatever Jehu's motives, his purge seems to have affected only the royal cult. The account in Kings is not concerned with the local cults of Palestinian Baals to which Hosea and the place names and the ostraca testify.[150] Still less does Kings notice the local cults of Yahweh, but we now have the seal of [Ze ka]ryahu, who was priest of Yahweh or Dor about 750.[150a]

Kings associates Jehu not only with Elijah and Elisha but also with Jehonadab ben Rekab, the founder of a sect distinguished by refusal to live in houses, plant fields and vineyards, and drink wine.[151] Such a sect clearly exemplifies the concern to preserve the desert way of life. (Wine is the most consequential and conspicuous characteristic of the diet of the well-watered lands and their peasant population, as opposed to the nomads; it was intimately connected with peasant worship, particularly with the fertility rites which the desert ethos found most offensive.)[152] We have seen that there is no necessary connection between such cultural purism and exclusive devotion to Yahweh, but that in Israelite Palestine the two could easily be joined.[153] That Jehonadab joined them is indicated by II Kings 10.15 ff. which represents Jehu as having persuaded Jehonadab to ride with him into Samaria (i.e., to support his revolt) by inviting him to 'come with me and see my jealousy on behalf of Yahweh'.[154] Jehonadab's 'house' survived as a sect to the time of Jeremiah, an example of the minor parties in the Yahweh-alone movement.[155]

The fall of Ahab's dynasty left his daughter Athalia isolated in Judah. Her sons, King Ahazyahu and his brothers, had been killed by Jehu.[156] She thereupon murdered her grandchildren and held the throne herself for six years.[157] At the end of this time Jehoyada, 'the priest' of the temple of Yahweh in Jerusalem, produced a seven-year-old boy named Joash whom he declared to be one of Ahazyahu's sons, saved as an infant from the massacre and since then concealed in the temple. He won over the Carian (?) mercenaries[158] and other troops of the royal guard, and with their protection anointed his candidate as king in a temple ceremony which secured support from the citizen body.[159] Athalia was murdered and Jehoyada made a contract between Yahweh, the king, and the people, 'to the end that they should be a people belonging to Yahweh', and (another contract?) between the king and the people.[160] 'All' the citizen body 'came to the temple of Baal and tore it down; they broke its altars and images into little pieces and they killed Mattan, the priest of Baal, in front of the altars.' 'And the priest [i.e., Jehoyada] set guards over the temple of Yahweh.' (To prevent reprisals? Or to secure military control of the fortified temple?) Then Jehoyada, with the citizen body and the military, took the king to the palace and set him on his throne.

It is hard to judge how far these proceedings were influenced by a desire to prevent the worship of gods other than Yahweh. Athalia's murders had probably made her unpopular and the rule of the country by a woman – and a foreign woman, at that – must have irritated the men of Judah. If the temple of Baal had been identified with her by her patronage, its destruction may have expressed political resentment.[161] It is reported as a spontaneous act of the citizen body; nothing is said of its having been inspired by Jehoyada, the priest of Yahweh. Also, the destruction stopped with the temple of Baal; Solomon's high places were not touched, nor is any other reform reported. Even if Jehoyada did instigate the destruction of the temple of Baal, this would not prove that he objected to the worship of other gods along with Yahweh in his own temple; he might simply have taken the opportunity to get rid of a competitor.[162] The strongest evidence for exclusiveness is therefore the contract that the people should belong to Yahweh, which looks like an attempt to provide legal foundation for something, possibly a limitation on enslavement (the claim is later used for this purpose in the priestly tradition).[163] Besides this there is a likelihood that a demand for all Israel to worship Yahweh alone would be supported by the priests of the chief temple of Yahweh. This likelihood cannot be pressed; other interests, particularly the concern to appeal to the syncretistic majority, must be reckoned against it. Nevertheless, it is plausible to suppose that at least a group of priests in the temple of Yahweh at Jerusalem was the centre of a party in the Yahweh-alone movement.

The account in Kings of the century following the revolutions of Jehu and Jehoyada (roughly 835–735) contains nothing to indicate the existence of the Yahweh-alone movement;[164] one may suppose that the revolutions satisfied most Yahwists, isolated the extremists, and led to a period of quiescence. Anyhow, the succession of bad kings in Israel and good kings (who did not suppress the high places) in Judah is uninterrupted until, with Ahaz of Judah (c. 735–715), there begins a new period of struggle in which royal policy fluctuates sharply, 'good' and 'bad' kings succeeding each other almost from reign to reign. Ahaz, in contrast to his predecessors, was conspicuously bad;[165] Hezekiah (715–686) was better than any of his predecessors or successors;[166] Manasseh (686–640) was not only worse than any preceding king but even worse than the Amorites dispossessed by Israel;[167] his son, Amon, who followed his policy, was murdered within two years;[168] Josiah (639–609) was again better than any of his predecessors or successors.[169] Josiah's defeat at Megiddo presumably discredited his policy, so the four kings who succeeded him in the last twenty-two years of the kingdom of Judah were all bad.[170]

A new trait in this list, besides the quick alternation of 'good' and 'bad' kings, is the extremity of their alleged goodness or badness. The tradition evidently derives from a period of immoderate party conflict. This conflict must be related to the change in the international situation, brought home to the Judaeans during the reign of Ahaz by the fall of Samaria in 722 to the Assyrians and the exile of thousands of north Israelites to Syria and Mesopotamia.[171] This was an incident in the expansion of Assyrian power which culminated in control of Egypt during the decade from 670 to 660.[172] Before and after these years Judah was a buffer state between Egypt and Assyria and the choice of alliance with one or the other was a matter of life or death. The danger presumably sharpened conflicts over foreign policy, and in the ancient world foreign policy was expressed in religious ceremonies. It is probably no accident that Hezekiah and Josiah, the heroes of the Yahweh-alone tradition, also attempted to maintain the country's independence,[173] while Ahaz, who initiated a policy of close alliance with Assyria, is the first in this series of 'bad' kings who followed the religious practices of the neighbouring peoples. Evidence of Assyrian influence has been found especially in the prominence which cults of the sun, moon, planets, and 'the host of heaven' (the stars?) now have in accounts in Kings.[174] But the sun and moon had long been worshipped in Palestine,[175] and the prominence of the planets and the heavenly host may be due to Babylonian rather than Assyrian influence.[176]

In any event the change cannot be explained entirely by Assyrian influence. On the one hand, the Palestinian cults of Baal and Asherah still take first place in the lists of abominations,[177] and there are newly prominent elements which point to Phoenicia rather than Assyria, notably the burning of children as offerings.[178] On the other hand, the Yahweh-alone party has now come to demand suppression of the high places and limitation of the sacrificial cult of Yahweh to the temple in Jerusalem.[179] This demand explains much of the bitterness of the conflict, which seems to have led to a persecution of the Yahweh-alone party by Manasseh, with numerous executions,[180] and to at least the report that Josiah 'sacrificed' all the priests of the high places in the district of Samaria[181] (this may reflect only the wishful thinking of a pious Yahwist).

Unfortunately, Kings says nothing of the development of this demand, and almost nothing of the parties which supported

it. There is little to indicate the background or supporters of
Hezekiah's reforms.[182] At most the stories of his friendly relations
with Isaiah[183] show that the party which remembered and exaggerated Hezekiah's escapes also preserved and improved Isaiah's
prophecies.[184] 'The men of Hezekiah' are credited with a collection
of proverbs,[185] but beyond this are unknown. Manasseh's
opponents are simply 'Yahweh's servants, the prophets' and
'innocent'.[186] Manasseh's son, Amon, was murdered, but there is
no indication whether or not the murder was motivated by religious
considerations.[187] For the reformation of Josiah we are told that
the text of the contract between the people and Yahweh, which
Josiah undertook to enforce, was 'found' in the temple by 'the
priest' – that is, the chief priest – Hilkiah, who reported the find
to the royal secretary ('scribe') Shaphan, who reported it to the
King, who sent them and several other officials to the prophetess
Huldah, wife of the keeper of the (temple? or court?) wardrobe,
for Yahweh's opinion on the matter.[188] Thereafter the reformation
was begun by a temple ceremony (in which 'all' the elders of Judah
and Jerusalem and 'all' the people participated) and was carried
through by the king.[189] Here we glimpse elements from temple,
court, and prophetic circles acting together, but this is as far as
Kings enables us to go. It contains nothing which indicates that
the Yahweh-alone question was of importance after Josiah's death.
If his reforms were initially unpopular and later discredited by his
defeat, the groups which supported them, although continuing to
exist, were probably reduced to political unimportance.

3. *The material in the books of the prophets.* The development of
religious conflict in Judah, coincident with the rise of Assyrian
power, led to a new concern about prophetic support and written
propaganda for party demands, and hence to a new literature. We
saw above that the party which heroized Hezekiah also preserved
prophecies of Isaiah and made a collection of proverbs. Similarly,
the prophecies of other prophets who supported the Yahweh-alone
position were now (for the first time?) collected and preserved as
separate books. The earliest of the prophets from whom such books
are preserved, Amos, who prophesied about 750, and Hosea, about
740, are almost contemporary with the accession in 745 of Tiglath-
pileser III, who began the Assyrian conquest of the west.[190] The
collection of their prophecies probably took place a generation
later. The party's collection of national legends (the combination

of the J and E material in the Pentateuch) is plausibly attributed to the same period, and we shall see reasons for attributing to it also the earliest of the legal codes which the Yahweh-alone movement produced and/or preserved.

The loose composition of the movement from independent groups of different social backgrounds has been shown by the material in Kings. There were circles in the Judaean court and the Jerusalem temple, among the followers of the prophets, and in isolated sects (the Rekabites). These groups and others whose existence is presumable (e.g., among the levites)[191] sometimes had in common only their exclusive devotion to Yahweh. This state of affairs is reflected by the 'party's' literature, which evidently derives from groups not closely related. Of the prophets credited with books, only Isaiah figures in the historical material used by Kings. This material and the prophets alike have little touch with the legends collected by J and E, and all three mostly ignore the law codes which, for their part, do not until the time of Deuteronomy (621) reflect the demand for limitation of the cult of Yahweh to Jerusalem.

Of the Yahweh-alone groups reflected by these all-but-indepen-dent bodies of literature, some not only preserved the writings of their own members but also adopted and adapted material from the world around, proverbs, for instance. Perhaps most important of these adoptions is the Book of Amos, a prophet of Yahweh, but indifferent to the worship of other gods. He may have referred to such worship incidentally, but seems never to have mentioned it as cause of the disasters he predicted. Those were to be punishments for social injustice.[192] That some prophetic circles of the Yahweh-alone movement adopted, edited and preserved a book of Amos' prophecies shows their approval of his social criticism, henceforth an important theme in their own prophetic literature (a theme of which the court and priestly circles probably did not approve). Another such theme preserved by the prophetic circles but almost certainly disapproved by the priestly ones was that of hostility to the temple, which may have come from the Rekabite group.[193]

The prophecies of Hosea (about 740) are our first evidence of the reasons alleged to justify the demand that Israelites worship Yahweh alone. Hosea's theory derives from the cult of Baal. Identification of Yahweh with Baal has gone so far that Yahweh is generally spoken of as the *ba'al* (husband) of the land and of the people.[194] But the husband of the land should be the giver of crops, that is, the rain god, an unlikely role for a desert deity. Accordingly the settled Israelites, although they identified Yahweh as their Baal, still prayed to the Canaanite Baals for crops.[195] Hosea, too, is convinced that Yahweh is the husband of the people. He does not merely accept this notion intellectually – still less derive it consciously from the Baal cult! For him (and this shows how far the assimilation of Yahweh to Baal must have gone in his childhood environment)[196] it is simply a fact, and a fact of which his conviction is psychopathically vivid. Consequently he sees the worship of other gods as adultery. Hence the violence and confusion of the original prophecies (whence, in part, the corruption of the present text), and Hosea's abnormal compulsion to objectify, by himself marrying an adulteress, Yahweh's marriage with the unfaithful people.[197] This conviction and compulsion are obviously akin to the practices of Palestinian peasant religion, which attempted, by ritual copulation, to objectify the god's relation to the land and so to produce fertility.[198]

Theologically, Hosea's delusion yielded two consequences, expressive of deep ambivalence. On the one hand, Yahweh, as husband, loves Israel, and Israel is to love him in return.[199] On the other hand, Israel is unfaithful and Yahweh's love therefore becomes hatred and is expressed in punishment.[200] The conjunction of these two themes gives the Book of Hosea – and much of later prophetic literature – its peculiar power and peculiar rhetoric. The sudden alternations of love and hatred, the sexual metaphors and the violence of them (Yahweh will strip Israel naked in the sight of her lovers, he will destroy her children, he will give her a miscarrying womb and dry breasts)[201] – these are the language of obsessive passion which has compelled the prophet to express with extraordinary intensity the combination of love and hatred, the need to be loved and to be punished, the will to love and to destroy.

Adultery is the human situation which both provokes and excuses the most intense expression of this disturbing ambivalence. Therefore Hosea's realization of Israel's relationship to Yahweh as adultery[202] appealed profoundly to those disturbed persons who, in ancient Judaea, became prophets.[203] From Hosea's time on, the metaphor is standard,[204] and in Jeremiah 3 and Ezekiel 16 and 23 it is developed with violence (not to say obscenity) recalling the speeches Shakespeare wrote for characters driven by jealousy to the verge of murder.[205]

Jealousy is constantly expressed in the prophetic treatment of the theme of adultery.[206] Curiously, the specific term is late in making its appearance, but once it has appeared it is made by the Deuteronomic school and by Ezekiel the outstanding attribute of Yahweh. Their development of this theme is without parallel from the ancient Near East.[207] It is Yahweh's jealousy which justifies the first of his commandments, 'Thou shalt have no other gods before my face. . . . for I, Yahweh, thy god, am a jealous god.'[208] It is by jealousy that Yahweh is moved to punish his people, and by jealousy he will be moved to restore them and to punish the heathen.[209] His jealousy thus becomes the cause of the End, the denouement of all history, and is declared, not an occasional state of mind, but the essence of his nature: 'Yahweh is a jealous god, his name is "Jealous".'[210]

Consequently the imitation and execution of his jealousy are the peculiar virtue of his followers. Here the meaning of the term goes over from 'jealousy' to 'zeal'; it is often impossible to decide which translation should be preferred. Jealousy is the motive attributed to Elijah.[211] Jehu is said to have represented his massacre of the worshippers of Baal as motivated by jealousy on behalf of Yahweh.[212] Similarly it is used to justify social distinctions: the putative descendants of Phineas claimed to have been promised by Yahweh 'an eternal priesthood' as a reward for a murder committed by Phineas because of such jealousy.[213] In the post-exilic period, this ambiguous virtue was repeatedly claimed by the psalmists.[214] The examples of Phineas and Elijah were specifically recalled by Ben Sira[215] and by the Maccabees,[216] who both claimed and advocated this same virtue. This tradition of the early Maccabees was revived by revolutionaries of the first century AD, 'the zealots'.[217] Both they and the early Maccabees followed the examples of Jehu and Phineas by murdering Jews who conspicuously adopted Gentile ways.[218]

In sum, the demand that Israel worship Yahweh alone was justified by the concept of Yahweh as a loving and therefore a jealous god; this, in turn, was used to justify actions intended to prevent Israelites from worshipping other gods. Therefore the refusal to worship other gods than Yahweh had a triply isolating effect. It prevented participation in Gentile ceremonies; it thus alienated the Gentiles, who expressed their resentment by ostracism, if nothing more; and it found its justification in a concept of Yahweh which in turn justified an attempt to segregate all Israelites, whether or not they wanted segregation.

These social potentialities of Hosea's thought were far from realization in his time. There is nothing in 'his' book, nor in that of any pre-exilic prophet, to indicate membership in an organized party, nor even an organization of prophets. Amos denied that he was a (professional) prophet or a 'son of a prophet' (a member of a prophetic organization).[219] In Jeremiah and Zephaniah 'the prophets' appear as a social class, beside 'the priests'.[220] Jeremiah was a critical member of both classes; had either been an organization he would have been expelled from it.[221]

On the other hand, we can occasionally see that the prophets were not wholly isolated, but had supporters in the society around them. Isaiah had friends to whom he could turn for assistance in prophetic actions, and he seems to have had disciples.[222] Jeremiah had a follower, Baruch, and was protected by individuals among the 'elders', royal officials and members of the royal household.[223] Of his supporters, Ahikam ben Shapan, Elasah ben Shaphan, Gemariah ben Shaphan and Gemariah ben Hilkiah[224] are probably the sons of Shaphan the royal secretary and Hilkiah the chief priest, who 'found' and brought to King Josiah's attention the contract which was the basis of his reforms.[225] Ahikam ben Shaphan had then been old enough to be a member, along with his father, of the delegation Josiah sent to the prophetess Huldah to get Yahweh's opinion of the document.[226] Another member of that delegation had been Achbor ben Micaiah, and we find an Elnathan ben Achbor, probably his son, among Jeremiah's protectors.[227] After the fall of Jerusalem the Babylonians entrusted Jeremiah for safekeeping to Gedaliah ben Ahikam ben Shaphan, whom they also made governor of Judah.[228] We may think of the families of Shaphan, Hilkiah and Achbor, and other great families, as the backbone of the Yahweh-alone party, much as the great Whig families of England were the backbone of that unorganized but definite party.[229]

Accordingly, Jeremiah's protestations that he stands alone are exaggerations.[230] But among the priests and particularly among the prophets he seems to have been almost a minority of one.[231] Here again the evidence is not conclusive; we have still to reckon with the independence of the groups from which our documents derive. Jeremiah and Ezekiel, for instance, though contemporary, ignore each other. Nevertheless, Jeremiah certainly felt almost isolated, and this confirms our judgment that the Yahweh-alone party was a small minority in relation to those who worshipped other gods as well as Yahweh.

From this fact follows what should be obvious, that the whole of Israelite religious and political history cannot be accounted for merely by the conflict between these two 'parties'. Many other factors were at work, and this book makes no pretence to give an account of them or to be a complete 'History of Israel'. Many persons, especially members of the majority, probably never thought of themselves as members of any party at all; they simply followed the customs of their own communities and the teachings of the religious figures they revered. But as Jeremiah's history clearly shows, there were some upper class circles, perhaps with popular followings, whose members were clearly aware of the conflict and co-operated with or opposed each other in ways most conveniently described by party terminology. What this chapter tries to show is that among such circles the Yahweh-alone party played a decisive role in shaping the Old Testament.

For example, the conflict between the Yahweh-alone party and the majority of the prophets, the priests and the people accounts for one of the most important, peculiar and neglected characteristics of the Old Testament: the representation of the Israelites as constantly in conflict with the demands of their own religion. This conflict is projected back to the beginning of Mosaic legislation and, indeed, before. As the speech of Stephen, in Acts 7, points out, Joseph is sold by his brethren and Moses is rejected by his people. Moses himself resists the command of Yahweh;[232] the stories of the wandering in the wilderness deal again and again with the people's refusal to obey the divine commands; the stories of the judges and of the kings treat the history of the settlement in Palestine as a constant recurrence of conflicts between the will of the people or the policy of their rulers and the will of Yahweh. And the prophets continually harp on the same theme. There is nothing comparable to this in any other religious literature from the ancient Mediterranean or Mesopotamian worlds. Occasional conflicts between rulers and gods are of course common, and divine punishment of a people for something or other is not rare.[233] But these are represented as occasional and exceptional events. That constantly recurrent national apostasy should be made the leit-motif of an entire literature is something unparalleled in antiquity; it requires explanation. Part of the explanation may be found in the necessity of explaining the Assyrian and Babylonian conquests, which shaped the selection of the prophets and the edition of the histories. But the tradition goes back farther than that. It is evidently the tradition of a minority party which has lived its life in conflict with the majority of its people and has seen its brief moments of victory again and again reversed by the return of the majority to their traditional ways. In this respect the material from the national legends (of which the collection and development ran from the Assyrian period far down into post-exilic times)[234] confirms the impression derived from the material in Kings and in the books of the prophets.

Nevertheless, we must beware of exaggerating the import of the evidence, and particularly of that from the Book of Jeremiah, for in his time the division between syncretists and worshippers of Yahweh alone was crossed by a political split between pro-Babylonians and pro-Egyptians. Many of the Yahweh-alone groups may have belonged to the pro-Egyptian political party, to which Jeremiah was anathema.[235] And other groups, the Rekabites for instance, although certainly adherents of the Yahweh-alone movement, and in touch with Jeremiah,[236] represented positions so extreme that they scarcely counted for much in the political struggle. Accordingly we must think of the movement, down to the exile, as composed of a number of groups differing in political policy and social affiliation, but agreed that Israelites should worship only Yahweh and therefore able to co-operate for this purpose and to compromise on other matters.

4. *The material in the pre-exilic law codes.* The first great document of this capacity for co-operation is the core of the Book of Deuteronomy (at least some parts of the introductory chapters and much of chapters 12–26 and 28).[237] This was not, indeed, the first law code produced or adopted within the Yahweh-alone movement; the 'covenant code' in Exodus 21–23 is certainly older,[238] and brief, mnemonic collections of precepts like the ten commandments may be older yet. But as their phraseology shows, these older collections have been so glossed by Deuteronomic editors that it would be foolhardy to rely on their details as evidence

of the make-up or doctrine of the Yahweh-alone party before the rise of the Deuteronomic school.[239] The Yahweh-alone material in them is suspect, and the undoubtedly ancient material does not illuminate the history of the party.

Similarly, secure results are hardly to be reached by source analysis of the core of Deuteronomy. Although secondary developments can sometimes be clearly distinguished,[240] they are generally so close to the original in outlook, style and, probably, time[241] that we had better be content to take the whole of the core as evidence of the make-up and objectives of the Yahweh-alone movement during the century before the document was 'found' in the reign of Josiah (in 621 BC). That it was drastically edited just before being 'found' is probable, and the edition probably reflected the interests and opinions of the chief priest Hilkiah, who 'found' it.[242]

These suppositions are confirmed by the content of the work. In the interest of the Jerusalem priesthood all shrines outside Jerusalem were outlawed, the duty of pilgrimage to Jerusalem was emphasized, the perquisites of the priesthood were confirmed, and the Jerusalem priesthood was declared the highest judicial authority in the land.[243]

But the work was planned to appeal to other circles of the Yahweh-alone party, too. The common party concern was represented by the provision that the high places should be suppressed and by repeated prohibition of the worship of other gods and orders to destroy their sanctuaries and exterminate their worshippers (not an unimportant provision if made when Josiah was about to attempt the conquest of Palestine).[244]

Ever since their adoption of Amos, some groups of the Yahweh-alone party had been concerned for the poor; their interest is reflected in Deuteronomy by many charitable laws[245] – no doubt intended to secure the support of the lower classes for the proposed reform.

The Yahweh-alone movement probably had followers among the levites – a *soi-disant* Israelite tribe which had come to claim a monopoly of the priestly functions – since Deuteronomic laws regularly insist that all priests must be levites,[246] and also provide for the levites along with the poor. This provision may in part anticipate the consequences of the closing of the rural shrines, where many of the levites were priests, but it probably in larger part reflects the existence of an extensive class of unemployed levites whose priesthood was only potential.[247] There is also a provision that levites who wish to come to Jerusalem may officiate at the temple there.[248] (This provision the Jerusalem priesthood – once it had secured the suppression of the other shrines – refused to honour.[249])

The nomadic-ascetic circles in the Yahweh-alone party, with their hostility to Canaanite culture, must have been gratified by the Deuteronomic prohibition of images and of peasant fertility rites,[250] and by the charitable laws so hard on landowners and so careful to protect the migratory labourer.[251] From these circles, too, may have come the appeal to Moses, the great figure of nomadic legend (as opposed to the patriarchs, who were associated with the Palestinian peasant shrines), and the emphasis on the deliverance from Egypt (a tradition of the nomads). The appeal to antiquity and to ancient national traditions was typical of the time.[252]

The interests of the party's prophetic circles are represented by the prohibition of means other than prophecy for divining the future.[253] Moses is made the example of the true prophet and it is foretold that another prophet like him will be raised (presumably, in each generation)[254] as the spokesman of Yahweh for the guidance of the people. But punishment of anyone who disobeys a prophet is left to Yahweh, and a prophet whose prophecies do not come true is to be put to death.[255] Evidently this code came from the Jerusalem priesthood rather than the prophets; no major prophet, but only an obscure prophetess (wife of a temple or court official), could be found to approve it.[256]

Finally, besides the Yahweh-alone party, the whole population of Jerusalem stood to profit from the centralization of the cult there and particularly from a law requiring that one tenth of the nation's agricultural income be consumed there. If the food could not be brought in kind it must be sold and the money spent in Jerusalem, to the obvious advantage of the Jerusalem merchants.[257]

The absence of any provision obviously designed to appeal to the court is surprising. King Josiah may have had a practical interest in the centralization of the cult as a means of strengthening his control of the country,[258] he may have needed the support of the Jerusalem priesthood and the Yahweh-alone party, or he may have been moved by superstitious fear, as the text reports.[259] He was only twenty-six and, if we can judge from his later attempt to stop the Egyptian army, not very intelligent.[260]

This fusion of practical interests produced only a temporary alliance; after Josiah's death the temple and court went back to syncretism. More important was the fusion of religious themes effected by the Deuteronomist and the writers of the Deuteronomic school – writers who imitated the style of the Deuteronomist and continued, through the following centuries, to edit and expand both his work and other documents of pre-exilic literature. The exact limits of the documents these writers used and of the collections they produced are disputed,[261] but the general result of their work is clear: it built into a single system (if not into a single literary structure) the legends and history of the people, their laws and customs, and the teachings of those prophets who had demanded the worship of Yahweh alone.

At the heart of the system is the teaching of the Yahweh-alone prophets: Yahweh's jealous love for Israel.[262]

The history and legends of the people were made proofs by example of this prophetic teaching: they were made to show Yahweh's love, jealousy, power, and determination to reward or punish as the people did or did not worship him alone. The moral – therefore it is best to worship him alone – was drawn at length.[263] The great examples of Israel's unfaithfulness and Yahweh's revenge were the history and destruction of the northern kingdom.[264] Therefore, even before the Babylonian conquest, the Deuteronomists had an apologetic theodicy, explaining why Israel fared so badly in spite of Yahweh's love for her. A special application of this theodicy is to be seen in the passages which put the blame for the fall of Judah on the wickedness of Manasseh.[265] These are attempts to explain why the reforms of Josiah did not succeed – Manasseh's wickedness had already made Yahweh's determination to destroy the country irrevocable. It seems that the syncretistic party said similar things about Josiah's wickedness: the wrath of the gods whose worship he prohibited was not appeased even by the resumption of their cults in the following reigns.[266] After the Babylonian conquest this apologetic concern was strengthened[267] and the whole of the people's history, from Sinai on, was represented by the Yahweh-alone party as repeated provocations of Yahweh's anger. As remarked above, this representation was not mere theological invention. It reflected the experience of a repeatedly disappointed minority. But once the theory was enunciated it lived on independently and continued to be expressed in Deuteronomic language (for instance, in the post-exilic confessions of sin).[268]

The laws and customs of the people were also subordinated, in the Deuteronomic system, to the demand that the people love and worship Yahweh alone. They were conceived as the means by which love was to be expressed and exclusive worship maintained. To conjoin them with the history of the people, the Deuteronomist resorted to legends of a contract between the people and Yahweh. Such legends seem to have been common in Palestine; the Old Testament contains many stories of contracts of similar forms of relationship between various deities and the Israelites or their alleged ancestors.[269] The Deuteronomist seems to have taken advantage of one of these stories (that of a contract made at Horeb)[270] to represent his work as the content of the contract – a review by Moses of the laws which the people had undertaken to observe, the rewards Yahweh had undertaken to give for observance, and the penalties which would follow Israel's non-performance.[271] Thus the relationship between the people and the god, though conceived as love, came to be expressed as law.

The laws which the people were obligated to observe by this Deuteronomic contract were of various origins. Mentioned above were those which reflected the immediate interests of the Jerusalem priesthood, the poor, the levites, the nomadic-ascetic circles, the prophets, and the population of Jerusalem. Besides these there are many laws which apparently served nobody's immediate interests and are therefore more likely to represent tradition. Outstanding among these are elements from priestly law – provisions about purity, sacrificial practices, festivals, marriage and sexual offences, inheritance, asylum and atonement for murder, legal evidence, and so on. These strengthen the impression that the compilers and editors of the code were members of the Jerusalem priesthood.

All the laws in Deuteronomy are dominated by the Yahweh-alone tradition. It has encased them in a framework which declares, at the beginning and end of the code, that their object is to ensure the love of Yahweh and the worship of him alone.[272] It has interpolated and expounded them with a string of comments to the same effect.[273] It has added many laws from its own tradition or invention, and of these the most elaborated and most emphatically repeated are the laws which prohibit the worship of other gods and order the destruction of their shrines, the extermination of their worshippers, and the execution of any Israelite who either practises or recommends their worship.[274]

Moreover, the Deuteronomist sets out to make Israel a separate and peculiar people. Intermarriage with Gentiles is prohibited when it may lead to worship of alien gods.[275] The peculiar customs of Israelites are to be observed in order to set them off from the peoples round about.[276] Here is the reason for taking over so much of the priestly law, especially of its taboos and purity rules. The intent to separate Israel from the Gentiles is also one expression of a concern for purity as the condition and result of the people's relation to Yahweh.[277] To pertetuate this relation and preserve this purity the legislator intends to create a peculiar, Israelite, Yahwist, and only Yahwist way of life. For this purpose he remodels the liturgy as well as the law. The passover and the presentation of the first fruits are made commemorations of the love of Yahweh for his people, whence his deliverance of them, whence their duty to worship him alone.[278]

This purpose of the legislator accounts for much of the hortatory material in Deuteronomy and for the code's failure to cover the whole field of law. It is presented as a sermon; it has – in main outline and in many brief passages – the literary form of one: the laws are subordinated to the preacher's purpose.[279] They are therefore limited to the cult law, that is, the rules which the deity requires his worshippers to observe; they are not intended to be a complete code of civil law. They are, however, intended to be a code – the code of a way of life for which sufficient prescriptions are given to ensure its peculiarity. This purpose is shown by the introduction, which requires that these commandments be repeated morning and night, meditated and memorized, and taught to one's children.[280] The concern for memorization and teaching suggests[281] a legal tradition which differed from that of the surrounding society. The laws must be preserved with such effort because they will not be taught by the day-to-day routine of the surrounding world. Knowledge of them will distinguish the followers of this legislator from ordinary men.[282]

Whether or not such a sectarian legal tradition lay behind the original core of Deuteronomy, or was anticipated by its author, it was certainly produced by his work. Within a dozen years Josiah was dead and his reform with him (609 BC). Within forty years the kingdom of Judah was destroyed by the Babylonians (587 BC) and the Judaeans became a sprinkling of minority groups in a world of alien ways and alien gods. In this world, the commandment to learn and to teach the law became all-important for the preservation of the law and for the preservation of the Judaeans' peculiarity. Most of them, probably, did not try to preserve their peculiarity. But those determined to worship only Yahweh, and especially those who accepted the Deuteronomic rule limiting his sacrificial cult to Jerusalem, now found in the study and teaching of the law the backbone of their religion. Abstention from work every seventh day was one of the Israelite customs of which observance was required by the law. On this free day they began to meet in private houses for prayer to Yahweh, praise of him, and reading of his law.[283]

With this appearance of the beginnings of synagogue worship – a type of worship quite different from the sacrificial cult of the temples – the Yahweh-alone party became in effect a new religion, and a new kind of religion. From the Israelites had emerged that peculiar people who called themselves *Israel* and were later to be called *the Jews* – a people of many different social groups and political affiliations, united by compromise in minor matters, but united essentially by its agreement to worship Yahweh alone, united by its contempt for all other gods (a contempt soon expressed as denial of their existence), united by its consequent alienation from all other peoples (and by their consequent hostility), united by its conviction of Yahweh's love and of his jealousy, united by its consequent self-imposed segregation, united by its legendary and historical tradition (treated as a series of examples of Yahweh's love and punishment), and united by its peculiar customs and its law – a law conceived as the declaration of Yahweh's will, as the terms of a contract with him which Israel is obligated to obey, as the rules of a discipline by which Israel is purified for his love, as the rules of a life which manifests and celebrates his love, and as the central element of a literary and oral tradition which each succeeding generation must successively learn and teach.[284]

3

'Hellenization'

The four hundred and twenty years between Nebuchadnezzar's destruction of Jerusalem (587) and the outbreak of the Maccabaean revolt (167) saw an immense cultural change, not only in Palestine, but throughout the Near East. This change is usually described as 'hellenization'. The term is unfortunate, since it suggests that the change was due entirely to imitation of Greek ways. That was not the case, but much of the change was due to Greek influence and the dominant elements in some aspects of the resultant culture – notably in language, in design and decoration, in business, in scholarship, and in technology – were Greek. Therefore we shall begin our study of the hellenization of Palestine with an account of the ways in which Greek influence was exercised in the country.

Trade between Palestine and Greek lands began in remote antiquity and was considerable in the late bronze age.[1] The invasions at the end of the second millennium doubtless interfered with it, but did not wholly interrupt it.[2] Among the invaders, the Philistines were themselves a seagoing people in touch with the Greeks.[3] Gaza is persistently associated by legend with Crete, and there is linguistic and archaeological evidence to support the legend.[4]

Throughout the first millennium BC trade was supplemented by the continuous emigration of Greeks and other Aegaean peoples to serve as mercenaries in the pay of Near Eastern rulers. David's mercenaries 'the Cherethites and the Pelethites' have been conjecturally identified as 'the Cretans and the Philistines' and the conjecture is not implausible.[5] The Carian (or Cretan?) mercenaries of Athalia put Joash on the throne about 840,[6] and two centuries later Greek adventurers probably played a considerable part in Egyptian resistance to Assyria.[7] A legend in Herodotus reports that the Egyptian king Psammetichus I, in the second half of the seventh century, owed his conquest of the country to his alliance with them.[8] There were undoubtedly many Greeks in the army with which Necho, the son of Psammetichus, defeated and killed King Josiah of Judah in 609. (Josiah's death, as we saw above, put an end to the Deuteronomic reform. And Josiah himself had some Greek mercenaries. There were 'Kittim' in the Judaean fortress at Arad in Josiah's time, and seventh-century Greek pottery has been found in the central Negeb.[9]). Necho celebrated his victories by sending an offering to the temple of Apollo in the territory of Miletus.[10] Necho's grandson, Apries, who tried to relieve the siege of Jerusalem by sending an army into Palestine in 588,[11] had some 30,000 Greeks in his service, if Herodotus (II.163) is to be believed. The Jews who fled from Palestine to Egypt after the fall of Jerusalem, therefore, fled to a land where Greek influence was long-established and of great importance. Moreover, in one particular town to which they fled (Tahpanhes) the Pharaoh Psammetichus had established a settlement of Greek mercenaries.[12] Nor was Greek influence absent from Mesopotamia. Nebuchadnezzar, too, had Greek mercenaries in his army, one of them the brother of the poet Alcaeus, who returned to tell of the fall of Ascalon, of which the capture by Nebuchadnezzar in 604 was also celebrated by Jeremiah.[13] A Babylonian text recording a payment of oil to Jehoiakin, 'the son of the King of Judah', records similar payments to seven Greek carpenters.[14]

With the Persian conquest, Palestine became part of an empire which included Greek territories in Asia Minor and raised its army by conscription from its territories. Greek conscripts certainly played a large part in the Persian army.[15] Some were probably stationed in Palestine, since Palestine was important in Persian military history.[16] The country became the line of communications for the Persians when they conquered Egypt (525-521) and, thereafter, whenever they had to suppress revolts there (520?, 486–484, 460–449, 445?, 414–404).[17] In spite of the Persian conquest Greek influence remained strong in Egypt and Greek traders, mercenaries, and tourists were common there.[18] The revolt of 460–449 was supported by the Athenians who were for some time masters of the country and held out for six years; the minimal figure for their expeditionary force in Egypt is 8,000; the maximal, 50,000.[19] They were also fighting on the Palestine-Syrian coast; it has even been suggested, albeit on dubious evidence, that they seized Dora, about 60 miles north-west of Jerusalem, as a base for their operations.[20] Though eventually defeated, the Athenians continued to have important connections with Egypt and probably supported Egyptian rebels again in the 440s.[21] The Persians finally lost Egypt in 404–401;[22] thereafter, Palestine was frontier territory and was garrisoned accordingly.[23] The remains of a string of Persian forts run for some fifteen miles across country south of Gaza.[24] The Persian garrison at Gaza was strong enough and loyal enough to hold up Alexander by three months of suicidal resistance.[25] But Palestine was not only a frontier district for the Persians, it was also their base for repeated attempts to reconquer Egypt (385–383, 374–370, 357[?],[26] 350), which succeeded only in 343.

About 420 the Persians began the practice of employing Greek mercenaries, as well as Greek conscripts.[27] These mercenary forces soon became large. During the years from 379 to 374, some 12,000 mercenaries (at least)[28] were collected in Galilee, in preparation for the campaign against Egypt. The campaign, based on Akko, dragged on for several years, then failed, and the Greek forces were left in Akko under the command of a Greek general.[29] Egypt, at the same time, was using large numbers of Greeks in its forces. In 360 the Spartan king, Agesilaus, with 1,000 Spartans, 10,000 other Greek mercenaries, and a supporting Greek fleet, took part in a Graeco-Egyptian occupation of Palestine.[30] Jerusalem probably participated in this revolt, since it seems to have issued silver coinage in the name of its own territory and authorities; in the Achaemenid empire such coinage was normally issued only by Persian authorities and autonomous cities.[31] Some time within the next ten or fifteen years both Jerusalem and Jericho were taken and punished by Artaxerxes III,[32] whose forces probably included a large Greek contingent – at his conquest of Egypt in 343 he had 1,000 Thebans, 3,000 Argives, and 6,000 Asian Greeks, besides 4,000 Greeks of unspecified origin.[33]

Along with this military penetration by Greek forces went economic and cultural penetration by Greek traders, Greek merchandise, and Greek ways. Palestine was criss-crossed by trade routes – not only those from Egypt to Phoenicia, Syria, and Babylonia, but also those from Damascus, Gerrha on the Persian Gulf, and South Arabia, to the coastal ports of the Mediterranean. Travel was slow and any town or village along the way might serve as an overnight stopping place. The land through which these routes ran could hardly preserve an uncontaminated population or an isolated cultural tradition.

The penetration of the country by foreign elements is demonstrated by the archaeological evidence, which shows that there were Greek settlements along the coast in the late seventh century,[34] and even the small towns of the central part of the country had trading connections with Greece in the seventh century.[35] Such connections became frequent in the sixth century.[36] Summarizing the finds at Beth Zur – a few miles south of Jerusalem – Sellers writes: 'Culturally, from the early part of the fifth century on, Palestine was dominated by Greece. The few objects showing Persian influence are almost negligible. There is no change in pottery forms or other objects at the coming of Alexander. That conqueror did not introduce Greek culture into Palestine . . . he found . . . it there.'[37] That Beth Zur was not exceptional has been shown by Rostovtzeff's survey of the evidence from the whole Near East, which led him to conclude that the demand for Greek wares in Palestine, Phoenicia, and Syria reached a peak in the fifth century BC. Thereafter, local manufacturers in these countries took to producing goods of Hellenistic style, and the imports from Greece declined until, after Alexander's conquest, the large-scale settlement of Greeks throughout the area led to a renewed demand for genuine Greek merchandise.[38]

Where Greek merchandise went, Greek merchants followed. Some were resident in Akko in the days of Demosthenes (384–322),[39] and Joel, perhaps a contemporary of Demosthenes, complains of the frequency of foreigners passing through Jerusalem (4.17b). Probably for their trade, but also for domestic use, the authorities of Jerusalem (?) began in the fifth century to issue coins modelled on Hellenistic and Greek types.[40] Issuance was continued in the fourth century.[41] It is now generally recognized 'that Alexander chose the Attic standard [of currency] not only in view of its popularity in the Aegaean world, but also because it was widely used alongside of the Persian in the Persian Empire, especially in Palestine'.[42]

Pottery and coinage were not the only means by which Greek iconography was introduced to the country. Along with coins went seals. A representative group from the Persian period, in the Palestine Archaeological Museum, Jerusalem, includes three representations of Heracles, one of a dancing satyr, two of males 'half-running' in Greek archaic style (one of them winged), and one of a Persian holding a phallus (Gallery Book: 'an object like a stick').[43] Commenting on the bullae and signets from Wadi Daliyeh, Cross writes: 'One is particularly struck with the vivacity of Attic Greek influences in the glyptic art of Samaria in the era before the coming of Alexander.'[44] Besides such glyptic representations, Greek statuettes of deities were popular. The same museum displays, from the sixth and early fifth centuries, a seated goddess of Greek style (Demeter?), a head of Athena, a reclining male holding a rhyton (like the representations of the heroized dead on Greek tomb reliefs), two heads of Heracles, a mask of Kore (Rhodian), two 'Astarte' figurines showing Greek influence, two 'mother goddesses' (pregnant woman, Cypriot-Egyptian), and an Isis with Horus who holds a stalk of wheat reminiscent of Eleusinian symbolism.[45] These figurines come not only from the coastal area (Athlit, Tell es-Safi) but also from inland sites (Lachish, Megiddo, Beth Shan). A number of them show Greek influence mediated through or combined with traits from near eastern countries; of this we shall speak later.

After Alexander's conquest in 332, both military and economic penetration were intensified. As an example of military penetration, consider the history of Jerusalem. The city must have made its submission to some body of Alexander's forces and have been occupied by them for a short time, at least.[46] After Alexander's death in 323, his empire was carved up by his generals, and Ptolemy, who got Egypt, acquired Palestine. His descendants held it until 198. In the Ptolemaic period Jerusalem was captured ten or twelve times,[47] and was often occupied for considerable periods by Greek garrisons. In particular, it almost certainly had a garrison in the years from 320 to 290: Josephus speaks of Ptolemy I as governing the city harshly, which supposes some body of troops to enforce his decrees.[48] Other garrisons in 218 and 199 are mentioned.[49] A garrison was there in the time of Antiochus Epiphanes – sometime after 175 – *before* the troubles leading to the Maccabaean revolt began.[50] Further, the city was presumably an important base for the Ptolemaic forces – and therefore garrisoned by them – during their chronic war with their northern neighbours, the Seleucids, a war which raged intermittently from 280 to 241.[51] Launey, from exhaustive studies of Hellenistic military methods, has concluded that 'the presence of a garrison composed of aliens is a characteristic and quasi-permanent trait of Hellenistic cities', not only of those in Asia Minor, Syria, Palestine, and Egypt (where he takes the presence of a part of the royal army as 'normal'), but even of the cities in Greece – and from the histories of these he demonstrates his rule.[52]

The breakdown of established standards which accompanies military occupation by aliens need hardly be mentioned. It seems worth while, however, to emphasize that armies travelled – on land – almost entirely by foot, and consequently spread all over the country, and were in intimate contact with the population. This was inevitable, for even friendly armies had to live off the country – like friendly swarms of locusts.[53] Launey remarks the frequency with which soldiers acquired civic rights in the area where they were stationed, the custom of camping and even wintering in the countryside, which brought the armies in close touch with the rural population, and the custom by which both passing armies and permanent garrisons billeted their soldiers in civilian families.[54] A general of Antiochus III shortly after 200 protests the billeting of royal troops in his villages in Galilee by Ptolemy, son of Thraseas, and also complains of the damage done by transient troops who stopped to rest in the villages.[55]

Further, the Hellenistic army was not an exclusively military group. Rather – especially in the Seleucid Empire – it was an international organization, composed of troops from all peoples, centred upon a Graeco-Macedonian core and commanded in Greek. These troops formed an economic and social centre, followed by purchasers (of booty, slaves, etc.) and vendors and money-changers and women and their children and servants and slaves and miscellaneous hangers-on. An army was a nomadic city, constantly interchanging its population with that of the countries through which it travelled, receiving both individuals and groups as accretions, and giving back both individual deserters and whole colonies, which were detached from it to form or reform cities in strategic points.[56] In the 260 years from Alexander's death to the conquest of Jerusalem by the Roman general Pompey, there were at least 200 campaigns fought in or across Palestine.[57] This military history alone shows that no part of the country can have escaped Greek influence.

But this military history was now supplemented by the Greek[58] policies of military colonization and the foundation of cities. The importance of these has not always been understood correctly.[39] 'Foundation' was often no more than a legal and financial transaction: the city, for a price, got the right to call itself after some member of the royal family, to revise its constitution along Greek lines, and to govern itself by its own representatives, elected according to the revised system. It thus got rid of the royal civil governor and his staff – no small saving, both in money and in face, even though the royal military commander, treasury officials, and the like remained.[60] Also, the opportunity to revise the constitution was an opportunity to change the franchise and so diminish the civil rights of the opposition. Since factional quarrels were endemic in Hellenistic cities, this opportunity was not overlooked. Kings who needed money were therefore able to persuade many cities to accept such 'foundation'. Antiochus Epiphanes founded half a dozen cities in Palestine and Trans-Jordan alone, most of them self-governing before his foundation.[61] His efforts were not always taken kindly. In II Maccabees 4.7–5.26 and I Maccabees 1.11–64 we have accounts (from the opposition!) of the events which attended his foundation of Antioch-in-Judaea (formerly Jerusalem).[62]

On the other hand, foundation might mean the creation of an entirely new city on a site formerly empty or occupied only by a village. The great examples of this were Alexandria and Antioch. It seems that no Palestinian city of the first importance was founded in this way before the Herodian period,[63] but a number of minor places[64] – and, in Trans-Jordan, some considerable cities, notably Dium, Pella, and Gerasa[65] – may have been. Also, Gaza and Samaria were destroyed by the forces of Alexander or his successors and re-built, so as to be practically new foundations.[66]

Between these extremes, many procedures were possible. In general, however, a city might hope to get, by 'foundation', not only a Greek (usually dynastic) name, a constitution of Greek form providing for government by elected representatives, and autonomy in domestic, civil affairs, but also help with municipal building (especially fortification) and perhaps a grant of territory around the city.[67] However, many cities without either Greek or dynastic names seemed to have enjoyed these privileges (Ascalon, Joppa, etc.). In particular, almost all of them seem to have had considerable territories under their authority and therefore subject to the influence of their citizens. Moreover, when records become sufficient to make a check possible, we find similar privileges extended even to villages, which often were fortified, held public lands from which they received income, had important buildings (baths, markets, etc.), and had a good deal to say as to the administration of their own affairs – their inscriptions refer not only to the royal officer in charge but also to a series of municipal magistrates and occasionally to a local council or assembly.[68] We find such fortified villages already in the first century AD,[69] and from the earlier period we find a string of Greek place names for places which can never have been more than villages, but which evidently had Greek settlers and therefore may have had Greek cultural forms.[70] This suggests that the difference between 'cities' and towns cannot have been sharp, and the same conclusion is suggested by Josephus' carelessness in describing places now as cities and again as villages,[71] and by the fact that rabbinic Hebrew never developed or adopted a special word for 'city' in the Greek sense, but used 'ir for cities, towns, and villages alike.[72]

Thus the cities founded by the Hellenistic dynasts formed no distinct class by themselves – nothing like the later Roman colonies – but were only one aspect of a policy intended to provide for the Greek followers of the kings and to establish centres of loyal population throughout the land. That there was no intention of limiting such centres to the cities is proved by the settlement of old soldiers through the countryside as small landholders – *cleruchs* – in rural colonies. The Ptolemies used this method widely in Egypt and (probably) in Palestine. We know of one such colony in Trans-Jordan, at Birta; Rostovtzeff has inferred another, somewhere near Gaza, and he remarks that Ptolemy III Euergetes threatened to turn the city land of Jerusalem into small holdings and send cleruchs to occupy it.[73]

Therefore the contrast commonly drawn between the Greek cities and the Semitic countryside has been exaggerated. The countryside was permeated by Greek elements and influences. They came to it not only through military operations and military and municipal settlements but also through economic and administrative channels. Both administrative and economic interests were represented for example, by Zeno, an agent of Apollonius, the finance minister of Ptolemy II. In 259–258 BC Zeno visited Gaza, Marisa, Jamnia, Strato's Tower, Jerusalem, Jericho, Birta, Abila, several towns in the Hauran, Kadesh, Beth Anath,[74] and Ptolemais. Further, his correspondence shows him in touch with Ascalon, Joppa, Pegai, Tyre, Sidon, Berytos, Tripolis, Adora, and Philadelphia.[75] In many of these places he had agents. In so far as these represented the government (and not the private interests of Apollonius and Zeno) they were probably members of the special staff of the royal department of finance, and so apart from the regular administration, which was itself threefold: the country seems to have been divided into a number of major districts, each of which had a civil administrator and his subordinates, a military commander in charge of the troops quartered there, and a revenue officer in charge of the tax collectors.[76] (This last branch of the government was by no means the least. The activities of tax collectors sometimes amounted to small military campaigns: Josephus gives us a picture of one setting out with 2,000 troops and beginning his operations by the capture of Ascalon.)[77] Besides these three main branches, there were: 1. special officers of the king or of his great ministers – as remarked above, Zeno belonged to this class; 2. a judiciary system of some sort;[78] 3. officials of special royal institutions, for example, the royal bank; 4. the secret service, using a body of informers to whose efficiency Tarn attributes Ecclesiastes 10.20, 'Even in your thought (?) do not curse the King, . . . for a bird of the air will carry your voice'; 5. officials of the local administrative units (cities, temples, etc.) who were either appointed or confirmed by the royal government. Thus in Jerusalem, just before the outbreak of the Maccabaean revolt, the government's chief officers were a civil administrator (Philip, the Phrygian), a military commander (Appollonius) with 22,000 men, a chief tax collector (this same Apollonius), a special royal commissioner to oversee the religious reformation, and the high priest (Menelaus) who was a royal appointee.[79] In Jamnia (?) in 259 BC we find a special royal representative, two officers of the garrison, the chief paymaster, a judge, and a clerk.[80] The papyrus which gives us the information for Jamnia is not a complete roster of the officials of the town but merely a business document which happens to mention a few of them.

Zeno's letters testify not only to this omnipresent administrative system but to business and banking connections equally extensive. Wherever he went, he acted as a purchasing agent. He also kept an eye on the interests of Egyptian Greeks who had loaned money to Palestinian villagers. All this business, of course, was conducted in Greek, and Bickerman has admirably summed up the gist of the linguistic evidence in his statement that 'even in the villages there must have been persons able to draft a contract in Greek, or to write a request in the style required for a Greek petition'.[81]

Many of the villages must have been located in estates owned by the king or by great courtiers and managed, therefore, by their enterprising Greek appointees. Such estates had been given already by the Persian kings to persons they wished to favour, among them Greeks.[82] In Zeno's day we know of an estate owned by Apollonius at Beth Anath in Galilee.[83] Evidence for many other such estates, from the Maccabaean and later periods, has been collected by Herz, *Grossgrundbesitz*.[84] Estate management was made a science in the Hellenistic period; consequently these large holdings and the larger royal domains, which were managed by similar appointees, served as centres for the dissemination of the Greek language, Greek technical advances and the Greek businessman's attitude.[85]

In all this we have discussed only the direct ways by which Greek influence came to Palestine. But in the Persian period, especially, the indirect influence of Greek culture – that exercised through neighbouring peoples – must have been even greater than that exercised directly by Greeks. To the north of Palestine, Tyre and Sidon had been profoundly penetrated by Greek influence long before the fifth century (when, for instance, they began to buy even their copies of Egyptian sarcophagi from Greek factories).[86] Prior to Alexander's conquest they seem to have controlled the coastal plain of Palestine and to have established trading colonies in the cities of the central mountains.[87] There was a Tyrian colony in Jerusalem in the days of Nehemiah (13.16). In Marisa there was a colony of *soi disant* Sidonians, of which the preserved remains date from the third to second centuries BC and are full of imitations of Greek material.[88] The Samaritans of Shechem are represented by Josephus as calling themselves Sidonians – especially when they asked permission to dedicate the temple on Mt Gerizim to Zeus Hellenios.[89] Whatever truth there is in the story,[90] it testifies to a tradition of Sidonian influence on the city. Coins minted in Phoenicia – especially in Tyre – and in the Palestinian coastal cities are frequent in Palestinian and Transjordanian sites from the end of the fifth century on.[91] Tyrian coins are prominent in the recent finds from fourth-century Samaria, and they were the customary currency both in Palestine and in Trans-Jordan throughout the Ptolemaic period (300–200 BC).[92] From a yet later period, a hoard of them has been found at Qumran. For Palestinian Judaism the general rabbinic rule reads: 'The money mentioned by the Law [in specifying penalties, etc.] is always Tyrian money. What is Tyrian money? It is Jerusalem money.'[93]

To the south of Palestine the Greek influence was even stronger in Egypt than it was in Phoenicia to the north. The Phoenicians, it is true, were supported by the Greeks in their revolts against Persia in 385–381 and 351–350.[94] But Egypt, as we saw above, already relied on large-scale Greek assistance in its struggle against the Assyrians in the seventh century BC. By the beginning of the sixth century the Greeks there reportedly numbered in the thousands. Driven out by the Persians, they came back again and again to support the revolts of the fifth century. When those revolts succeeded they came in even greater numbers and were the strength of the Egyptian armies which beat off the repeated Persian attacks throughout the fourth century. In 343, when Artaxerxes III finally conquered the country, the Egyptians opposing him had 20,000 Greeks in their service, there were Greek garrisons in 'all the cities' of the Delta, and Pelusium, the key fortress on the east mouth of the Nile, seems to have been predominantly Greek.[95]

To the north and to the south, then, Palestine was bordered by countries where the Greeks were numerous and Greek influence important. Even to the east, the Arabs had felt the effects of Greek influence in statuary as early as the fifth century and by the third century were minting coins after Greek models.[96] Each of these countries exercised its influence on Palestine, but, as far as the Palestinian Jews were concerned, the most influential foreign group were presumably the Jews of the diaspora, which had begun in northern Syria already in the eighth century, in Egypt at the latest in the seventh.[97] During the fourth and third centuries, especially, vast numbers of Jews were carried abroad by repeated deportations (we hear of five),[98] constant enslavement (not only in military campaigns; slaves were one of the country's main exports throughout the Ptolemaic period and the trade had already been considerable in Persian times),[99] military conscription (which they often welcomed),[100] and more or less voluntary emigration (Palestine was a country oppressed by constant movements of armies and naturally poor).[101] The Jews thus carried abroad soon adopted the language and ways of thought of their Greek neighbours. Their continued loyalty to Jerusalem linked that city by the closest ties of financial interest, as well as kinship, to the great centres of Greek influence, especially Alexandria, Antioch and the Aegean.

Gifts from the diaspora to Jerusalem began with the return of the exiles in the late sixth century, if not before.[102] Some time after the canonization of the Law came the payment of regular taxes prescribed by its interpreters. By the first century this tribute was customarily sent every year from every province of the Roman Republic and from Mesopotamia.[103] With these gifts came tens of thousands of pilgrims whose expenditures in Jerusalem were a substantial part of the city's income.[104] Tacitus[105] thought the importance of the Jewish state due to these contributions from abroad, and Josephus[106] attributed to the Emperor Titus the opinion that the right to collect them was the greatest of the many great privileges the Romans had given the Jews. Only this external support can account for the recurrent recovery of the city after its recurrent lootings. Can one suppose that so important a source of income as the diaspora did not make its intellectual and religious influence felt?[107]

When all these factors are considered – repeated military conquest, constant military occupation, Greek settlement both in cities and in the countryside, economic and administrative penetration which reached every village, systematic exploitation of the countryside through landed estates, Palestinians' dealings with Phoenicians and Egyptians, and Jewish ties with Jews of the diaspora – when all these factors are considered it is clear that the cultural history of Palestine from the beginning of the Persian period is one of constant subjection to Greek influence, and that already in the Ptolemaic period every sector of the country must have been shaped by that influence more or less. 'More or less' implies differences of degree which were undoubtedly important, but they were only differences of degree. As the evidence has shown, some of the most important elements of Greek culture had everywhere come to be taken for granted: typically Greek artefacts and techniques were everywhere in use; the country had a monetary economy, foreign trade was a major concern, the frame of thought had ceased to be the land of Palestine and become the civilized world, and Greek had become – as it was throughout that world – the normal language of business and politics.

Yet in spite of all this it would be a serious error to ascribe merely to imitation of Greek ways the great cultural change which took place, throughout the Near East, between the sixth and second centuries BC. To understand this change we must realise that the world of the Greeks and Persians, Jews and Philistines, was a world of invaders. The invasions had taken place chiefly in the period from 1250 to 950 BC. Before that time, there had existed, throughout some two thousand years, a more ancient world, that of the Babylonians and Egyptians, the Semitic-speaking empires of the great river valleys, essentially concerned to maintain systems of irrigation, conservative as the law of real property, and stabilized by the landed endowments and hereditary personnel of the immense temples. This more ancient world had been weakened and transformed, but not wholly destroyed, by the invasions. In Mesopotamia, especially, it retained the strength for a final effort to restore the old order. This effort continued to the sixth century, and Nebuchadnezzar was its last great figure. Within fifty years after his destruction of Jerusalem (587) the Neo-Babylonian empire was itself destroyed by the Persians (539).

It was the Persian, not the Greek, conquest which marked the beginning of a new era in the Near East. Admittedly, Cyrus made no drastic changes. In religious affairs he came as a restorer of the old order; his conquest of Babylon was welcomed by the priesthood of the great temple of Marduk.[108] In political matters he permitted much local independence.[109] Political reorganization came only with Darius, and the power of the Babylonian priesthood was not broken until the reign of Xerxes (486–465).[110] Even after Darius and Xerxes the Persians left local institutions generally undisturbed and governed largely through local officials who were not Persians.[111] And even to decorate their own palaces they employed artists from their subject peoples who most often repeated and refined the clichés of ancient Near East tradition.[112] Nevertheless, the mere fact of their conquest resulted in differences from the old order which were of epoch-making importance.

In the first place, the new empire they created was of vastly greater extent than any previous one. The biggest of the previous ones – those of Egypt and Assyria – had been river valley empires, which pushed beyond their valleys to conquer neighbouring territories, but remained practically and psychologically centred in their valleys with their central river transport and irrigation systems. With the Persian conquest these valleys became merely parts of a much greater empire, stretching from the Danube across Thrace, Anatolia, Armenia, Media, eastern Persia and Afghanistan to the upper Indus. The lifelines of this new empire were overland trade and military routes, and its psychological as well as its geographical centre was not in the river valleys but in the uplands along the Zagros and the other mountain ranges that formed its skeleton. Its population was far more numerous and more various than that of any previous empire, and the ruling people, instead of being the largest body of people in their own territories, were a military minority spread thin over the multitude of their diverse subjects.

In the second place, from the Persian conquest on, for the next thousand years, the great powers of the Near East were Indo-Europeans (Persians, Greeks, Parthians, and Romans) whose languages never replaced completely the Semitic tongues of masses of their subjects.[113] This difference of language exacerbated natural conflicts of interest. Even when, as in the Persian empire, the scribes employed by the rulers used a semitic language – Aramaic – for their official correspondence, this was not the mother tongue of most of the governed, and the resultant tension between the rulers and the various native populations was henceforth (until some time after the Arab conquest in the seventh century AD) characteristic of this area and was one of the major factors which shaped its history.

Moreover, the new rulers did not establish their seats of government usually – or, at least, exclusively – in the river valleys where had formerly been the chief centres of population. Even the Ptolemies called the city from which they ruled 'Alexandria *by* (not *in*)[114] Egypt' and their interest (as opposed to their interests) was often in the Aegean area. The new locations and concerns of the governing groups contributed further to the differences between them and the native populations. In these differences the priest-hoods of the great temples located in the former centres of population found themselves on the side of the natives. Their endowments were usually maintained and sometimes extended, but they had become groups alien to the ruling class.[115]

Thus the political and institutional foundations of the old

order were undermined by the Persian conquest. Similarly the
development of trade fostered by the Persian empire – by road
building, establishment of a gold currency of universal circulation,
and so on[116] – diminished the relative importance of the agricultural
interests in the state, impoverished many small farmers, produced
a landless proletariat in the cities it financed, and resulted in a
uniform pattern of social and religious adjustments.[117] Although
this process had already begun in the Assyrian empire, it was
much accelerated by the enormous extension of unified political
control and the consequent facilitation of travel under the Persians.
That Greeks played a large part in the development of trade
and that the universal circulation of Greek silver matched and
supplemented that of Persian gold[118] is true, but the social and
religious changes resulted from the trade, not from the Greeks'
part in it, let alone from their personal influence as Greeks.

Thus the forces which produced the changes called 'Hellenization' were not universally nor even primarily Greek. As for the
forces which conditioned the change, they were often not only
independent of Greek influence but resistant to it – so, for instance,
the institutional inertia of the Near East[119] and the self-perpetuating
pattern of peasant life. Even when a change can be attributed to
Greek influence – as, for instance, the spread of silver coinage
along the Phoenician and Palestinian coasts[120] – it remains a
question whether the cultural element diffused by the Greeks was
of Greek origin (coinage, for example, seems to have been originally
Lydian).[121] And it was not only the Greeks who appropriated and
disseminated elements of neighbouring cultures. We have seen that
Greek influence came to Palestine largely through the Phoenicians;
Palestine, in its turn, must have been a centre from which Greek
influence spread through Arabia. At the same time, within the
Greek tradition some important developments which mark the
change from the classical to Hellenistic culture were due to oriental
influence (for instance, the rise of the cults of Adonis, Isis and
Sarapis). As the people of the Near East changed both by adoption
of Greek ways and by resistance to them, so the Greeks changed
both by adoption of oriental ways, and by careful efforts to preserve
classical usages which, when classical, had been spontaneous.

Thus 'Hellenization' in the Near East and Greece[122] cannot be
described simply as the adoption of Greek ways by the peoples of
the Near East and of oriental ways by the Greeks, though both

these processes were parts of it. Instead, we have a vast tissue of change, in which innumerable strands of independent, but parallel, development are interwoven with a woof of influence and reaction to produce a single, new culture, the Hellenistic, which is no less different from classical Greek culture than from the cultures of the more ancient Near East. To mention only the most important differences from classical Greek culture: 1. In the classical world the principal form of land tenure was the relatively small holding of the ordinary citizen; in the Hellenistic world it was the large estate of the king, the temple, or the great official. 2. In the classical world the chief political form was the city-state of small extent and homogeneous population, with some form of conciliar government; in the Hellenistic world – though the appearance of legal autonomy was often preserved, and the fact occasionally survived – the chief political form was the absolute monarchy ruling various peoples and a vast territory. 3. In the classical world the structure of society was regulated chiefly by local custom and tradition; in the Hellenistic world a much larger part than before was played by explicit, written laws.[123] 4. In the classical world the cult of the gods of the city was the centre of both petition and patriotism; in the Hellenistic world patriotism found expression in the cult of the divine ruler, while petitions were more often directed to deities whose political affiliations, if any, were of minor importance. 5. In the classical world, because the economic and political units were so small, private individuals were of relatively great importance; this both encouraged their concern for the state and made their activities matters of public concern; consequently the artistic and philosophical life of the period was closely connected with politics and politics was a major concern of the average man. In the Hellenistic world, because the units were so big, private persons were generally of no importance; accordingly they neglected the state and the state them; therefore the artistic and philosophic life of this period was generally non-political (except when inspired by patronage or the hope of patronage) and the average man was less interested in politics, more in his private affairs. 6. In the classical world the civil administration and the army were both run largely by amateurs (citizens ordinarily employed in private occupations) and professionals were rarely used except as subordinates; therefore the internal histories of the states were full of struggles between political factions. In the Hellenistic world both the administration and the army were staffed almost entirely by professionals and the internal history was therefore one of bureaucratic intrigues and palace revolutions. 7. In the humanities, arts and sciences, too, the Hellenistic world was distinguished by the growth of professionalism and the consequences of the professional approach.[124] These consequences were: collection of previous knowledge, systematization and consequent discoveries (mostly minor), reduction of the system to a handbook and a set of rules, consequent standardization of product and decline of originality.

In all the above points except 3. (the importance of written law) the Hellenistic world resembled Persia or Egypt rather than classical Greece. This resemblance is not accidental, nor was Hellenistic culture an imitation of the classical, which failed, in these points, to achieve its goal. The Hellenistic rulers had no intention of imitating the political forms of the classical city-states.[125] The religious changes, which took place also in Greece, were due to deliberate adoption. The growth of professionalism was already begun in the classical world, but was there felt to be incompatible with the ideal of the gentleman and was attacked accordingly.[126] It is true that Hellenistic culture comes to include among its *new* elements the recognition of bodies of 'classics' and the deliberate imitation of 'classical' models: the canonization of the plays of the Greek tragedians, the chapters of the Book of the Dead[127] and the books of the Old Testament,[128] the imitation of Homer by Apollonius Rhodius, of Ramesside documents by the Bentresh stele, and of Judges by the author of I Maccabees, are cases in point. But the culture as a whole was not, and was not intended to be, an imitation of the classical. It was a new way of life, with its own structural unity.[129] We can trace the social and cultural changes which were to produce this way of life, we can see them at work before the new culture emerges as a totality, and therefore we can speak of the process of Hellenization as at work even in the Persian period, or even in classical Greece.

An important element in Hellenistic culture was the tension already remarked between the primarily Semitic-speaking masses of the population (many of whom, as we have seen, must have understood some Greek) and the primarily Greek-speaking upper class (most of whose members could probably understand a little Semitic).[130] But this was not the only tension in the society. Another existed between the city dwellers and the village dwellers, and yet another between those who lived in Greek fashion and those concerned to preserve native ways. We have seen that not all the primarily Greek-speaking were city dwellers. No doubt many of the primarily Semitic-speaking lived in cities, and many of them liked Greek ways and were determined to follow them, just as some Greeks went native.[131] So the common equations: Greek-speaking = city-dwelling = graecizing, and Semitic-speaking = village-dwelling = anti-Greek, are true only as loose generalizations. Semitic languages continued to be used in and by some of the cities where Greek customs were most generally adopted: Sidon, until 150 BC, issued coins bearing only semitic inscriptions; its coinage was bilingual until AD 75; Tyre's coinage remained bilingual until the city was made a Roman colony, AD 198;[132] numerous Phoenician inscriptions from these cities date from the last three centuries BC.[133] On the other hand, some of the most violent anti-Greek propaganda was written in or translated into Greek, not only by Jews (the Books of the Maccabees, the Sibylline Oracles),[134] but also by pagans (the Potter's Oracle, which happily prophesies the ruin of Alexandria).[135]

Thus the cultural tensions within the society – to say nothing of the political – were complex and are misrepresented when simplified to a single conflict. But such oversimplification errs more seriously when it represents the whole society as the result of a conflict between 'Greek' and 'oriental' cultures,[136] and neglects the existence of Hellenistic culture as a thing in itself, different from either of its sources. The resultant confusion can be illustrated by a passage from Rostovtzeff – the more striking because it occurs in the works of so great a scholar. In discussing the policy of Antiochus Epiphanes which occasioned the Maccabaean revolt, he writes: 'The existence of Greco-Semites, either Hellenised Semites or orientalized Greeks, was a fact, and Epiphanes endeavoured to make use of it . . . to transform his realm . . . into a network of cities with Greek organization and a Greek mentality.' The religious aspect of this programme was the introduction of the cult of Zeus Olympios, 'a counterpart of the Ptolemaic Sarapis . . . bearing a Greek name . . . worshipped in semi-oriental temples . . . represented in a semi-oriental dress and with semi-oriental attributes . . . as much the Pansemitic Baalshamin as the Greek Zeus, the symbol as it were of the growing Syrian solar henotheism'.[137] This is an amazing series of statements: Epiphanes hoped, by using 'Hellenized' and 'orientalized' subjects, to produce a *'Greek'* mentality, therefore he introduced a 'semi-oriental' religion. This confusion underlies Rostovtzeff's further statements that the break-up of the Seleucid empire was due to rural reaction against Hellenism, yet 'the new rulers [who replaced the Seleucids] were certainly not hostile to Greek civilization as such. Most of them belonged to the Hellenized upper class of the native population . . . therefore . . . the states they set up were of the Hellenistic pattern.'[138] We shall do better to recognize 'Hellenistic' as a cultural classification distinct both from 'Greek' and from 'oriental', and to see the civil conflicts of the Seleucid and Ptolemaic empires as conflicts between various groups of a single cultural continuum – the Hellenistic.

The gradual development in Palestine of this Hellenistic culture forms the environment within which, from the Persian period on, the members of the Yahweh-alone party resumed their struggle to control the Jerusalem temple and to make their form of the cult of Yahweh the law of the land.

4

The Survival of the Syncretistic Cult of Yahweh

The Assyrian and Babylonian conquests put an end to the royal patronage of the cult of Yahweh,[1] but the popular, syncretistic piety on the one hand and the exclusive devotion of the Yahweh-alone party on the other continued and extended the cult. Accordingly, there were two phases of the extension. One the one hand, the syncretistic form of the cult was spread widely by Israelite deportation and/or emigration from the eighth century on, and evidently secured considerable adherence from Gentiles (if we can judge from the claims of the prophets and the enormous increase in worshippers of Yahweh during the Persian and early Hellenistic periods). On the other hand, the leaders of the Yahweh-alone party seem to have been mostly carried off to Babylonia. There the party secured a strong and wealthy following among the exiles. At the time of the Persian conquest, it supported the Persians and thereafter succeeded in placing some of its members in high positions in the Persian court. With Persian support it eventually gained control of the rebuilt Jerusalem temple and then won over the populace, first of Jerusalem, later of Judaea. This made it the largest and politically the most important group within the cult of Yahweh. Its pre-eminence was enhanced by the success of the literature which it produced or edited (most of the books now in the Old Testament) and by the traditional prestige of Jerusalem.[2] Consequently, the adherents of the old, popular form of the cult gradually assimilated their claims and practices to those of Jerusalem, and in effect were converted to the Yahweh-alone position. This process is traceable in Palestine before the Maccabaean period. It was enormously accelerated, both in Palestine and abroad, by the success of the Maccabees, but it became substantially complete only with the triumphs of Christianity and of rabbinic Judaism in the fourth century and later. (And even then isolated groups of the old syncretistic cult may have survived in magical, gnostic, or pagan circles.) This is, in outline, the history of which this book studies the beginning. In the present chapter we shall discuss briefly the survival of the syncretistic cult of Yahweh, beginning with some remarks on its ethnic background.

The Assyrian and Babylonian conquests increased, if anything, the mixture of ethnic groups in Palestine. The Assyrians, towards the end of the eighth century, carried off large numbers of Israelites and replaced them by settlers from Syria and Mesopotamia. Both the Assyrian records and the Book of Kings speak of the exile of 'all the people' of parts of the northern kingdom,[3] but this is probably a loose generalization. The more specific accounts of Sargon, the Assyrian conqueror, say he took some 27,000 from Samaria.[4] But II Kings 15.19f. indicates that twenty-six years earlier there had been 60,000 wealthy men in Israel.[5] Supposing the poor were only three to one, this would indicate a population of 240,000 adult males. The intervening years had seen two Assyrian conquests and the deportation of much of the population of Transjordan and Galilee,[6] but these had been the less densely populated parts of the country. Even if the men of the territory from which Sargon's exiles came numbered only a third of the former total – about 80,000, and this is a low estimate – his deportation would have taken less than half of them. And his 'annals' have been read as stating that he made the 'remaining' inhabitants assume the responsibility of ruling the district and collecting tribute for him.[7] Presumably, therefore, a considerable Israelite population was left in the northern part of the country.

The deported Israelites carried the syncretistic cult of Yahweh with them to northern Mesopotamia, where both Yahwist names and Baal names – and perhaps a temple of Yahweh and other deities – survived for centuries.[8] The Syrians and Mesopotamians who were transplanted into northern Palestine brought their native cults with them, but soon adopted the cult of Yahweh as well. We are told (perhaps by malicious misrepresentation) that the cult at the northern shrine of Bethel was restored by Israelite priests at the behest of the Assyrians.[9] Probably it was restored (or never interrupted) at other shrines, too. The temples of Beth Shan continued in use down to the Persian period.[10] Worshippers from the north still made pilgrimages to the holy places of Yahweh in the south, most probably to Jerusalem.[11] The Assyrian conquest, therefore, seems to have made no basic difference to the essential ethnic and religious picture of northern Palestine, that of a mixture of peoples worshipping a number of gods, among whom the most prominent was Yahweh.

Even less change seems to have been effected in the south by the Babylonian deportations of 597 and 587.[12] The figures given for these are small, the largest being about 10,000 – II Kings 24.14, but this figure is suspiciously round and may be a gloss. Further, the account in Kings is discredited by differing in its dating of events from the account in Jeremiah 52.28ff., of which the dating is confirmed by the Babylonian records.[13] Jeremiah 52.28ff. says 3,023 were carried away in the first exile; 832 in the second. Probably only men were counted. At any rate, many people were left in the country under a governor appointed by the Babylonians. The governor was murdered, and both Kings and Jeremiah say the whole population then fled to Egypt.[14] This must be an exaggeration, since the Babylonians thereafter deported some 700 more, no doubt as punishment for the murder.[15] Besides these specifically reported deportations, a good many Israelites were probably carried off from the minor Judaean cities, of which many were destroyed.[16] But the destruction of a city does not imply the disappearance of its population (as the case of Jerusalem shows); many fled to the hills and caves,[17] more were left by the conquerors to raise crops and taxes. We are told that the Babylonians took care for this;[18] it was not to their interest that their lands should lie idle. Nothing is said of importations to repopulate the country. What repopulation took place was probably due to the return of refugees or exiles, to the moving in of neighbouring peoples (many of them, doubtless, half-Israelite already), and to the natural increase of the remnant left in the land. Neither singly nor together were these causes apt to produce a sudden, profound change in the ethnic or religious character of the country.

It is clear, too, that intermarriage between the various ethnic and religious groups in the country continued after the exiles. We hear many reports of it.[19] In these reports most attention is given to influential persons whose marriages doubtless served as examples, but it is presumable that the common people, too, were marrying outsiders; the complaints that the aristocracy had taken the lead imply that others had followed.[20] In the fifth century, Ezra and Nehemiah successively tried to put a stop to the practice, but their efforts were limited to Jerusalem and not successful – not, at least, if we accept the preserved sequence of their stories, which puts Nehemiah after Ezra.[21] In that event Ezra's attack on mixed marriages seems to have completely lost its effect by Nehemiah's time, for Nehemiah found intermarriage common among the people. Even a grandson of the high priest was married to a daughter of the governor of Samaria.[22] Nehemiah evidently was not able to compel a divorce. The report of the incident by Josephus declares that 'many priests and Israelites were involved in such marriages'.[23] The report is popular story-telling, but it seems to reflect the common state of affairs in the pre-Maccabaean period. In this period the high priestly family of Jerusalem intermarried with a prominent family of Ammonites:[24] cf. Deuteronomy 23.4: 'An Ammonite or a Moabite shall not enter the assembly of Yahweh, not even to the tenth generation.'

From the Jerusalem priesthood it is plausible to argue *a fortiori* about non-priestly families in towns closer to non-Israelite territory. Such argument is justified by other reports. The Greek historian Hecataeus speaks of Jewish intermarriage with aliens as prevalent from the Persian period on.[25] In the Ptolemaic period, cohabitation of Greek soldiers with Palestinian women was so frequent that legislation in defence of persons unjustly enslaved recognized the resultant connection as a peculiar class of slavery.[26] Somewhat later, Jewish names appear in the Gentile tombs of Marisa, presumably as a result of Jewish intermarriage with Gentile families there.[27] Later yet, the poet Meleager of Gadara complained of his mistress' relations with Jews.[28] The increase within Judaism of emphasis on the laws against exogamy doubtless did something to discourage the practice of intermarriage,[29] but something more to discourage the practice of Judaism.[30] Rabbinic law recognized that there was such a large Israelite admixture among the Samaritans, the Palmyrenes and other peoples that their ethnic status was, for legal purposes, uncertain.[31] At the end of the first century BC, the geographer Strabo found the territory around Jerusalem 'inhabited in general, as is each place in particular, by mixed stocks of people from Egyptian [by which he means Jewish] and Arabian and Phoenician tribes; such, moreover, are those who occupy Galilee and Jericho and Philadelphia and Samaria'.[32] At the outbreak of the Jewish revolt in AD 66, persons of mixed stock, as well as Judaizers and persons equally friendly with Gentiles and Jews, formed an important element in every town of Syria (and, *a fortiori*, of Palestine).[33]

In sum, the ethnic history of the country seems to have been that expectable from the political and economic history reviewed in the previous chapter – a history of conquests and reconquests, of deportations of native stock and importations of aliens, of campaigns and encampments of armies, billeting of garrisons, penetration of the country by foreign traders and government agents, and the establishment of estates, agricultural colonies and entire cities dominated by aliens. To suppose that throughout such a history the native population retained its ethnic purity (which it probably never had) would be fantastic, even if there were no specific evidence to the contrary. But there is specific evidence – that reviewed above – which consistently reports the fusion of the Israelites with the surrounding peoples.

This fusion was accompanied by a dissemination of the cult of Yahweh. The destruction of Jerusalem did not put an end to the syncretistic form of the cult. As the north Israelites had carried it with them in exile to northern Mesopotamia,[34] so the Judaeans in exile carried it with them to Egypt and Babylonia; along with Yahweh they continued to worship the other gods of the common religion which they had practised in Judaea, and they began to worship the gods of their new environments, too. This is the testimony both of the literary and of the archaeological material.

From the literary material, we see Jeremiah in Egypt addressing to the Judaeans there a typical Jeremiad, only to have 'all the men who knew their wives had offered incense to other gods, and all the women who stood by, a great assembly, all the people who dwelt in Pathros in the land of Egypt', answer him, 'As for the word which you have spoken unto us in the name of Yahweh, we will not listen to you. But we will . . . burn incense to the Queen of Heaven and pour out libations to her, as we did, both we and our fathers, our kings and our princes, in the cities of Judah and in the streets of Jerusalem; for then we had plenty of food and prospered and saw no evil. But since we left off burning incense to the Queen of Heaven and pouring out libations to her we have lacked everything and have been consumed by the sword and by famine.'[35] In Babylonia we have Ezekiel declaring that even the men who come to consult him are still worshipping idols and

burning their children as offerings.[36] Accordingly, the Deuteronomic editors made Moses 'prophesy' that the Israelites in exile
would turn to idolatry.[37] And the priestly legislators, resigning
themselves to the facts, ruled that 'if any man curses his [own, as
opposed to the people's] gods, he shall bear [the punishment
inflicted for] his sins [by those gods, but he shall not be liable to
criminal action]; however, he who affixes [a curse to] the name of
Yahweh shall, without exception, be put to death.'[38] Or, again, 'If
any man . . . gives [sacrifices] a child of his to Molek, he shall
surely be put to death; the citizens shall stone him . . . but if the
citizens absolutely refuse to attend [to the matter] . . . I [Yahweh]
will . . . destroy him.'[39]

Similarly, from the archaeological material, we have in Babylonia the Murashu documents, in which the names show that
worshippers of Yahweh also worshipped Nīnarta, Bel, Nana, Sin
and Shamash.[40] In Egypt we have the Elephantine papyri and
associated ostraca, showing that Yahweh shared his temple there
with Anath and Bethel,[41] while the Judaeans who were his worshippers probably worshipped also Chnum or Han, Sati, Bel, Nabu,
Shamash and Nergal.[42] This material, both Babylonian and Egyptian, continues to the end of the fifth century, and proves that the
syncretistic cult of Yahweh flourished in both countries to that
time, as one element in a more complex and inclusive religion.

As for Palestine, Ezekiel prophesied, after the destruction of
Jerusalem, against 'the inhabitants of the waste places in the land
of Israel' who expected to acquire the land from which the previous
owners had been exiled: 'Thus saith the Lord Yahweh, "You eat
flesh with blood and lift up your eyes to your idols and shed blood;
shall you then possess the land?"'[43] From the following century we
have the attacks in 'Third Isaiah' (i.e. Isaiah chs. 56–66) on those
who 'burn with lust among the oaks, under every green tree; who
slay . . . children in the valleys, under the clefts of the rocks'; who
pour libations and bring offerings to baetyls, sacrifice and hold
religious feasts on the mountains, practise ritual prostitution and
worship idols.[44] They provoke Yahweh to his face continually,
'sacrificing in gardens and burning incense on bricks', they 'sit in
tombs and spend the night in secret places; . . . eat swine's flesh
and broth of abominable things, . . . set a table for Fortune and fill
cups of mixed wine for Destiny',[45] and so on. Solicitation of oracles
from the teraphim and worship of other gods ('idols') continued

to the time of the late additions to Zechariah (10.2; 13.2). At the same time the succession of syncretistic seals with Yahwist names on them and the succession of human remains under the door-sills or the foundations of houses[46] – presumably from foundation sacrifices – continue uninterrupted until the end of the fourth century. The excavations at Ramath Rahel yielded 'numerous Astarte figurines', both pre- and post-exilic, as well as the (pandemic) winged sun disc[47] and the bull of Apis (or Yahweh?) with the sun disc between his horns.[48] The excavations at En Gedi yielded personal seals representing priests worshipping Marduk.[49]

The syncretistic cult of Yahweh, to which this evidence testifies, was carried on at a number of temples or holy places outside Palestine. We have already mentioned the biblical account of the establishment of an altar to Yahweh in Damascus. There is dubious evidence for a north Israelite temple in northern Syria, near Haran, and certain evidence for a Judaean one in southern Egypt, at Elephantine, where the cult seems not to have been connected with the biblical tradition – at least, no fragments of biblical books have been found. The Elephantine temple was destroyed by the Egyptians in 410, but the Judaeans promptly set about negotiations to rebuild it, and a century later there was probably an altar to Yahweh in the middle of Egypt and a pillar sacred to him (and probably connected with sacrifice) on the border between Egypt and Judaea.[50] It has been thought, and is not impossible, that 'the place' in Babylonia to which Ezra sent for temple personnel was a temple.[51] Yet more likely is the notion that another temple was built in Babylonia at the time of the rebuilding of the one in Jerusalem (520 BC), for Zechariah, at that time, declared he had a vision of wickedness being carried by two demons from the land of Judaea to the land of Shinar (Babylonia) where *a house* (i.e., temple) *was to be built for it* and it was to be established.[52] This vision probably expressed the prophet's hope for the purification of Judaea by the rebuilding of the Jerusalem temple, and his disapproval of the building of another temple in Babylonia. The Babylonian building may have been pushed by syncretistic exiles in opposition to the propaganda for return to Palestine and the appeals for money to finance the building in Jerusalem. Professor Bickerman called my attention to the Epistle of Jeremiah which in Hellenistic times attacked Jews attracted to Babylonian worship by its impressive ceremonies.

Similarly in Palestine the sacrificial worship of Yahweh continued after the destruction of the Jerusalem temple (Jeremiah 41.5) and prior to its rebuilding (Ezra 3.1ff.). Ezra 4.1ff. declares that such sacrificial worship was also carried on by the neighbouring peoples.[53] In the Hellenistic period a temple, of the same type as that at Arad, seems to have been built at Lachish and has been taken as evidence of a long-established Yahwist cult there.[54] That the cult existed already in the Persian period is shown by the other finds at the same site, notably an altar for incense dedicated by someone with a name like Joash ben Machir, most likely 'to Yah, his [?] Lord'.[55] Other such altars were frequent at Lachish, and seem to have been deliberately polluted at the time of the Jewish capture of the city. Some of them were decorated with human figures in relief.[56] They have been plausibly identified as the *hammanim* which many post-exilic texts attack in connection with the high places and the cult of Asherah.[57] That they appear only in post-exilic texts shows that the ritual of the syncretistic cult not only lived on but continued to develop after the exile. It also indicates that the post-exilic attacks on high places and Asherah with which the attacks on these incense altars are almost always associated were not mere literary reminiscences but reflect the survival of these forms of the cult. Another such altar, of late Persian or early Hellenistic period, incised with the name Yakino and pictures of a man and a horse, has recently been found at Tell es-Sa'idiyeh.[58]

Occasionally we get bits of information which indicate particular centres of this survival. In the mid-fifth century there were devotees of Yahweh both in Samaria – where the two sons of the governor, Sanballat, had Yahwist names[59] – and in Ammon – as evidenced by Tobias ('My good is Yahweh') and his son Jehohanan ('Yahweh was gracious').[60] (However, the name Sanballat ['Sin gives life'] was recurrent in the Samaritan family; the papyri from fourth-century Samaria shows a predominance of Yahwish names, but many names compounded with those of pagan deities [Qos, Sahar, Kemosh, Baal, Nabu]. As for the Tobiad family, we have a letter from a descendant, also named Tobias, giving thanks to 'the gods'.)[61] The Samaritan cult on Mt Gerizim is probably a survival of one practised during the Israelite monarchy.[62] (As opposed to the cult, the *temple* on Gerizim came later.)[63] The Israelite cults at Tabor, Carmel, Hermon, Hebron and, just outside Hebron,

Mamre continued until Roman times.[64] Joshua 22 is apparently an apology for an altar in Israelite Transjordan.[65] It now appears that there was not only an altar but a temple there at Deir 'Alla;[66] it is not unlikely that there was a cult centre in Ammon, also: a little after 200 BC, when a member of the Tobiad family quarrelled with his relatives, including the high priest of Jerusalem, he withdrew in dudgeon to his own territories and built himself a capital at 'Araq el-Emir.[67] The most prominent of the buildings he put up has been thought a temple.[68] In the middle of the second century, when the legitimate representative of the Jerusalem high priesthood was deprived of his position, he went to Leontopolis in Egypt and built a temple there.[69] So the cult of Yahweh was disseminated from a number of centres known to us – Haran, Elephantine, Babylonia, Lachish, Samaria, Gerizim, Tabor, Carmel, Hermon, Hebron and Mamre, Deir 'Alla, Tell es-Sa'idiyeh, 'Araq el-Emir, Leontopolis – and probably from others of which we have no record. (Consequently, post-exilic 'Israel' cannot be equated with the adherents of the Jerusalem temple.[70] The term was claimed also by other worshippers of Yahweh, both those who had other temples and those who had none.)[71]

That these centres attracted non-Israelites is argued by the many prophecies that all nations will eventually come to worship Yahweh[72] – an idea which would hardly have occurred to the prophets had not many individual foreigners already come to serve him. Such prophecies are so prominent in exilic and post-exilic periods, and so rare in material which might be pre-exilic that it is plausible to take them as evidence of exilic or later origin. In many psalms they appear as exhortations to immediate action[73] and may reflect symbolic participation by groups of Gentiles in the worship of the second temple.[74] While they no doubt had some root in the official support of the Yahweh cult by Persian and later governments,[75] yet their chief basis was probably an extensive private cult of Yahweh carried on by Gentiles. Malachi declares that from the east to the west the name of Yahweh is great among the Gentiles, and that everywhere incense and cakes of pure flour are offered to his name.[76] Malachi's object here is to prove that the second-rate offerings of Jerusalem are contemptible by comparison. This comparison proves that the Gentiles' offerings were being made at that time, and the emphasis on the greatness of Yahweh's *name* rules out the suggestion that the worship was virtual, that is, that what the Gentiles worshipped in other gods was really Yahweh (a notion extremely rare in Jewish thought).[77]

There are numerous traces, both in imaginative literature and in historical record, of such Gentile worship. A story concerning it is told as automatically credible in Jonah 1.16. The coming of individual Gentiles to worship at the temple is contemplated in I Kings 8.41ff. (post-exilic material). The sacrifices of Gentiles are explicitly declared acceptable in Isaiah 56.7, and the declaration is so made as to suggest that the question was one of practical, immediate concern. Many particular Gentiles are said to have offered sacrifices,[78] and at the outbreak of the war with Rome we find the chief priests pleading with the rebels to remember that the temple owed most of its wealth to the offerings of non-Jews.[79] These non-Jews did not impose on themselves the limitation of the cult of Yahweh to Jerusalem, nor did Jewish law impose it on them; the oldest rabbinic commentary (Siphra) on Leviticus 17.3ff. explicitly declares: 'Gentiles may build altars and offer sacrifices to Heaven [i.e., Yahweh] anywhere.'[80] Nor were Gentile worshippers of Yahweh bound, like Israelites, to worship him alone. For the law of the second temple this is immediately clear from the acceptance of offerings made by pagan officials. For private cults the principle was recognized by some groups within the Yahweh-alone party already in the monarchic period. When Naaman, the Syrian general, declared his intention to worship only Yahweh and (when he had to) Rimmon, Elisha dismissed him with a blessing.[81] The story is reliable at least as evidence of the opinion of the group which preserved it. In the post-exilic period this opinion not only survived, but prevailed.[82]

The consequent expansion of the syncretistic cult of Yahweh is the most likely explanation of the discrepancy between the number of 'Jews' (whatever that term means) in the ancient world in the time of Nehemiah and their number in Maccabaean times. For Nehemiah (444-c.432 BC) they are a handful settled in the province of Judaea (roughly twenty-five miles square).[83] Together with these he would have reckoned, no doubt, the Yahweh-alone party in Babylonia and at the Persian court. Should we add to these the other exiles and emigrants from Judaea, in Babylonia and in Egypt and possibly in Arabia,[84] we should find it difficult to justify an estimate of more than 200,000 for the total.[85] But four hundred years later (in 30 BC, at the end of the Maccabaean age) not only have the Jews of Judaea conquered and converted most of Palestine and much of Transjordan, but Jerusalem is the centre of an enormous diaspora, extending not only to Babylonia, Arabia and Egypt (where the Jews make up a quarter of Alexandria), but also to upper Mesopotamia, Persia, Media, Syria, southern Anatolia, Cyprus, the Greek islands, Athens, southern Italy, Rome and Cyrene, and a likely estimate for the total would hardly be less than 3,000,000.[86] Given the infant mortality rate of antiquity, and the frequency of wars throughout the Near East during these three hundred years, it is hardly possible to explain this increase as the result of physical multiplication. Nor can much of it be explained by conversion to the Yahweh-alone party, which seems to have made little progress even in Palestine until its faith was propagated by the Maccabaean armies: at the beginning of the revolt the true believers in Trans-Jordan and Palestine outside Judaea were so few that it was possible to evacuate them all.[87] And we have no evidence nor literary remains of a major missionary effort in these centuries, but we should have had them if such an effort had been made by the Yahweh-alone party from which our preserved records come. Accordingly, the most likely explanation of the increase is that the syncretistic cult of Yahweh spread widely through the countries listed above, and that later the exclusive form of the cult spread – as did Christianity – through groups who were already worshippers of the god. The successes of the Maccabees may have done as much to spread their form of the cult as the destruction of Jerusalem did later to spread Christianity.[88] As with the spread of Christianity, however, though we can be sure it occurred, we have only occasional glimpses of the process.[89]

In the second century, when Onias (the ousted but legitimate representative of the Jerusalem high priesthood) wrote to King Ptolemy Philometor requesting permission to found a temple in Egypt, he is reported to have said, 'I have been in Coele Syria and Phoenicia and in Leontopolis [in Egypt] . . . where the Judaean settlement is, and have visited other centres of my people, and have found them to have many [different] forms of sacrificial [?] worship, contrary to what is fitting, and have found them hostile to each other on account of this – as also happens in the case of the Egyptians by reason of the multitude of their forms of sacrifice and of their disagreement about religious matters.'[90] He requests, therefore, that he be permitted to build a temple as a means of uniting his people. The word here translated 'forms of sacrificial worship' (*hiera*) has that meaning normally, but not necessarily. It can refer merely to 'religious acts', but had this reference been the one intended, Onias' parallel with Egyptian practices[91] and his argument for the institution of an authorized *sacrificial* cult would be surprising. Since sacrifices were certainly to be offered in the new temple, it is presumable that they were already being offered in Egypt, and that they represented a survival there of the cult of Yahweh, which, as we have seen, was already practised in the country during the fifth and fourth centuries. Unfortunately, the text of the letter of Onias has probably been to some extent corrupted[92] and its original wording is therefore dubious. But even if it were wholly a forgery, it would be evidence that the forger believed the situation he described would seem credible to his readers.

Moreover, a similar survival appears in Asia Minor where, in the time of Hyrcanus II (63–40 BC), the Assembly of Sardis granted the Judaeans a place in which to perform their 'sacrifices' (as distinguished from the accompanying prayers).[93] The word here translated 'sacrifices' (*thysias*) is normally specific. Again, the Judaeans who were expelled from Rome in 139 BC for corrupting Roman mores with the cult of Zeus Sabazius (presumably an *interpretatio graeca* of Yahweh) had probably erected altars for his cult.[94] Not only was Yahweh often associated with Dionysus-Sabazius, but he was also worshipped as 'Hypsistos', that is, 'the highest', the title of a Syrian god often identified with Zeus.[95] This deity was worshipped especially at Palmyra as the unnamed God, whose name is blessed, who hears prayer –[96] attributes also prominent in the Jewish cult of Yahweh, and possibly derived by both cults from a common source.

Another body of evidence for the survival of the syncretistic cult of Yahweh may be found in the magical papyri and the cognate material (for instance, amulets and gnostic documents generally taken as evidence of Jewish syncretism).[97] This is not to say that there was no Jewish syncretism, but the question raised by such data must be restudied with the possibility of Yahwist survivals in mind. The evidence for such survivals is sufficient to justify the conclusion that the spread of the exclusive cult of Yahweh alone, from the Persian period on, took place through an environment permeated by the syncretistic cult of Yahweh. In Palestine, more-

over, this environment was largely composed of descendants of the
Israelite stock which had fused with the other peoples of the land.
This religious and physical kinship with its environment must
have done much to open Jerusalem to outside influences of the sort
which were probably exerted by the Samaritan and Ammonite in-
laws of the high priests.

5

From Nebuchadnezzar to Nehemiah

Most of the leaders of the Yahweh-alone party were probably among the upper classes of Jerusalem whom Nebuchadnezzar carried off to Babylon. The Old Testament contains very little from Palestine during the half century between the fall of Jerusalem to Nebuchadnezzar (587) and the fall of Babylon to Cyrus (539). The Palestinian source of Kings continued for a few years after 587; Lamentations 5 may have been written in Palestine about this time, and there may be a few fragments of Palestinian prophecies from the next fifty years; but both the attributions and the original contents are uncertain.[1] This lack of material is explained by the prophecies in Ezekiel, from the beginning of this period, and in 'Third Isaiah' (Isaiah 56–66) and Zechariah from the period following, which denounce the Israelites of Palestine for their continued worship of other gods.[2] Yet Ezekiel 11.15 also denounces them for claiming they had a monopoly of the cult of Yahweh and telling the exiles to give it up. It appears from the context that participation in the cult was somehow connected with the legal right to the land – a fact that was to be important when the exiles returned. Ezekiel then goes on to prophesy that they will return and put an end to the idolatry and abominable practices of the Israelites who have remained there.[3] Hence it would seem that, for the most part, the religion which survived in Judaea was not that of the Deuteronomic tradition but the syncretistic cult of Yahweh described in the preceding chapter.

From Babylonia, during the same half century, come some of the largest and most important bodies of Old Testament material: the prophecies of Ezekiel and 'Second Isaiah' (Isaiah 40–55),[4] the 'Holiness Code' (Leviticus 17–26) and other elements of the 'Priestly' collection of traditions and laws which bulks large in Genesis, Exodus, Leviticus, Numbers and probably Joshua,[5] also a number of psalms and of prophecies scattered as interpolations through the larger books, for example, Isaiah 13f. – all these are commonly assigned to Babylonia. But it seems likely, besides, that much of the editorial work of the Deuteronomic school in the Pentateuch, Joshua, Judges, Samuel and Kings, was done there. This is suggested by the differences between the earlier and later work of the school. The original author of Kings, for instance, was very close to the events, personalities and issues of Josiah's time. But when Nebuchadnezzar carried off the upper classes and gave the farms of Judaea to 'the poor of the land' (II Kings 25.12) he created a group whose members had reason to oppose the return of the exiles (the former owners). Consequently we should expect that the upper-class leaders of the Yahweh-alone party in Babylonia would lose touch with the Judaean lower class. And in fact this loss of touch appears in the later work of the Deuteronomic school, which lacks the social concern and sense of the actual Judaean situation characteristic of the original Deuteronomists and the pre-exilic prophets. In the later strata of Kings, social injustice is almost never mentioned; worship of alien deities is usually the sole cause of Yahweh's anger; almost the sole criterion by which kings are judged 'good' or 'bad' is their religious policy; the political tensions and practical considerations of the actual history have been forgotten. All this is presumably the work of aristocratic exiles in Babylonia, separated by one or two generations from the Judaean environment.[6]

Even more surprising than the amount of the material produced in Babylonia is the variety of it: the differences of mentality and style between Ezekiel and Second Isaiah, between the Deuteronomic and the Priestly legal traditions, and even within the Priestly tradition between the Holiness Code, the laws in Ezekiel, and the other P material. And yet more surprising is the fact that this various and indeed contradictory material is now preserved in a single collection.

The quantity of the material testifies to the importance of this period in the history of the party. It seems to have been the time of formation. The national disaster is plausibly supposed to have made the survivors collect and edit those few written texts which had survived, and write their own accounts of the material of texts which had been lost and of material which had hitherto been preserved orally by institutional groups like the priesthoods of the various holy places.[7] At the same time some groups of the party reacted to the disaster by stronger assertions of their devotion to Yahweh alone. By these the party position was carried to its illogical conclusions in the Holiness Code's conception of Israel as a holy people isolated by its peculiar purity[8] and in Second Isaiah's denial of the existence of any god save Yahweh (a denial which was eventually to transform the cult of Yahweh alone, from the duty of Israelites, to the only true religion).

The variety of this material confirms what was said in Chapter 2 as to the various groups within the movement, and indicates that such groups survived, distinct, into exilic times. The fact that works from all these groups, in spite of their differences, are preserved cheek by jowl in the Old Testament reflects a history of compromises and alliances, and presupposes the development of harmonistic exegesis which must have drawn on the background of oral law.[9] It is plausible to connect this material with the development of synagogues, which is often supposed to have taken place in Babylonia.[10] In the absence of evidence, we can only speculate, but it is a likely speculation that the various groups of the Yahweh-alone party formed, in the diaspora, various synagogues, or chains of synagogues; that these were the environments for which the diasporic authors wrote and which preserved their writings; and that alliances between synagogues – involving compromise on both sides – gradually built up in Babylonia a network of like-minded communities within which a good deal of literature (probably much more than has come down to us) found copyists and readers. This literature was not wholly traditional and/or prophetic. Synagogue worship had its own literary needs. The absence of sacrifice increased the importance of psalms and of prayers (like those put into the mouths of David and Solomon)[11] and, above all, of homiletic material, which now fills much of Deuteronomy, Jeremiah and Ezekiel, and is scattered through all the prophets.[12]

These substantial literary developments must have had a basis in satisfactory social and economic adjustments. At least one group of the Yahweh-alone party, that represented by Jeremiah, had been strongly pro-Babylonian. It doubtless won many converts after the Babylonian triumph, which could be represented as proof of its prophecies. The Babylonians were aware of its propaganda on their behalf and protected its members, for example, Gedaliah and Jeremiah.[13] They also protected King Jehoiakin and eventually recognized him again as king of Judah.[14] Jeremiah's exhortation to the exiles to build houses and plant gardens[15] implies that they were not enslaved nor in utter poverty. However, many remained hostile to the Babylonians; when the Persian conquest appeared imminent the author of Second Isaiah joyfully prophesied it. Consequently his circle of the party, at least, was probably in the good graces of the Persians.

The founder of the Persian Empire, Cyrus the Great, after his conquest of Babylon in 539 reportedly issued two edicts, one permitting the worshippers of Yahweh to collect money in their own communities, return to Jerusalem, and use the money thus collected to rebuild the temple, the other ordering the return of the temple treasures and the rebuilding of the temple from royal funds.[16] Both decrees are probably fakes, but sooner or later[17] some exiles did return and the temple was rebuilt – about twenty years after Cyrus' pretended orders. As to the details, Ezra 1–6 contains a hodge-podge of traditions and inventions[18] in which the following elements can be identified:

1. a return in Cyrus' time, led by one Sheshbazzar, 'prince of Juda';[19]

2. laying of the foundations of the temple by Sheshbazzar;[20]

3. a return led by Zerubbabel, whom the Persians had appointed governor, and by the high priest Joshua;[21]

4. the building of the altar, beginning of sacrifices, and celebration of the feast of booths (*Sukkot*), also by Zerubbabel and Joshua;

5. laying of the foundations of the temple, also by Zerubbabel and Joshua;

6. an offer by 'the rivals of Judah and Benjamin'[22] to help build the temple, repulsed by Zerubbabel and Joshua;

7. consequent interruption of the building by 'the people of the land' until the time of Darius (521-486);

8. charges against the Jerusalem community in the time of *'Ah ashwerosh* – possibly Xerxes (486–465);[23]

9. an attempt to rebuild *the walls* of Jerusalem, in the time of Artaxerxes I (464–424), stopped by royal order;

10. thereafter, laying of the foundations of the temple, at the

instigation of Haggai and Zechariah, by Zerubbabel and Joshua, in the time of Darius (521–486);

11. investigation of their right to rebuild, by the satrap of the province;

12. completion of the temple, with the help of the provincial officials, in accordance with the orders of Cyrus, Darius, and Artaxerxes (464–424);

13. completion of the temple in the sixth year of Darius (516–515).

Of these, 12. is probably harmonistic, 9. is intrusive, 8. is obscure, 7. and 2. are contradicted by the fact that Haggai, in the second year of Darius, speaks of the time before that date as the time 'when one stone was not yet laid upon another in the temple of Yahweh'.[24] Further, the references to Zerubbabel and Joshua in 3. and 4. are suspicious, since they were the leaders in the actual rebuilding and may have been the only famous names to which stray material could be attached. But if the reference to Zerubbabel and Joshua be eliminated, there is nothing to 'the return under Zerubbabel' but a list, allegedly of returned exiles, without indication of the date of the return.[25] Thus we are left with a return under Sheshbazzar, in the time of Cyrus, perhaps another return at some time later; establishment of an altar, beginning of sacrifices, and celebration of Sukkot, reportedly by Zerubbabel and Joshua; laying of the foundations of the temple, by Zerubbabel and Joshua, in the second year of Darius (520–519), trouble with the Judaeans and investigation by the provincial officials; and completion of the temple, with the help of the provincial officials, in the last month of the sixth year of Darius (515). Even this remainder may be too large, for the long delay between the return and the rebuilding casts doubt on the story of a return under Cyrus,[26] and the story of the celebration of Sukkot 'as it is written'[27] is paralleled by the Ezra narrative which tells of a celebration of the feast of the seventh month (— Sukkot) in which huts were made 'as written' in Ezra's law, 'as the children of Israel had not done from the time of Joshua the son of Nun to that day'.[28] These look like two reports of a single event. Similarly we have two reports of the founding of the temple by Zerubbabel and Joshua, two lists of the returned exiles, and so on.

Such sandwiching of slightly contradictory reports of identical events is a well-known editorial procedure (e.g., in the Pentateuch) and invites source analysis. But here analysis is made uncertain by the fact that, except for the remains of Nehemiah's 'memoirs', the books of Ezra and Nehemiah show everywhere the conspicuous style of 'the Chronicler'. 'The Chronicler' was formerly the author-editor supposed to have produced Chronicles-Ezra-Nehemiah by excerpting earlier sources and adding a framework and stories, genealogies and comments of his own.[29] These secondary elements have now been shown to come from several hands, so we must suppose, if not a second editor, at least a series of glossators who imitated the first editor's style.[30] These writers (whose number and precise contributions we need not here try to determine) can best be seen at work where Chronicles parallels Kings, since they used as one of their sources a text of Kings only slightly different from that preserved.[31] This text they usually quoted almost verbatim, except for excision of details they found offensive. Between quotations they added comments or entire stories, sometimes taken from other sources, but mostly in their own well-marked style, so the resultant work is clearly stratified. In Ezra, on the other hand, the traits of their style appear everywhere, therefore the whole is their original composition. Such, at least, was the contention of Torrey and, with more or less modification, of Pfeiffer, Noth and others. However, the Chroniclers have given us, in their additions to Kings, many examples of their own compositions. These show a passion for edifying miracles, but also the ability to tell a well-connected story. Therefore, had Ezra been their own composition, it would certainly have been more miraculous and less muddled. The present realistic and occasionally unedifying jumble must have been produced from a variety of sources, extensively rewritten and glossed by the editors. So Eissfeldt, Rudolph, Mowinckel and others have argued. It must be granted that the use of sources is *a priori* more probable. At the same time it must be admitted that attempts to distinguish and delimit the sources have not been wholly convincing. Therefore, instead of continuing this familiar debate, it seems more profitable to turn from source analysis to the essential elements of the historical situation and try, from these, to reconstruct the course of events from which the present account, through whatever channels, is eventually derived.

Granted that in the reigns of Cyrus and/or his successors many exiles did return to Palestine, we may suppose that there came to be at least three parties in Jerusalem: a local party, and two important groups of former exiles.

The local party, composed of descendants of the men who had been left in the country in 582 or come back to it soon thereafter,[32] was made up for the most part of adherents to the syncretistic cult of Yahweh. The people continued to sacrifice to Yahweh (Ezra 4.2), they fasted on the anniversary of the destruction of the temple (Zechariah 7.4), but they also worshipped the other deities, whose cults Ezekiel and Third Isaiah denounced so vividly (about, p. 75). We have already seen that those to whom the land had been given by Nebuchadnezzar could be relied on to be hostile to the returned exiles (the former owners). Moreover, they had close ties to the surrounding peoples, for both Ezra and Nehemiah were to polemize against such connections.[33] Consequently the term 'the people of the land' (*'am ha'arez*) is now for the first time used to refer to the syncretistic population[34] as opposed to the members of the Yahweh-alone party who, by contrast, are often referred to as 'the exiles' (*benē haggolah*).[35]

This suggests that the majority of the returned exiles were devoted to Yahweh alone. The suggestion is probable, since the followers of the Deuteronomic tradition had a reason which most Judaeans did not have for returning to the city – Deuteronomy had both required sacrificial worship and limited it to Jerusalem.[36] However, it is probable that the Yahweh-alone party was never one of exiles alone; Ezra 6.21, if reliable, would indicate that they had a small following from the local population.

A second group of returned exiles were the priests of the Jerusalem temple, who had an economic interest in its restoration. Some of the priestly group may have been members of the Yahweh-alone party, but others certainly were not, as shown by their marriages with aliens.[37]

These various groups did not live at peace with each other. Zechariah 8.10 reports that before the building of the temple there was no safety in the city because every man's hand was against his neighbour. Such factional conflicts – *staseis* – were conspicuous in the history of the Greek cities of the same time. Their causes lay not only in religious but also in economic tensions of which we shall see more in the next chapter. Both religious and economic tensions would have been aggravated, when the rebuilding of the temple became imminent, if membership in the cult community carried some sort of claim to the land, as Ezekiel 11.15, 17 suggests it did – compare the claim in the priestly legal tradition that the land belonged to Yahweh and could not be sold, all 'owners' being merely tenants holding from him (Leviticus 25.23). The existence of such a claim – even if it were not, for the moment, accepted by the Persian government – would make all residents of the district anxious to participate in the rebuilding of the temple and thus to establish their right to share in the god's property. Hence, too, when the returned exiles refused to let 'the people of the land' take part in the rebuilding, it would not be surprising that the rejected group did all they could to stop it. In the resultant struggle the temple priesthood would have found itself in an excellent bargaining position between the two parties.

Such is, in fact, the state of affairs which emerges in the first period about which we have information – that of the rebuilding of the temple in the years 520–515. For this we have, besides the traditions in Ezra, the prophecies of Haggai in the second year of Darius (520) and those of Zechariah (520–518). These confirm the Ezra traditions in representing as the foremost figures of the time Zerubbabel, the Judaean appointed by the Persians as governor,[38] and Joshua, the high priest.[39] These works, of course, are all Yahweh-alone documents, as appears not only from their content in general but also from their frequent reminiscences of Deuteronomy.[40] Of course the party did not preserve the oracles of the syncretistic prophets of Yahweh,[41] nor the stories told by the opposition. Therefore, since the traditions in Ezra represent Zerubbabel as the leader of the Babylonian exiles and of the opposition to 'the people of the land',[42] and since Zechariah and Haggai saw in him the coming Messiah,[43] it is presumable that he was the leader of the Yahweh-alone party.

This enables us to understand his relationship to the high priest Joshua in Zechariah 6.9–15, the report of a compromise between Zerubbabel's followers and the priestly party. Though the text is corrupt,[44] the general terms of the agreement are clear. Zerubbabel is to be crowned as civil ruler,[45] he is to be in charge of the rebuilding of the temple (or, he undertakes to rebuild it, or both), and the high priest consents to be associated with his messianic claims; in return, the high priest is to be next to him in rank[46] and 'a plan for peace shall be between them both', that is, they agree to define and respect each other's rights (v. 13, evidence of previous rivalry).[47]

Further, a contribution is made by wealthy members of Zerubbabel's following (returned exiles, vv. 10–11) to the temple treasury. This contribution, in the form of a gold and silver crown (or crowns), is to be hung up in the temple as a witness to the agreement (v. 14).[48] Finally, the exiles in Jerusalem will use their influence to persuade others to return and/or help build the temple (v. 15; there is a hint that if the scheme does not go through, diasporic help will not be forthcoming).[49] Zechariah adds that his prophetic mission will be demonstrated by the success of this agreement, which (as the text now reads, in a saving clause, v. 15c) will in turn depend on both parties' obedience to Yahweh's directions.

This same agreement[50] is probably reflected by Zechariah 3 and perhaps by Haggai 2.10–19.[51] From these it appears that previously the sacrificial cult maintained at the restored altar in Jerusalem, and in particular the High Priest Joshua, had been attacked by the Yahweh-alone party as unclean.[52] These attacks are now to be dropped. The shift in the party line is justified by the story that Yahweh intervened to change the status of Joshua, and by the argument that Joshua is, at least, 'a brand plucked from fire' – dirty and damaged, but better than nothing.[53] For his part, the high priest is assured that *if* he will keep the law (i.e., will follow the legal interpretations of the Yahweh-alone party) he will be recognized as the legal authority in control of the temple area, as judge in cases affecting the temple and its staff, and as having, himself, direct access to the court of Yahweh (perhaps this implies recognition of a priestly claim to be an independent source of divine revelation).[54] At the same time, he and his colleagues are warned of the authority possessed by Zerubbabel as Servant of the Lord.

This agreement is particularly interesting because it shows that the objective of the Yahweh-alone party had changed. What it wanted of the high priest was no longer a purge of the cults of other gods. Evidently these were not officially practised; we may assume that the party's influence had been strong enough to prevent their resumption when the city's cult of Yahweh was restored. As the Solomonic temple had always been primarily Yahweh's, the priesthood had no commitment to the cult of any other deity. But now a new issue had developed, a question of purity law. From Haggai 2.13ff. it seems that the Yahweh-alone party had ruled that an idol, or perhaps any object used in the cult of an alien god, was as impure as a dead body.[55] Consequently priests who practised in private the syncretistic worship attacked by Third Isaiah and Ezekiel, or who married or associated with worshippers of alien gods, would themselves be impure and would render the offerings of the official cult impure and unacceptable. The established cult and the high priest had therefore been attacked on the ground of *impurity*,[56] and what was now demanded of the high priest was observance of 'the law', that is, this new purity law of the Yahweh-alone party. Since the priests were the traditional authorities on purity law and on the rules of the cult, this demand reflects invasion of their domain by the party, with its different legal tradition. From now on the conflict in Jerusalem centres on such legal questions, and converts to the party are described as 'those who have separated themselves from the *impurity* of the peoples of the land'. That is, the characteristic act of conversion and the thing which most certainly differentiates a party member from his neighbours now becomes acceptance of the party's peculiar purity law.[57]

That the High Priest Joshua agreed to observe 'the Law' (as interpreted by the Yahweh-alone party) was probably due to Zerubbabel's authority as Persian governor. The priesthood had some sort of legal authority[58] and the priests' exercise of it, as well as their control of the temple, might be interfered with by the Persian administration.[59] So long as Zerubbabel was governor, therefore, the Yahweh-alone party had three strings to its bow: the governor's influence, its own capacity to carry on helpful or harmful propaganda, and the priesthood's need for financial support, especially for rebuilding the temple. The priestly party, on the other hand, had an even stronger position. First, it had control, both *de facto* and *de jure*, of the place and procedure of worship; if the Yahweh-alone party wanted its legally 'pure' worship it would have to come to terms with the priests. Second, because of this control the priests could choose between the support offered by the Yahweh-alone party and that offered by the syncretistic adherents of the cult of Yahweh. Accordingly they were in a good bargaining position, as shown by the terms they got in the compromise described above: recognition of legal and even, perhaps, prophetic authority, cessation of hostile criticism, the second place in the government, assurance of support for the building programme and a substantial gift of ready capital – all this in return for a promise to perform their functions according to the party's Law, and token support of Zerubbabel's messianic pretensions.

It is even possible that under priestly influence some effort was made to work out a further compromise which would include the syncretistic party also, for we find Haggai exhorting 'all the people of the land' to help with the rebuilding of the temple.[60] What the basis might have been for such a compromise is a matter of speculation. We may suppose that the practice of syncretistic worship had much declined in Judaea, as a result of the destruction of shrines in the Babylonian conquest. This is suggested by the fact that Ezra, Haggai, genuine Zechariah and Malachi do not attack syncretism. But there is no other indication that this relative decline did anything to diminish the hostility between the parties, and if any compromise was contemplated, it did not succeed, for Ezra reports that 'the rivals of [the tribes of] Judah and Benjamin' offered to help build the temple, but were repulsed by Zerubbabel (Ezra 4.1ff.), whereupon 'the people of the land' hindered the building (Ezra 4.4).[61] That a group urged to participate by Haggai should have been repulsed by Zerubbabel is not impossible. We have seen that the Yahweh-alone party was composed of different groups whose opinions on legal questions differed widely. Nor is this diversity of legal opinion within the party incompatible with the legal nature of the conflict between the party and the priesthood, and the new definition of conversion to the party as acceptance of the (party's) Law. Similar diversity of legal opinions is later found among the Pharisees, although the essential of their party was undoubtedly their peculiar legal tradition.

Numerous scholars have supposed that the group referred to by Ezra were the Samaritans,[62] and the present story clearly identifies as Samaritans at least the 'rivals' of 4.1. But the story is, in this respect, unlikely; the 'rivals' of the returned exiles would be the Judaeans with whom they were competing for control of the land. Ezra's tradition represented them as living within earshot of the temple,[63] and as claiming to have been worshipping Yahweh 'here'. The rebuilding of the temple was a local Judaean concern; we have already remarked its possible implications for real-estate rights.[64] The Samaritans had no reason to oppose it[65] and, apart from 4.2b, there is no sign that they did oppose it. But 4.2b is a polemic anachronism invented by the editor: the real Samaritans were not the Assyrian importees of two centuries earlier. And the editor was working after Nehemiah's time (he used the story of Nehemiah).[66] Under Nehemiah the Judaeans had been won over to the Yahweh-alone party and the Samaritans antagonized. The editor therefore has replaced the Judaean enemies, whom his tradition reported, by a caricature of the Samaritans, to whom he was hostile.

He has also taken as evidence of hostility the following report of a neutral investigation by the officers of the trans-Euphratine satrapy (5.3–6.13) who inquired whether or not the work had been authorized by the Persian court. They wrote a memorandum to the court, reporting the work and the claims of the authorization, and asking that the claims be checked and a reply stating the royal policy be sent. But, pending the reply, they permitted the building to continue, and their memorandum is a matter-of-fact report which shows no hostility. It does not mention a governor of Judaea. The investigation may have been occasioned by the disappearance of Zerubbabel, of which we shall speak below. But, if so, the report (as it now stands!) says nothing of this occasion. According to Ezra 6.1ff., a record was found of a decree by Cyrus not merely authorizing but subsidizing the building – the record may have been planted in the imperial archives by some Judaean in the secretariat; the decree it records is not likely to have been genuine since the order given was never carried out. At all events the reply from the court is said to have been favourable and to have ordered the officials to assist the building, and the officials are said to have assisted.[67] There is no record of any opposition to their assistance – either the opposition to 'the rivals' had not been based on objection to Gentiles as such, or the ruling group in Jerusalem had changed. At all events it would seem that the initial hostility to the returned exiles came neither from the Samaritans nor from the Persian administration of the satrapy, but from the local Judaean population. The neighbouring peoples outside Judaea were drawn into the quarrel later when Ezra's attack on mixed marriages threatened their daughters who had married Judaeans.

The rebuff to 'the people of the land' reported in Ezra most likely went hand in hand with the alliance reported in Haggai and Zechariah between the priesthood of the Jerusalem temple, headed by Josiah, and the Yahweh-alone party, headed by Zerubbabel. These events seem to have produced a good deal of resentment (especially in the country districts, where the syncretistic cult of

Yahweh had been strong) against both parties in the alliance, and even against the city of Jerusalem, which these parties controlled. This resentment doubtless augmented that rural hostility to cities which becomes chronic in the hellenistic history of the Near East. The result may perhaps be reflected in Zechariah 11.14 if the breaking of the staff of union signifies (or effects) the severance of Judah from Jerusalem.[68]

The expected consequences of this rupture are foretold by the prophecy in Zechariah 12.2–10: in the coming 'End', 'the people of Judah will also be in the siege against Jerusalem'.[69] Then Yahweh will smite the horses of the Gentiles with panic, 'but, as for the house of Judah', he will open its eyes.[70] 'And the clans of Judah say to themselves, "The dwellers of Jerusalem have prevailed against me[71] through Yahweh of hosts, their god."' Thereupon the Judaeans will go over to the side of the Jerusalemites and will destroy the Gentiles on every hand, 'while [the men of] Jerusalem still stay where they are, in Jerusalem'.[72] Thus Yahweh will give the victory to the Judaeans first, so that the glory of the house of David and the men of Jerusalem shall not embarrass them, but he will protect the Jerusalemites and make the feeblest of them like David and the house of David like a god, and the Gentiles shall be destroyed.

Wellhausen pointed out that the hostility between Judaea and Jerusalem is a historical element in the prophecy and one so unusual that it must refer to some particular situation.[73] The prophecy as a whole, because of the prominence it gives to the Davidic dynasty, suggests the time of Zerubbabel, who is reported to have been a member of that dynasty and was probably its last important figure.[74] Also, the hostility which it reports (and which Zerubbabel's policy provoked) may explain the sudden disappearance of Zerubbabel. For the prophecy suddenly, at the moment it reports the Judaean triumph, concludes: 'And I shall pour out on the house of David and the inhabitants of Jerusalem a spirit of compassion and supplication and they shall look [back?] to him whom they pierced and they shall mourn him as one mourns for an only son, and weep bitterly over him as one weeps over a first-born.'[75] This transition would make sense if Zerubbabel, the leader of the party to whom victory was to be due, had been assassinated as the result of a conspiracy led by other members of the Davidic family, who might have decided, either from ambition or from caution, to ally themselves with the syncretistic party and get rid of a relative whose messianic pretensions would involve them in his ruin if he failed, and might result in their destruction if he succeeded. Further, the supposition that the work on the temple, and Zerubbabel's career, were cut short by some hostile action of 'the people of the land' would explain the tradition to this effect in Ezra 4.1–5, as well as the tradition in Ezra 6.8–15 that the temple was completed with the help of outsiders[76] (whereas Zerubbabel and his associates had rebuffed an offer of help).[77] Nothing is said of Zerubbabel in the report of the celebrations at the completion (Ezra 6.16–end).[78] But the government did not forget his plot; before the time of Artaxerxes I the Persian dossier on Jerusalem contained records of attempted revolts.[79]

Whatever happened, Zerubbabel disappears from the documents and probably disappeared from the scene. His disappearance may perhaps have occasioned the visit of the satrapal authorities (5.3–6.13) who therefore found no governor on hand, but otherwise nothing untoward. They sent the court a report on the rebuilding of the temple, and when the court gave its approval they themselves assisted in the rebuilding. Its completion, with their help, in 515, was therefore probably a triumph for the syncretists. And it is unlikely that these did not report to the Persians anything they thought would damage the separatist party, their local opponents. The messianic expectations which had centred on Zerubbabel would have been conspicuous in such reports. Once the Persians learned of these, the party with which Zerubbabel had been associated probably went under a cloud. The next fifty-seven years (515–458) seem to have been a period of syncretist control.[80] We cited above the denunciation of idolatry from Third Isaiah and the additions to Zechariah which probably come from this period.[81] Zechariah 14.21 complains that there are 'Canaanites'[82] in the temple, and looks forward to the End, when they shall be ousted. But the preceding verses prophesy that in the End all the peoples of Palestine and the Egyptians shall come up to Jerusalem to worship. Therefore the objection to 'Canaanites' – that is Palestinians other than 'Israelites' (party members) – in the temple is probably an objection to their being attached to the temple staff, not their coming to worship. It may, indeed, be a veiled attack on the high priestly family because of their intermarriage with the neighbouring Palestinian gentry (cf. Ezra 9.1f.) The

Book of Malachi, which was probably written early in the period,[83] denounces – or was soon made to denounce – intermarriage with Gentiles, misinterpretation of the law by the priests, and the indifference to religion of both priesthood and laity.

Malachi is the last of the preserved books of the prophets, therefore much has been written about the cessation of prophecy at this time. However, it was not prophecy which ceased. There were still prophets in Nehemiah's day and in the days of the Maccabees. What ceased was the preservation, by the Yahweh-alone party, of new collections of prophecies. The party had begun preserving prophecies as documents in support of its position during its battle for control of the Judaean government in the Assyrian period. The fulfilment of the political prophecies of Jeremiah, Ezekiel, and Second Isaiah had doubtless been used as 'proof' of their theological pronouncements, so their prophecies were collected and preserved as propaganda to further the growth of the party in the diaspora. Now, however, the essential position had been formulated in Deuteronomic law and its consequences worked out in the Deuteronomic histories. The works of the prophets already preserved gave these ample support. What was needed now was not further prophecy but practical application. Legal revision, editing, combination and compromise are henceforth the major concerns, and new prophecies, when preserved at all, are preserved as interpolations in older books, or as pseudepigraphic works, like the Book of Jonah, saved by its pretended antiquity.[84] In this respect the Yahweh-alone party followed fashion. In Egypt and in Babylon, for a century past, the 'classicism' which was to be so prominent in the Hellenistic world had already begun to develop.

Closer than Egypt and Babylon, Arabia seems to have exerted an important influence on Judaea during the period of syncretistic control in the first half of the fifth century. On the one hand, the pressure of the Arabian tribes to the south probably required co-operation with the authorities of the neighbouring districts. On the other hand, the Arabs maintained the trade routes which provided the goods and raw materials for the merchants, goldsmiths and perfumers of Jerusalem – the only groups of its businessmen important enough to be mentioned in the list of wall-builders in Nehemiah 3.[85] The increase of Arabian trade in this period probably accounts for the increased importance of incense in the worship of Yahweh.[86] Further, in Nehemiah's time we find the Arabs on the best of terms with the Samaritans who, for their part, were friends of the Jerusalem priesthood.[87] Some evidence suggests that Arab expansion may have resulted in immigration to Judaea of many descendants of Israelites who had formerly lived further south. These immigrants had assimilated with the Edomites to such an extent that their claim to Israelite ancestry was often tenuous; their influx may account for much of the Edomite material in the Old Testament.[88]

At the same time, dealings with the peoples to the north, east and west established misalliances like those which Ezra and Nehemiah found shocking,[89] set under way that abandonment of ancestral customs which the Greek historian Hecataeus attributed to the Judaeans of this period,[90] and may have produced such artefacts as the half-shekel with male and female heads (of deities?) which Reifenberg attributed to mid-fifth-century Jerusalem.[91] Down to rabbinic times it was reported that idolatry remained in the temple until the days of Ezra and Nehemiah.[92]

After the accession of Artaxerxes I, in 464, the Yahweh-alone party evidently recovered its influence in the Persian court, for during the reign of this king it made, from that base, two attempts to reform both the cult of Yahweh in Jerusalem and the life of the Judaeans. The leaders of these attempts were Ezra and Nehemiah.

Ezra is one of the most controversial figures of the Old Testament.[93] As a result of the controversy, certain points can be listed as established (though certain authors will of course continue to dispute them). Whatever remains of the original story of Ezra must be embedded in Ezra 7–8, Nehemiah 8 and Ezra 9–10.[94] It was not invented by the editor of Ezra-Nehemiah, but was partly touched up, partly rewritten, disarranged, and mutilated by him.[95] The tale it tells is not incredible – Persian policy extended to the support and supervision of non-Persian cults; Ezra was sent to Jerusalem as a Persian official for these purposes.[96] This original story of Ezra said nothing of Nehemiah; Nehemiah's memoirs said nothing of Ezra. That the two men are now occasionally mentioned together is due to the editor.[97] The silence of each document about the other man (since both men were concerned about the same aspects of the affairs of a small city) makes it incredible that the two men should have been active at the same time. Nehemiah's activity is dated by his conflict with the High Priest Eliashib, the grandfather of the High Priest Jehohanan, and with Sanballat, the governor of Samaria, since both Sanballat and Jehohanan appear in the Elephantine papyri.[98] Therefore Nehemiah functioned under Artaxerxes I; 2.1 states that his first governorship began in 445–444 and 5.14 suggests that his second ended in 433–432 (the twentieth and thirty-second years of the king).[99]

Ezra must be placed either before Nehemiah's first governorship, or in the interval between his two governorships, or after his second. But the proposal to place him in the interval can be eliminated.[100] It contradicts the date in the text and is itself contradicted by the events. Ezra tried to force the people to divorce their alien wives.[101] When Nehemiah returned for his second governorship – and the text suggests that he was not absent for more than two or three years[102] – he found many marriages with aliens.[103] This can be explained – if Ezra's activity be dated with Nehemiah's absence – only by supposing Ezra's attempt to impose divorce made so much trouble that he was recalled in disgrace and matters were allowed to lapse to the *status quo ante*. But in that event the court would scarcely have sent out, immediately afterwards, a man likely to stir up again the same hornet's nest; any man sent out under such circumstances would probably have avoided the question; and a man who deliberately raised it – as Nehemiah did – could hardly have avoided mentioning the crisis just past.

Therefore we have the alternative: before or after. The text places Ezra before Nehemiah. This merely shows how the editor arranged his disconnected material, and the editor's arrangement is not good historical evidence.[104] Nevertheless, any proposal to contradict an apparently historical document must carry the burden of proof.

The weighty reasons for dating Ezra after Nehemiah are the facts that Nehemiah says nothing of Ezra and finds mixed marriages going on. But if Ezra made his attempt and failed in 458–457, Nehemiah did not arrive till thirteen or fourteen years later. After so long an interval he would have no compelling reason to mention the previous failure and might understandably have preferred to say nothing about it. The Book of Ezra does not say that Ezra failed, but the editor would never have reported the failure of one of his heroes. Moreover, the book's account of Ezra's work is manifestly incomplete.[105] It tells of the appointment of a commission to determine which men have taken alien wives, it

lists the men found to have done so, and it stops abruptly with
verse 10.44, which seems to say: 'All these man married foreign
wives and wives of theirs are extant and they have had sons.' What,
if anything, was done about them is never stated. Therefore,
although II Esdras 10.44 followed the Hebrew, the translator of I
Esdras 9.36 changed the verse to a report that they sent away their
wives and sons – an edifying emendation. The abrupt and obscure
ending suggests that what was not preserved was not edifying.
This suggestion is supported by the fact that, outside the traditions
which preserved Chronicles and I Esdras, Ezra cuts no great figure
in *early* Jewish legend. The author of Ecclesiasticus, in his list of
heroes, does not mention him, but praises Nehemiah; so does II
Maccabees.[106] Therefore it seems likely that Ezra's attempt at
reform failed and the reason for the failure can easily be guessed –
the complaints to the Persian court, not only by the Judaeans, but
also by the officials of neighbouring provinces whose daughters,
married to Judaean notables, were threatened by Ezra's policy.
But if Ezra's reform failed, then the conditions found by Nehemiah
and his silence about Ezra are no proof that Ezra came at a later
date.[107]

The other arguments advanced for dating Ezra after Nehemiah
are trivial[108] and do not justify a change from the order of the
text of Ezra,[109] since the history which the text recounts is not
implausible. From it we can reconstruct the following course of
events:

Ezra, a priest,[110] was a member of a Yahweh-alone group in
Babylonia which secured his appointment in the seventh year of
Artaxerxes I (458 BC) as a special royal commissioner[111] to visit
Judaea, enforce there a law[112] which they had represented to the
Persian court as the law of the local deity,[113] take to the temple the
offerings of the court and such other funds as he might be able to
raise, and supervise their expenditure. He was also authorized to
lead back a company of Babylonian exiles – who certainly would
be members of his own party.

In thus appointing, financing, and authorizing Ezra, the Persian
court was not motivated by pure piety; it had practical reasons.
In 458 Egypt was in the throes of a major revolt, supported by
200(?) Athenian galleys.[114] The Athenians were also fighting on
the Syro-Palestinian coast, and the coast is only fifty miles from
Jerusalem.[115] If an important inland city like Jerusalem were to

revolt and call in the Athenians, the Persian line of communications would be cut, Egypt would be lost, and Palestine might be. This is said, in fact, to have been the plan of the Athenian general Cimon, who had master-minded and begun the Athenian action (Plutarch, *Cimon*, 490 end). Therefore the Persian court was anxious, just at this time, to please its Palestinian subjects.[116] Unfortunately, however, it had been misinformed – evidently by the Yahweh-alone party – as to the state of affairs in Jerusalem. In sending Ezra and empowering him to enforce his law, it acted on misinformation.

Ezra is said to have arrived in Jerusalem in early August of 458[117] with a company of supporters, generous offerings to win over priesthood and populace, and a text he called 'The Book of the Law of Moses'. (Whatever this may have contained, it was not the present Pentateuch, nor even the whole of the preserved priestly material, since it did not provide for observance of the Day of Atonement.)[118] After conciliatory preparations, he held on Rosh Hashanah (New Year's Day, which that year fell on 2 October) a public reading of this new law, and tried to make the occasion a festival.[119] But when the content of the law became known, 'all the people' wept openly. Among the causes of their tears may have been rules intended to cut them off from their Palestinian neighbours, particularly a prohibition of marriage with non-Judaeans. In view of the general grief, Ezra chose to begin with more amiable innovations of his law – some allegedly novel observances for the feast of booths (Sukkot), which was now celebrated as prescribed.[120] About eight or nine weeks after the celebration, however, he had himself 'informed' that many of the people had married alien wives.[121] He thereupon made a great display of mourning; a crowd gathered and were moved – reportedly – to tears by his eloquence (the story recalls the stories of Greek and Roman demagogues).[122] Somebody suggested divorce and Ezra thereupon demanded of the leaders of the people that they swear 'to do so'. They – in front of the crowd – swore. An assembly was called to deal with the matter and met on the second day thereafter (19 December),[123] but was rained out (a realistic detail the editor would never have invented!). Consequently a committee was appointed to determine which men had married aliens. The committee met on 29 December and finished its work on 27 March, 457;[124] a list of offenders is given. With this the text breaks off, as described above.

Something must have happened to interrupt Ezra's rule. It was probably his recall by the Persian government. The trouble he was creating with his divorce programme would by itself, in such a situation, have been enough to get him recalled, but he seems to have given aid and comfort to his enemies by starting to rebuild the city walls. The Book of Ezra reports that such an attempt was made in the reign of Artaxerxes, and that it was denounced to the Persian government by the neighbouring authorities as likely to lead to revolt.[125] This led to a royal order to stop the rebuilding. Now Nehemiah was given permission to rebuild the wall in the twentieth year of Artaxerxes, and in spite of denunciations was permitted to go through with the rebuilding in the following year. That the government reversed its policy within a short period is unlikely. Therefore, the first attempt at rebuilding took place early in the reign, that is, about the time of Ezra's governorship. That the Book of Ezra knows so little about this first attempt, and buries it in the reign of Darius – where it does not belong – is curious.[126] Its ignorance of the end of Ezra's career is also curious. These two curious cases of ignorance concern events which happened at the same time; it is not unlikely they are results of the same cause. Daughters of the neighbouring authorities must have been among those concerned by Ezra's programme of divorce (as they were later concerned by the reforms of Nehemiah).[127] If so, the neighbouring authorities would have welcomed the opportunity given by the wall building to denounce Ezra (as they did Nehemiah)[128] for sedition. Their denunciations would have seconded the complaints and accusations from citizens of Jerusalem who did not wish to be divorced – or who had some other reason to dislike Ezra or the Yahweh-alone party. They probably raked up the stories of Zerubbabel's messianic expectations (which provided models for their later attempts to discredit Nehemiah)[129] and described the Yahweh-alone party as a perpetual source of hostility both toward its neighbours and toward the empire. The court was persuaded to send back an order prohibiting further construction and the neighbouring authorities promptly enforced it. What happened to Ezra was something his party preferred not to report, though they did keep the account of his mission, which he sent back to them in Babylon. His 'Book of the Law of Moses' disappeared with him. When Nehemiah arrived, some dozen years later, he found the walls in ruins, the assimilationist party in power, and the alien marriages continuing.[130]

6

Nehemiah

It is generally admitted that chapters 1.1–7.5a and 13.4–31 of the Book of Nehemiah are sections of the genuine 'memoirs' of its hero.[1] There are a few minor interpolations; much of chapter 13 may be excerpts from a longer original; certainly a good deal has been omitted.[2] Some fragments of the omitted material are often thought to be found in 11.1f. and in the narrative parts of chapter 12, but as to these supplements there is considerable difference of opinion.[3]

Nehemiah's book was a political tract, obviously intended to recall his accomplishments not only to his god[4] but also to his contemporaries. It was an attempt to win support by appealing to 'my record', to discredit his opponents with the people by revealing their traitorous plots, and to bring down on them the curse of his god by recalling their wickedness.[5] One may compare the poems written, a century earlier, by Solon, who likewise appealed to his record in an attempt to win support for his legal reforms,[6] and the 'autobiographical' propaganda put out, only fifty years before, by Darius I in the Behistun inscription, of which the Persian court had circulated manuscript copies that even in Nehemiah's time were read in Jewish communities.[7] This political motivation, however, affords no reason to doubt Nehemiah's report of the main course of events, as distinct from the interpretation he puts on them. Propaganda of this sort usually tries to win credence by accuracy in reporting what is generally known.

The reliability of these sections of Nehemiah's memoirs is of the greatest importance to the history of the cult of Yahweh. They are the longest piece of original historical[8] writing (as opposed to compilation) which we have from Palestine between the restoration of the temple and the Maccabaean revolt. The events they report were crucial in the development of the cult and the report they give comes from the principal actor in those events. Therefore they must be the touchstone of all histories of the cult during this period. The gaps and uncertainties of the evidence make it necessary that other parts of such histories must be largely conjectural. In the memoirs of Nehemiah are the facts with which all conjectures must agree.

Nehemiah was a cup-bearer of Artaxerxes I who profited by his favour with the king to ask and be granted permission to rebuild Jerusalem. This was in 444.[9] The Persians had driven the Athenians out of Egypt and had finally suppressed the Egyptian revolt so thoroughly that Egypt was exhausted. A subsequent revolt in Syria by the satrap Megabyzus had ended with a pardon for the rebel,[10] but must have left the country deeply disturbed, so Artaxerxes would be glad to establish a trusted servant in a strong position. Also, the Arabs to the south of Judaea were becoming a considerable power and raids by bands of Bedouin may have made fortification of the city desirable.[11] I Esdras 4.45 and 50 speaks of the Idumaeans (who were subject to the Arabs and often equated with them)[12] as having burned Jerusalem and seized a number of Judaean villages. The Book of Nehemiah begins with his learning that 'those who were not carried off as booty are there [in Judaea] in extreme hardship and disgrace and the wall of Jerusalem is breached and its gates destroyed by fire'.[13] It is absurd to suppose that this news, which reportedly caused Nehemiah to burst into tears, referred to the consequences of the Babylonian conquest, 150 years earlier. Even the interruption of Ezra's wall building, some thirteen years earlier, could no longer be news at the Persian court. Moreover, that was enforced by local Persian officials[14] and was probably not attended by any considerable carrying off of captives; indeed, even the partially built wall seems to have been left standing (since Nehemiah learned of its having been breached, and was later able to repair it in fifty-two days).[15] Therefore the supposition of an Arab raid is not unlikely, and this could have explained the king's willingness to have the city fortified. But the story knows nothing of such considerations. It represents the matter as a personal favour motivated solely by personal favouritism.[16] In this it may be correct. In spite of the modern fashion of finding valid *raisons d'état* for the actions of ancient monarchs, matters of policy at the Persian court seem often to have been settled by *raisons de coeur*.[17] It is possible, however, that Nehemiah may have omitted reference to contributory considerations, in order to increase the apparent importance of his favour with the king and make it seem that the permission to rebuild the walls was entirely due to his influence.[18]

Similarly, when he tells of coming to the city, he says nothing of any companions, but only of a military escort. However, after his arrival, he has 'a few men with me' and later on he speaks of himself as a member of a party (to which the gentry and officials of Jerusalem did not belong).[19] This party was, of course, the Yahweh-alone party,[20] which evidently had maintained its footholds both at the Persian court and at Jerusalem, in spite of the debacle under Ezra. Nehemiah's connection with it explains both his expectation of hostility from the rulers of the neighbouring provinces and the fulfilment of this expectation even before he began his reforms.[21] He reports their hostility, of course, as directed against all Jerusalem. But he also reports that they maintained most friendly relationships with the people of Jerusalem.[22] These reports can be reconciled by supposing the hostility resulted from Ezra's efforts and was directed, not against all Jerusalemites, but against the Yahweh-alone party. When Nehemiah arrived as leader of this party, its enemies were at once anxious to discredit the new leader by ensuring the failure of any project he initiated.[23] Therefore his secrecy as to his plans, the speed of his actions[24] and the choice and order of his projects, which suggest that his supporters and his determined enemies were both, at first, minorities of the people and that the majority was neutral. (He did not, of course, rely entirely – perhaps not even principally – on civilian support. He was the Persian governor and, like all Persian governors, had at his disposal a military force of men alien to the city in which he was stationed.[25] But if the majority of the people had been with him he could have begun his religious reforms at once, and if the majority had been bitterly hostile he could never have succeeded as he did.)

As things were, he did not at first attempt any of the reforms required by Deuteronomic or Priestly law. Instead, in spite of his piety, he prudently began with an action calculated to appeal to the common interest – restoration of the city walls. He authorized and protected the project, while wealthy individuals, singly or in groups, undertook the rebuilding of certain stretches; the same system was used, fifty years later, by Conon when the Persians sent him back to Athens and he rebuilt the long walls.[26] The system required the co-operation of the priesthood and gentry of Judaea, and they co-operated – perhaps compelled by public opinion, perhaps persuaded by memory of the Arab raid. All that Nehemiah's domestic opponents dared attempt, to hinder the project at this stage, was a little passive resistance and the circulation of defeatist verses.[27] Nehemiah alleges that the rulers of the neighbouring provinces planned to stop the work by a surprise military attack (4.2, 5f.). Whether or not they did is uncertain. United, they doubtless had the strength to carry through such a project, in spite of Nehemiah's preparations to meet them. What restrained them was probably the thought of repercussions in the Persian court. Therefore, Nehemiah's reports of their plot were most likely exaggerated, and this not only by the projection of his own hostility but also by policy. The repair of the walls required considerable sacrifice by the population of Judaea (4.4; 5.19). Such sacrifice would be felt less and borne more willingly if the people were both distracted and motivated by threats of surprise attacks and stories of the hostility of their neighbours. Accordingly, complaints about the difficulty of the building and threats of foreign attack appear simultaneously in Nehemiah's account (4.2–6). Then, too, such threats and stories would throw suspicion on persons who had married aliens and were therefore prominent in the political and religious party opposed to Nehemiah.[28] And yet more – the necessity of meeting the military emergency was a convenient excuse for drastic exercise of his powers as governor, especially for using his troops to 'protect' the builders (4.10) and taking other measures to prevent any from getting away (4.16).

But military power was not enough; he needed popular support. Therefore he next undertook that sole Deuteronomic reform most likely to increase his popularity with the majority of the people: he compelled abolition of interest, release of land and other property already seized for debt, and remission of debts.[29] The lenders were, as it happened, the local gentry – the leaders of the assimilationist party.[30] It is to be noticed that Nehemiah did not act quietly, by mere official order (as, being governor, he might have done). Instead he called a great assembly, confronted the offenders before all the people (most of whom, no doubt, were debtors), and made a speech (5.7–11). He dwelt on the efforts of his party to ransom Judaeans sold into slavery; he contrasted this with the local gentry's practice of selling Judaeans for debt; he paused dramatically to hear what his opponents had to say; without pausing too long, he pointed out that they were silent;[31] he denounced their practices, emphasizing their impiety and the disgrace to which they had exposed the Judaeans in the eyes of the neighbouring peoples; he slipped in the admission that he and his family and staff had also been lending money and grain at interest; and he demanded the abolition of interest and the return of the properties seized.[32] Of course – in front of the crowd – the offenders consented. He made them swear to it on the spot. The consequent increase of his popularity can be imagined.

He further increased it by remitting the taxes formerly imposed for the support of the governor and his staff. The expense of his establishment he met out of his own pocket – he must have had large private means.[33] He entertained daily at his table – which was a good one – a hundred and fifty Judaeans and lesser officials (but none of the local gentry!)[34] and numerous visitors from abroad (5.14–17). In spite of the opposition of the local gentry – whose members plotted against him with his opponents in the neighbouring provinces (6.17ff.) – he was able to complete the walls and perhaps to strengthen the city by drafting additional population from the surrounding towns.[35] Here his memoirs are broken off by large insertions of alien material. A good deal of the original text seems to have been lost. The narrative in chapter 12 – though much of it is obviously from the editor – suggests that some of the lost material contained an account of an elaborate religious ceremony organized to celebrate the completion of the walls. II Maccabees 1.18 and 2.13 say that Nehemiah rebuilt the temple and collected the books concerning the kings and the prophets and David; this may be true: he speaks of requesting large timbers to use in the temple (2.8). The tradition in II Maccabees would explain the way temple and walls are linked in Isaiah 56.5, the possible reference in Ecclesiasticus 49.13d to other building by Nehemiah in addition to the walls, and the tradition in Ezra 6.14 that the temple was not finally completed till the time of Artaxerxes. Josephus, *Antiquities* XI.181, reports that he built houses in Jerusalem for 'the priests and levites' to facilitate their resettlement in the city; this may be truth or plausible invention.

When Nehemiah's account resumes he says of the interval only that he returned to the Persian court, spent some time there, and then came back to Jerusalem (13.6–7). As to the date of these journeys we have no reliable evidence.[36] The wall building had led to charges by his enemies that he was plotting to revolt (2.19; 6.5ff.); some of his admirers, too, may have been so foolish as to see in him the Messiah.[37] Therefore it seems likely that he was recalled, or got permission to go back to defend himself, shortly after the walls were completed. He may have been gone some years – the Persian court moved slowly. But eventually he was vindicated, came back secure of his power, and immediately began to carry out a drastic programme of religious reform. He first struck at the prestige of his opponents by expelling from the temple an important ally of the assimilationist party – Tobias the Ammonite[38] – who had been given his room there by the high priest. Moreover, he had the rooms purified of the pollution which Tobias' establishment there had occasioned (13.4–9).[39]

Here we see again a conflict with the priesthood over purity law, like that already remarked in the time of Zerubbabel. By all traditions of ancient religion the high priest was the final authority on cult law, especially on purity law, and above all on purity law as it applied to his own temple. Yet here is Nehemiah, not a priest at all, a layman who could not even enter the holy area reserved to the priests (6.10f.), not only declaring unclean and forbidden what the high priest had declared clean and permitted, but also overriding the high priest's ruling and cleansing the temple of the pollution which he said the high priest had introduced into it. This cannot be explained as the off-hand action of a private individual, nor even a Persian governor. Unless Nehemiah had some legal tradition to which he could appeal, the high priest's complaint to the court over his violation of the temple law would have led to trouble. Accordingly, we must suppose that Nehemiah would appeal for justification to legal traditions preserved (or invented) by the Yahweh-alone party, and we must see him as the representative of that party's attempt to enforce its legal opinions in the Jerusalem temple, in contradiction to those of the established priesthood who, although not syncretists themselves (not, at least, in their official worship), held much more liberal views as to the permissibility of associating with the syncretistic worshippers of Yahweh from the neighbouring districts of Palestine.[40] (We may remark in passing that Nehemiah, if challenged, would almost certainly have justified his contradiction of the high priest by appeal to some written law code *interpreted* according to the traditions of his party. Here is the first conspicuous instance of the clash between priestly authority and pious laymen's traditions of scriptural interpretation. The Maccabees, the Essenes, the Pharisees, the early Christians and the leaders of the Reformation will spring from this root.)

Since control of the temple and final authority in questions of cult and of purity were basic to the priests' social position and income, Nehemiah's attack on these was a declaration of war, and he immediately followed it by striking at the priests' *de facto* control of the temple. He gathered the levites into Jerusalem, established them in the temple, and financed them by a 10% tax on the agricultural produce of the country (13.10–14). To judge from the many charitable provisions on their behalf,[41] the levites had been a poor class even before Deuteronomy closed the rural shrines at which many of them had been priests. Their fellow levites, the priests in Jerusalem, had refused to permit them to share in the income of the temple there (II Kings 23.9), and the destruction of minor holy places at the time of the Babylonian conquest had perpetuated their poverty. After the restoration of the Jerusalem temple, the priests there had permitted some of them to serve on the staff in inferior positions, for which service they were to receive unspecified 'portions', but these portions had not been given, so the levites generally had left the temple service and lived, scattered about the land, as one of the poorest classes of the population.[42]

Nehemiah, by securing their position in the temple and their income, must have won for himself and his party a body of devoted adherents. Their presence in the temple counter-balanced the power of the priests. Being present there, they could insist on the observance of the purity law of Nehemiah's party. And they could also be useful in the city. The Sabbath was not generally observed in Judaea;[43] the country people and the Tyrians brought their wares to the city and sold them on the Sabbath (13.15–16). This practice was under the protection of (again!) the local gentry, who presumably owned estates in the country[44] and had interests in the market places (13.17). Nehemiah put a stop to the trade by having the city gates kept shut through the Sabbath and guarding them, at first, with his mercenaries. Later, when the initial crisis was over, he replaced the mercenaries with a guard of levites, who so assumed the function of municipal, as well as temple, police (13.19, 22).

With the city thus in hand, Nehemiah was able to approach the reform Ezra had been so foolish as to begin with: the prevention of mixed marriages. Evidently he had no easy task – he had to resort to flogging and torture[45] to compel his opponents to swear that they would not permit such marriages to be contracted by members of their families. He drove into exile a grandson(?) of the high priest, who had married a daughter of the governor of Samaria, and a number of other priests and levites who had made such marriages.[46] At the same time, however, he tried to conciliate the remaining members of the priesthood by provisions for offerings to the temple (13.31). (It is to be supposed *a priori* that the priesthood, being a large collegiate body, was split by family and individual rivalries into more or less hostile cliques. Some of the high priest's opponents will have become Nehemiah's supporters, and his measures on behalf of the temple will have strengthened their hands.) With these events, and a prayer to be remembered for good, his memoirs close. They were written to defend his actions, so we can infer that the opposition remained strong and that he was never beyond the need of appealing for popular support. How long he remained in power is unknown, but 5.14 seems to indicate that his governorship ended in 432. He probably wrote shortly thereafter. He was not mentioned in a letter addressed to the authorities of Judaea in 408,[47] so he had probably died or been recalled sometime earlier.

Such was Nehemiah's career. To understand it we must try to see it first as a part of the general history of the times, and second, as a part of the special history of the cult of Yahweh.

The times of Nehemiah were those of Pericles and of Herodotus, of whom he was a younger contemporary. Herodotus visited Tyre, Gaza and Egypt sometime after 449,[48] that is to say, shortly before the beginning of Nehemiah's first governorship (444). Had he come back twenty years later, when Nehemiah's career had run its course, and had his attention been called to the events of the past twenty years in the little inland Persian province of Judaea, he would not have considered them extraordinary. He might have remarked that Judaea was a bit behind the times, that during his boyhood Persian governors of Nehemiah's sort – 'tyrants' he would have called them – had been common in the Greek cities along the

Aegean coast, but that the Persians had found them unreliable.[49] However, he might have added that their unreliability in the Aegean area was due to the existence of the Greek states as independent powers to which they could appeal for aid, that, consequently, their use in Palestine did not present the same dangers (not, at least, while Egypt was subdued), and that even in Asia Minor the Persians continued to use them, though mostly for the government of non-Greek peoples.[50]

To understand the word 'tyrant' which Herodotus would have used to describe Nehemiah, we must try to put out of our minds the pejorative sense which it had begun to acquire already in his time, and which later became almost universal, especially because of the influence of the Greek orators and of Plato.[51] Herodotus himself would not have used the word as a term of praise. He did not like tyrants.[52] But in his day, and for quite a while after, the word still had a wide range of meaning. Originally it had meant no more than 'sole ruler', and it retained this general sense even after Plato's time. However, from the seventh century on there had arisen a large number of sole rulers of a new sort, and the word had acquired a new reference to them.[53]

These new rulers were products of the economic and social change which was taking place all over the area. We must recall that at the end of the second millennium BC barbarian invasions had destroyed the order of the more ancient world, brought trade almost to a standstill, and reduced much of the Near East to a culture of mere local subsistence. As civilization gradually grew up again, the city-states of Greece, Asia Minor and Syria moved from an economy of subsistence farming and barter toward one of manufacture and farming for trade. This movement was accelerated by the development of the great Assyrian empire and the vast trade network of Greek cities in the ninth, eighth and seventh centuries. From the ninth century on a further acceleration was effected by the increasing use of precious metals as the common medium of exchange. This worked to the advantage of the rich who had them, against the small landowners and artisans, who now had to have them. The working was made more effective at the end of the seventh century when weights and qualities of metal began to be standardized in coinage, but even in areas where coinage was not soon introduced the movement followed the same pattern[54] and produced similar phenomena. Stabilization of society led to increase in population and foreign trade. Foreign trade increased venture capital and also produced a class of new rich, the traders, as opposed to the older aristocracy of landowners. Increases of capital, of population and, consequently, of need produced successively borrowing (at usurious rates), default, confiscation and enslavement. The resultant resentment and social instability was often used by ambitious political leaders to secure a following, seize control, and oust their opponents. Such revolutionary leaders, as distinct from the established rulers whom they replaced, were known as 'tyrants'. Neither their backgrounds nor their programmes were uniform. Some came from the new rich; many were maverick aristocrats; sometimes hereditary rulers – kings or dynasts – became tyrants by exceeding the traditional limits of their power.[55] Some tyrants drew their support from a small circle of wealthy friends, others from a particular ethnic group, others from private mercenary troops, many from the Persian government.[56] Some used their powers on behalf of the rich, others, of the poor, and many were pure opportunists with no social programmes, ready to adopt any policy to keep themselves in the saddle.

Perhaps the most common type, however, were those who got their following from the dispossessed and discontented lower class, and who therefore tried to satisfy their followers by such measures as public works programmes, cancellation of debts, release of persons enslaved for debt, confiscation of the property of their wealthy opponents, and redistribution of land.[57] In consequence of their programmes they were often extremely popular, though the accounts we have of them in the literature usually reflect the hatred with which they were regarded by the older aristocracy from which came most of the writers.[58] The pattern admitted of wide variation. Often lower-class support was only one factor in a tyrant's rise to power; of the many possible measures for relief of the poor, some were adopted in one case, others in another; it also happened that successful tyrants disappointed their poor supporters and, once in power, did nothing to help them.[59]

These economic, social and political developments were not limited to the Aegean area. The expansion of trade and growth of empire began in Phoenicia and Assyria. Before the end of the tenth century, the trading interests had reached Palestine; Solomon was already a partner in Phoenician ventures.[60] But Solomon's foreign trade was a royal monopoly; there is no sign of general mercantile development throughout the country. And things still moved slowly in the time after Solomon, when the land was looted by the Egyptians[61] and impoverished by internecine warfare between Judah and Israel. A recent survey of the pottery recovered from the sea off the Palestinian coast shows almost none – *ergo*, little coastwise trade – from the twelfth to the late ninth century; then a sharp rise beginning in the eighth.[62] In agreement with this, excavations show that by the middle of the eighth century a great change had taken place in Palestinian society: the division between rich and poor had become much sharper; the simple, uniform houses of the earlier centuries had been replaced by luxurious dwellings of the rich on the one hand, by hovels on the other.[63] In the mid-eighth century, accordingly, we encounter the prophecies of Amos, full of bitter attacks on the rich for their exploitation of the poor, and similar attacks are continued through the next century and a half by Micah, Isaiah and Jeremiah.

It is reasonable to assume that in Greece and in Palestine the movement followed the same lines, though the development in Palestine was somewhat earlier because of the proximity of Assyria, Phoenicia and Egypt. Therefore it is not surprising that we find in both Palestine and Greece similar literary and legal consequences of these social developments, taking place at almost the same time. Shortly after Yahweh had called the herdsman Amos[64] to prophesy in verse against the unjust rulers of Samaria and to proclaim that Yahweh would destroy Israel because of its neglect of justice,[65] the Muses called the herdsman Hesiod to attack in verse all rulers who perverted justice and to proclaim that any unjust city would be destroyed by Zeus.[66]

In the history of law, abuses usually come first, then complaints, and finally remedies. Particularly, the first codification of laws in a society is usually a somewhat tardy response to social development.[67] Accordingly, after the complaints of Amos and Hesiod, legal codification and specific reforms were only gradually effected in Greece and Palestine. And as the abuses (outlined above) were similar in both countries, so we find the same legal remedies being introduced in both, at about the same times. This deserves presentation in tabular form:

	Greece[68]	Palestine			
Legal reform	Athens 621, 594/2	Covenant code c.720[69]	Deutero- nomy 621	Holiness code 600–550[70]	Nehemiah 444
Usury prohibited	Megara 570–560	Ex. 22.24[71]	Deut. 23.30[72]	Lev. 25.35ff.	Neh. 5.10[73]
Debts cancelled	Athens 594/2		Deut. 15.2f.[74]		Neh. 5.10
Slaves released	Athens 594/2	Ex. 21.2f.	Deut. 15.12f. Jer. 34.8ff.	Lev. 25.29ff.[75]	Neh. 5.8[76]
Land re- assigned	Athens c.538			Lev. 25.13ff., 23ff.	Neh. 5.11

These parallels clearly show *independent* adjustment to the same social process. In Palestine the adjustment began by formalizing in the Covenant Code the probably immemorial traditions of Israelite society prohibiting interest and limiting the tenure of (Israelite) slaves. This proved insufficient, so the Deuteronomist went further by extending to debts the septennial limit on slavery (a plausible extension, since enslavement was the creditor's last resort). The authors of the Holiness Code felt this too was inadequate, and struck at the root of the matter by providing for a periodic redistribution of land (based on the notion said to have developed also in Sparta, that the tribesman's ancestral holding was inalienable).[77] This they could do more easily because (except for Josiah's brief enforcement of Deuteronomy and the isolated and unsuccessful instance of Jeremiah 34) none of this social legislation is known to have been enforced before Nehemiah's time – a fact which indicates the regard felt for this legal tradition by the ruling class of restored Jerusalem. When action did come, it came from a reformer seeking support against the established aristocracy. Just such a sequence, of just such measures, and just such a record of enforcement, fits exactly the sociological and economic history of the age of the tyrants – the seventh to fifth centuries.[78]

Against such a background of parallel social change it is impossible to dismiss as accidental the obvious similarity of Nehemiah's career to that of the typical tyrant. Moreover, that similarity is no mere matter of main outline. It extends to every detail: Nehemiah appeared at the time when coinage was first becoming important in his country; so did Cypselus of Corinth, Pisistratus of Athens, and, generally, the earlier tyrants along the Ionian coast.[79] He was wealthy in his own right, as most tyrants were.[80] He owned his position to appointment as Persian governor; so did a whole series of tyrants in Asia Minor.[81] He had formerly held a high position in the Persian court, but at his own request was sent back to his city to deal with local difficulties – and incidentally to ensure the city's loyalty to the Persians; exactly so was Histiaeus of Miletus. Nehemiah was maintained in power by his Persian garrison, but also had a party favouring him in the city; this was the typical situation of such tyrants.[82] He tried to increase his popularity, first of all, by a building programme which affected especially the religious centre and the fortifications of the city; so did Pisistratus of Athens, Polycrates of Samos, and many others. Such building was typical of tyrants; often it may have been used to provide employment (sometimes, perhaps, compulsory) as a means of economic relief and social stabilization.[83] The behaviour of Nehemiah's opponents, especially their intrigues with the rulers of neighbouring states, was no less typical than his own: disaffected factions in ancient Greece usually plotted with the neighbouring governments to overthrow, if necessary by invasion, those of their own cities.[84] Similarly, Nehemiah's use of these plots was typical: the tyrants regularly kept their people stirred up by threats of war, and used or invented surprise attacks as excuses for securing extraordinary powers.[85] We have already remarked that a number of tyrants made themselves leaders of tribal groups; Cleisthenes of Sicyon, in particular, tried to keep himself in power by stirring up hostility against opponents connected with his enemies abroad,[86] and even Pericles – who had many traits in common with the tyrants – put through a law discouraging marriage with aliens by disenfranchising children born of them.[87] That Nehemiah's economic reforms were those typical of the tyrants has already been shown, but it should be noticed that the way he put them through, the demagoguery of that assembly and that speech, was no less typical. In general, the stirring up of the poor against the rich was a regular procedure of the tyrants,[88] for their chief opponents, like Nehemiah's, were most often the members of the established aristocracies.[89] Accordingly, other tyrants, like Nehemiah, tried to make themselves popular by remitting taxes or fines due them[90] and by loans or direct gifts from their own funds to the needy.[91] Again, Nehemiah was like the tyrants in his lavish hospitality and entertainment of great numbers both of citizens and of guests from abroad. (Polycrates and the sons of Pisistratus were especially famous for this, but most tyrants made it a practice.)[92] When Nehemiah increased the population of Jerusalem by forcible recruitment from the surrounding towns, he was following a practice frequently used in his age – the Greek term is *synoikismos* – and especially favoured by the tyrants of Sicily.[93] The organization of elaborate religious ceremonies, the building of temples and the financing of the established religion were regular traits of the tyrant.[94] Pisistratus, in particular, patronized religion and is said to have had an official text of the Homeric poems prepared,[95] as Nehemiah reportedly had the sacred books collected. Collection of books is attributed also to Polycrates; of oracles, to Hippias.[96] Along with this patronage of religion goes the enforcement of religious taboos: Nehemiah purified the temple and enforced the Sabbath, Pisistratus purified the island of Delos and reorganized the Panathenaic festivals.[97] The constitution of a core of particularly devoted followers by special patronage of a group of the very poor was a manoeuvre to which many tyrants resorted.[98] The tithe on agricultural produce, by which Nehemiah financed his levites, was a tax also introduced by Pisistratus[99] and by Cypselus of Corinth (10% on all income, not only agricultural) for the benefit of their supporters.[100] With such support the tyrants were able, as Nehemiah was, to resort to acts of physical violence against their subjects. His floggings and hair pulling were examples of the acts of insolence and violence (*hybris*) by which tyrants regularly made their opponents hate them, and when he drove his opponents into exile he did what tyrants were expected to do.[101]

Given such an array of evidence, it is impossible to question Nehemiah's role in the general history of his times. Had Herodotus found reason to mention him, he would undoubtedly have described him as 'the tyrant of Jerusalem'.[102] We have now, therefore, to consider his role in the particular history of Judaism. What was accomplished by his tyranny?

He was remembered, of course, for the fortification of the city, as that was the accomplishment most prominent in the sections of his memoirs which the editor chose to preserve. Evidently the memory of his other building, too, lived on till the time of

Ecclesiasticus (c. 180 BC). Fortification must have made the city more attractive to merchants who wanted security. Consequently there will have been an increase of the alien mercantile influence. This Nehemiah may have foreseen. His lavish entertainment of foreigners suggested that he welcomed them, no doubt as strengthening the influence of the new-rich, mercantile class, in which he probably found support for his struggle against the landed gentry.[103] The influence of this class must have been increased by the growth of the city's population and its development as a centre of provincial government.[104] Greater wealth and size brought a greater sense of self-importance and independence; consequently the influence of the Mesopotamian diaspora declined.[105]

But far more important than his development of the city was Nehemiah's political and religious success. He seems to have won majority support for the programme of the Yahweh-alone party. With this achievement the party position becomes that of the Judaeans generally; for the first time it becomes a territorial, if not a national, religion in fact, as well as in ideal. This is not to say, of course, that all the Judaeans were won over. The landed gentry, the upper priesthood and those of the people who happened to have close ties with foreigners were no doubt bitterly hostile, and many of the country people were probably indifferent. As the subsequent history shows, the religious make-up of the province continued to be a union, necessitated by common interest and maintained by compromise, of competing parties. But from the caution of his early procedure we are justified in assuming that Nehemiah had won majority support before he attempted the reforms made in his second governorship. With that support and with those reforms the separation from the neighbouring peoples was now a *fait accompli*. The Judaeans had been made a peculiar people; the Yahweh-alone party had acquired a separate administrative district in the empire. Most of the people of that district were now marked off from those of neighbouring districts by exclusive devotion to Yahweh, limitation of their sacrifices to Jerusalem, peculiar customs (the observance of Sabbath), an attitude of hostility and a tradition of self-segregation. Whether the assimilationists liked it or not, they were in the same district with the rest, they were members of the same group, and they were bound to it by practical interests; as it moved they had to go along.

Now, therefore, the position of the Yahweh-alone party may first be called 'Judaism' – that is, the religion of (most) Judaeans. And from now on beings the gradual assimilation to it, by successive compromises, of the other forms of the cult of Yahweh. But the word *yehudi* (and its Greek transliteration *ioudaios*) long remained a territorial term (meaning *Judaean*). With the diffusion of the syncretistic cult of Yahweh,[106] persons who worshipped the god of the Judaeans came to be called, by extension of the term, 'Judaeans', so the word gradually became, in the Gentile world, a religious term meaning 'devotee of Yahweh'. When, after the triumph of the Maccabees, the other forms of the cult assimilated more and more to the teaching and practice of Jerusalem, the religious meaning of the term became more and more specific; by the end of the Maccabaean period it *usually* can be translated, with reasonable inaccuracy, 'Jew'.

The strength of Judaism, which compelled the other parties to assimilate to it, was primarily its tradition of lay study of the law, dating from Deuteronomy.[107] That was what kept it true to itself and set a limit to its compromises. But its further strength was its control of the temple, and this was Nehemiah's work. Not only had he won over the majority of the population of Jerusalem, but he had concentrated in the city – probably for this reason[108] – a considerable part of the population of Judaea, and he must also have had some following in the country districts. Thus he laid the foundation of popular support on which control of the temple had finally to rest. He drove out an assimilationist candidate for the high priesthood and so opened the way for a different successor – who later followed Yahweh-alone rather than assimilationist policies, no doubt because he had owed his place to Nehemiah and depended on Nehemiah's followers for continued support.[109] Finally, Nehemiah located in the temple a group – the levites – whose devotion to him and to the Yahweh-alone party was assured by the fact that their position and their income depended on it. They were made a police force and so gave the party an enduring instrument for control both of the temple and of the city. This was what made Nehemiah's reforms outlast his time. Majority support might change, the high priest would soon be succeeded, but the self-interest of an organized social group – that would endure.

Perhaps the importance of Nehemiah's achievements can best be indicated by speculation as to what would have happened had he failed. In that event the control of the temple would have remained in the hands of the assimilationist party and the Yahweh-alone party would have remained principally a religion of synagogue worship in the diaspora. How long it would have continued its efforts to gain control of the temple, and how long worship at the temple would have remained purely Yahwist, there is no telling. It is not unlikely, however, that in Palestine assimilation would soon have been followed by open syncretism. The Yahweh-alone party would then have had to abandon the temple, and the developments which actually took place after AD 70 would have begun in the Persian period, without the onus of hatred produced by the Maccabaean wars and the rebellion against Rome. Such speculations are not entirely worthless if they make it clear that the connection between Judaism and the worship of the restored temple was, in the philosophical sense of the word, 'accidental'. It was demanded, indeed, by the traditions and aspirations of the religion, but was not essential to its nature. The national, political, territorial side of Judaism, by which it differed from the other Hellenistic forms of oriental religions, was, as a practical matter, the work of Nehemiah. He secured to the religion that double character – local as well as universal – which was to endure, in fact, for five hundred years and, in its terrible consequences, yet endures.

7

From Nehemiah to Antiochus Epiphanes

The Old Testament contains no historical work dealing with the two hundred fifty and more years from the end of Nehemiah's regime (432?), to the beginning of the troubles under Antiochus Epiphanes (c. 170). This cannot be attributed to disuse of Hebrew during this time: the Song of Songs, Ruth, Ecclesiastes, Ecclesiasticus, many psalms, Chronicles, Ezra, Nehemiah, Jonah, Joel, many of the interpolations in the other books of the prophets, the earlier elements of Daniel, the later elements of Proverbs and Job, and the latest strata of the P material in the Pentateuch are commonly and more or less convincingly assigned to this period[1] and testify to the vigour and variety with which Hebrew lived on.[2] Nor can one suppose that historical writing as a genre was not practised at this time. On the contrary, this was the heyday of Hellenization, history was one of the genres most in fashion, and the many traits which Chronicles shares with Greek historical works[3] show that the fashion was influential in Hellenistic Palestine as it was in contemporary Babylon (Berossus) and Egypt (Manetho).

How can we explain, then, the disappearance of the historical works dealing with this period? It is tempting to answer that the Greek historical works of the Hellenistic age have also disappeared; of the writers who dealt with Alexander and his successors we have only fragments. This is a consequence of the triumph of classicism in later Hellenistic and, even more, in Roman times: certain ages and authors were selected as 'classical' for education; the rest were left to vanish from mere neglect. This process was paralleled in the history of Hebrew literature: in the Maccabaean period and later there was much imitation of early models – Judges by I Maccabees, the 'classical' prophets by Daniel,[4] 'the Psalms of David' by the Psalms of Solomon, Genesis 49 by the Testaments of the Twelve Patriarchs, I Samuel 1–2 by Luke 1–2, Elijah by John the Baptist. With this went neglect, and even rejection, of more recent works. The Pharisees, for instance, accepted in their collection of sacred books no work of which the alleged author was later than Nehemiah; that the books of the Maccabees and of Ben Sira recognizedly came from a more recent age had much to do with their being rejected.[5]

But this is scarcely enough to explain the almost total disappearance of all historical works dealing with a period of two hundred and fifty years in the life of a people which both before and after this period was outstanding among the nations of the ancient Near East for its production of histories.[6] And the disappearance had taken place before the triumph of 'classicism' in rabbinic education. Already in the first century AD Josephus knew so little about Palestine during this period that the items of his account can be listed briefly. He knew:[7]

1. the names of a few of the high priests (but not their succession);

2. the story of a murder committed in the temple by a high priest;

3. a story of the building of the Samaritan temple, intended to discredit the priesthood there;

4. two episodes from a Jewish Alexander legend (the first in defence of the privileges of Jerusalem, the second hostile to the Samaritans);

5. a reference from Agatharchides of Cnidus to Ptolemy I's capture of Jerusalem;

6. the references to Jerusalem in the (bogus) letter of Aristeas;

7. Polybius' account of the wars of Antiochus III;

8. a letter and a decree of Antiochus III granting privileges to Jerusalem;

9. a *chronique scandaleuse*[8] about the later Tobiads;

10. a (bogus) letter from a king of Sparta, claiming kinship with the Judaeans.

The character of this material is significant. Those elements which come from Jewish tradition (as opposed to invention) are mostly hostile to the high priestly family and their in-laws, the Tobiads of Ammon and the leading families of the Samaritans. The legitimate high priestly family had been a constant reminder that the Maccabaean high priesthood was illegal, and the Ammonites and the Samaritans had been among the primary opponents of the Maccabaean expansion. Since the little historical material which survived to Josephus' time was hostile to the opponents of the Maccabees, it is a likely guess that the larger bulk which did not survive had been favourable to their opponents, above all to the legitimate high priestly family which had been pre-eminent in Jerusalem during those two and a half centuries. It is reported that Judas Maccabaeus made a collection of books; it is not reported that he collected some and destroyed others, but the two activities are likely to go together.[9] The fact that the preserved historical works break off when the opponents of the Maccabees came to power and resume (in the Septuagint) with the events which led the Maccabees' rebellion and eventual triumph makes it seem likely that the Maccabaean collection was the source of the preserved material, and Maccabaean censorship the source of the surprising lacuna.

Consequently there is almost no direct evidence to determine which parties produced and perpetuated Old Testament material during the two and a half centuries between Nehemiah and Antiochus Epiphanes. Therefore discussion of the problem must be based on indirect evidence. We shall try, first, to determine the social divisions in Judaea during this period, then to describe, in terms of these, the religious divisions as they were at the end of Nehemiah's governorship. Next we shall outline those political events which would have contributed to party divisions, and shall indicate briefly some other factors which affected the formation of parties. Finally, we shall try to find in the Old Testament evidence of production or transmission by these parties, and so to determine the *Sitz im Leben* during these centuries of the Old Testament elements preserved from them.

The social divisions[10] most important in Judaea during Nehemiah's time can be discerned from his memoirs and from the list of wall builders in Nehemiah 3.[11] First there is the Persian governor (Nehemiah himself), his staff (including the commander of the citadel and the soldiers of the garrison) and his family.[12] (Like other tyrants and Greek generals in Persian employ, Nehemiah was looking out for his relations, and evidently had several brothers to assist him.)[13] Such a 'governor's circle' was a constant feature of city life through this period.

After the governor, the leading group is probably the priests –

at least they rank first when the groups are listed together (3.1). Their head is the high priest, who has a palace near the city wall (3.21). Attached to the temple, but inferior to the priests, are the levites, and there are yet lower ranking groups of temple personnel.[14] Neither priests nor levites, however, cut much figure outside the temple in the events Nehemiah has to report. Even in the temple the levites had been neglected prior to his reform (13.10), and their subsequent importance in the city was due to his initiative (13.22). They repaired only one section of the wall. The priests repaired many sections, and one of those was probably paid for by a priestly settlement in the Jordan valley,[15] but otherwise they appear outside the temple only to administer an oath (5.12). Prophets (and a prophetess) are important in the society,[16] but the evidence does not prove them a fixed social class, nor specially connected with the temple. A 'scribe' (*sopher*) is mentioned (13.13), but the meaning of the title is uncertain.

As opposed to all these probably religious figures, Nehemiah's main concern is usually with the laity, composed of the landed gentry (*horim*), the civil officials (*seganim*), 'the Judaeans' (possibly the heads of the families, regardless of wealth), and 'the rest of the people'.[17] As we saw in the previous chapter, the gentry were mostly the descendants of the Israelites left in the land by the Babylonians, and were leaders of the assimilationist party; they had close relations with the rulers of the neighbouring territories (6.17) and were interested in money-lending (5.7) and trade (13.17) as well as land. From them, presumably, came most of the thirty-odd individuals who undertook from their private means to repair portions of the wall. The officials were also among the money-lenders (5.7) and were blamed by Nehemiah for having neglected the support of the levites and, consequently, the upkeep of the temple (13.11). Nevertheless, he tried to win over by hospitality at least some of their members (5.17). He seems to have been on better terms with the heads of the families, perhaps because of his protection of the poor (5.17; 6.6). The title *sar*, which appears often in the list of wall builders, seems to be that of a territorial administrator (but also may be a military title);[18] how the persons who bore it were related to the gentry is uncertain. The people of the outlying towns had some sort of town organizations and could act through them independently of their local notables (3.5). In Jerusalem, when attack was supposedly imminent, the people were organized to fight by families (4.7), but after the wall had been completed shifts of guards were organized from the dwellers of Jerusalem without reference to families, each man being assigned to that portion of the walls nearest his own house (7.3). At least three trades were important in the city – the gold-smiths, the perfumers and the merchants.[19] We have seen that the Yahweh-alone party, mostly of diasporic background, was an im-portant element. Evidently, however, it no longer formed a distinct social class, since Nehemiah consistently writes of the people as a whole (contrast the reports from the preceding century in Ezra 1–6).

With this picture of the social structure of Judaea in Nehemiah's time (444), it is interesting to compare that implied by the letter of Antiochus III in 201.[20] The garrison (and, by implication, the commander of the citadel, if not the governor) is still there. The most important civic authority seems to be the lay council of elders (which the king twice names in first place).[21] After it come, in order, the priests, the scribes of the temple, the temple singers and the rest of the people. Evidently there has been a great increase in the number and importance of the scribes; 'the levites' have been replaced by or become 'the singers' (a change which also took place between P and the later strata of Chronicles!); but these differences are matched by the persistence of the garrison and the lay gentry, besides the priests, as the most important elements in the city. And along with the classes which Antiochus specified we must suppose the continuance of the bourgeoisie (Nehemiah's goldsmiths, perfumers, and merchants), the poor (city workmen and rural peasantry), a steadily increasing number of aliens (some resident, some on business visits, but mostly pilgrims), and the submerged four-fifths of all ancient cities – the women, the children and the slaves. These social classes were divided on religious, political and cultural questions, to say nothing of family and factional divisions. Hellenistic Jerusalem was a complex little city.

As to religious parties, our interpretation of Nehemiah's memoirs, presented in the preceding chapter, enables us to recon-struct at least roughly the situation at the end of his second governorship. There was no longer any question, in Jerusalem, of official syncretism as opposed to the worship of Yahweh alone. The conflict now was between Nehemiah's party, which we may call the separatists (who maintained that the worship of other gods was impure, therefore persons polluted by it should be barred from the temple and from marriage with Judaeans), and the assimilationists (who denied, perhaps the impurity, certainly the conclusions drawn from it).

The new separatist party was heir to the personnel and the legal and literary traditions of the Yahweh-alone party, but it was a different party. Its basis was not a circle of upper-class synagogues in the diaspora, but the bulk of the Jerusalem populace, especially the poor, whom Nehemiah had protected. Its leadership was no longer drawn from officials in the Persian administration, but from those few members of the Jerusalem priesthood and gentry who had gone over to Nehemiah's side and, mostly, from the levites whom Nehemiah had established as temple police and who had a vested interest in maintaining his tradition.

The assimilationist party, too, had changed as a result of Nehemiah's work. Along with the essential requirement of the Yahweh-alone party, it was coming to accept much of the party's literature – the Deuteronomic version of the national legend and history, the various collections of legal material preserved or produced during the exile, some of the books of the prophets, especially Second Isaiah, with its concern for the Gentiles. All of these the assimilationist party had adopted or soon would adopt for its own purposes and would interpret to suit its own position. On the other hand, Nehemiah's break with the high priest Eliashib had ended the priesthood's mediation between the Yahweh-alone group and the old Judaean families. Now the bulk of the priesthood and the gentry were united by opposition to the separatists. The union was made lasting by the priesthood's resentment of the levites' supervision in the temple, and by the gentry's intermarriage with the leading families of neighbouring territories, as well as by their hostility to the poor. Thus we can oppose the forces as follows:

Separatists	Assimilationists
A few priests	Most of the priests
Almost all the levites	
Most of the Jerusalem *plebs*	Almost all the gentry of Jerusalem and *Judaea*
Allied with the Yahweh-alone party in Mesopotamia and Persia	Allied with the Yahwist gentry of the territories around Judaea

Here certain groups are omitted. The lower temple personnel probably at first inclined toward the priests, their traditional authorities, rather than the levites, newly set above them. Most of the Judaean peasantry probably held to their old, syncretistic cult of Yahweh. The Jerusalem bourgeoisie were probably won over by Nehemiah; those of the smaller towns are an unknown quantity. But none of these figure in the earlier strata of the evidence.

To most of the people in the city, political party differences were doubtless as important as religious ones. When Egypt regained its independence in 401 and Jerusalem again found itself beside the frontier between Egypt and Asia, the city was presumably split between pro-Egyptian and pro-Persian parties. While the Persians were trying to reconquer Egypt, in the first quarter of the fourth century, the pro-Egyptian party must have kept out of sight,[22] but later on it succeeded in winning the city over to the Egyptian side – if not before, then almost certainly when Tachos invaded Palestine in 360. The reconquest by Artaxerxes III Ochus, some time within the next fifteen years,[23] resulted in a violent change: the pro-Persian party came back to power, many of the pro-Egyptian party were exiled.[24] The tables may (or may not) have been turned again, within another ten or fifteen years, by Alexander.[25] There is no indication whether or not the Judaeans took sides in the wars of the diadochi. The century of Ptolemaic rule (302–198) was mostly one of enforced political tranquillity,[26] until its last years, when the Seleucid conquest was in the offing. During this century, however, so many attachments to Egypt must have developed that the Seleucid conquest in 202–198 surely began by a period of renewed conflict between pro-Seleucid and pro-Ptolemaic factions, which probably contributed to the troubles under Antiochus Epiphanes.[27] Messianic expectations were also becoming important in this period, and seem to have led to an unsuccessful rising in the uncertain years between the second Seleucid invasion of 201 and the final conquest of 198.[28] Unfortunately we know almost nothing of the parties involved.

Besides religious and political divisions, a rift developed between persons who held to the old, Palestinian cultural forms (of language, decoration, costume, diet, exercise and so on) and those who adopted the newly fashionable Greek ones. The resultant differences, of which the complexity has been discussed in Chapter 3, were conspicuous among the causes of the Maccabaean revolt.

Further sources of divisions were the feuds of families and personal quarrels, of which we are told by Josephus (the murder in the temple, *Antiquities* XI.297ff.; the Tobiad scandals, *Antiquities* XII.160ff.) and II Maccabees 4.23ff. (the competition for the high priesthood). On a lower social level, the development of individualism produced teachers who sometimes wrote books, sometimes even founded sects expressing their own interpretations of the law. The Wisdom of Ben Sira is an example of the former, the contract in Nehemiah 10 and the passages in Enoch (89.73) and the Assumption of Moses (5.4f.) which declare all sacrifices of the second temple impure are traces of the latter.[29] But these minor causes of division are of little significance for the Old Testament material as a whole. That came down primarily from and through the major religious parties, and it reflects clearly the traditions of three leading social groups within those parties: the gentry, the levites, and the priests of the Jerusalem temple.

First, the gentry.[30] It was probably members of the upper-class laity who expanded with worldly-wise sayings the collection of proverbs dating from the time of Hezekiah, and attached to it the other minor collections which were used by the pious editor of our present book.[31] Such proverbial instruction was a familiar literary form throughout the ancient world: the Mesopotamian proverbs of Ahikar[32] (which were read in the Judaean colony at Elephantine), the use of the Egyptian sayings of Amenemopet by the Palestinian author of Proverbs 22,[33] and the Greek elegiac couplets of Theognis (whom ancient tradition dated about 540) are examples of its popularity in the sixth century. In Palestine as in Greece this popularity appears also from the importance of proverbial sayings in the dramatic dialogues of the fifth century.

Of these the great Palestinian example, Job 3–27, the remnant of the original Book of Job,[34] is evidently the work of a lay aristocrat. Job, like the heroes of the aristocratic Greek tradition, is – of course – a man of great wealth; that is taken for granted.[35] And the viewpoint of such a man is expressed in the book, which is entirely concerned with him and his relations to his peers and to God. There is much concern for the plight of man, but little for the plight of the lower classes. No less characteristic are the intensity of pride and the arrogant demand for justice – from God! – generated within the self-centered, aristocratic world. The problem here is essentially that which dominates Greek tragedy – the problem of *hybris*, that force which makes man overstep himself and challenge God. Since Job is roughly datable by its close relationship in style and contents to Second Isaiah (probably a relationship of dependence, especially in its conceptions of God and creation),[36] these fragments show that in Jerusalem, as in Athens, at about this time, agonized and revolutionary speculation on the nature of God and the problem of evil found expression in magnificent poetry cast in that form, dialogue, which was the ideal (if idealized) reflection of everyday conversation, the characteristic form of intellectual life in the early classical city-state.[37]

Another work of the same upper-class tradition was probably an answer to Job. It ridiculed the human pretension to speculate on such subjects. This answer – disfigured by innumerable pious interpolations – now forms the core of the Book of Ecclesiastes. In Jerusalem, as in Athens, the age of heroic speculation was evidently followed by one of criticism and practical morality, for which the goal of life was to live quietly and attain tranquillity.

Again, it was no doubt the gentry who produced or preserved the short stories of the Old Testament and the Apocrypha. Ruth and Jonah, Judith and Tobit, as we shall see, were written from the viewpoint of pious members of the assimilationist party. Esther, if not written in Palestine, was preserved there and probably by the same group which produced the other examples of this literary form – the Hellenistic romance.[38] Finally, we probably owe to the gentry the exquisite love poetry of the Song of Songs.[39]

All this material – Proverbs, Job, Ecclesiastes, Ruth, Jonah, Judith, Tobit, Esther and the Song of Songs – is essentially belletristic and as such is sharply distinguished from the national legend and history, laws and prophecies, preserved by the earlier Yahweh-alone tradition. This belletristic material testifies to the continued existence from the sixth to the second century of a lay circle enjoying wealth, leisure, and considerable culture (and of lay scribes and teachers who copied this material and perpetuated it as part of a humane literary education). This circle cared little for the old Israelite literature which had been preserved by the Yahweh-alone party. From all of that it took over and developed only the nucleus of Proverbs – *if* that was a party product. The author of Job was deeply influenced by Second Isaiah, and the authors of the short stories imitated or echoed – some more, some less – the historical books, but on the whole the most remarkable characteristic of this upper-class material, *vis-à-vis* the earlier Israelite literature, is its independence and originality, the reflection of a social clique which, as we should expect of one at the centre of the Jewish diaspora, was in close touch with the civilization of the surrounding pagan world. Its tastes, interests and literary products changed with the changes of international fashion: gnomic verses in the sixth century, poetic drama in the fifth, philosophic reflection in the fourth, romances and erotic poetry in the third and later, succeeded each other here as they did in Greece and Asia Minor and, presumably, in Syria and Egypt. As in Greece, too, the high point of the series is the poetic drama. The relation of the earlier collections in Proverbs to Job is clearly that of an archaic work to a classical one, and by comparison with Job we see in Ecclesiastes the decline of emotional intensity, the increasingly subjective concern, the pervasion of the poetry by an elegiac tone, which are typical of the Greek works of the late fourth century. It is no accident that the author has so often been compared with Epicurus; though there is no reason to suppose that he knew Epicurus' work, the similarities of temper and attitude are unmistakable.[40] As for the romances, their relation to Job is unquestionably that of pretty, little Hellenistic works (with fine touches of pathos, well-managed dramatic scenes, and circumstantial accounts of divine deliverance) to a masterpiece of the fifth century.

Thus the Judaean aristocracy, for which this literature was produced, kept in touch with the intellectual and artistic developments of the Hellenistic world. At the same time, however, as the same literature shows, it progressively came to terms with the law of the Jerusalem priesthood and the belief and practice of the Judaean populace – in a word, with Judaism.

The early material in Proverbs and the remains of the original book of Job (chs. 3–27) simply ignore Judaism:[41] they do not mention its special practices nor its festivals, they say nothing of worship at Jerusalem, they never refer to Israelite tradition,[42] and they know nothing of Israel as the peculiar people of Yahweh. The god of the worldly-wise strata of Proverbs is Yahweh, as the god of Ahikar is Shamash; but for Proverbs, as for Ahikar, the god governs all men alike. So does the god of Job 3–27, who is the universal deity (*ho theos*) of the theological speculation of the preceding century,[43] and therefore is not identified with Yahweh.[44]

(This complete indifference to Judaism is a good reason for dating Job in the period prior to Nehemiah.)[45]

The author of Ecclesiastes[46] has reconciled himself not only to the inadequacy of human reason but also – thereby – to a popular piety which is an important element in his world (though he never discusses it directly) and which he practises though he does not believe.[47] This is the typical adjustment of Hellenistic philosophers to the cults of the city-states. The canonization of his work was no mistake – here, as so often, the sceptic turns out to be the defender of (conformity to) the faith.[48]

By the time of Ruth and Jonah the authors have moved yet nearer their opponents, though they are still opposed to the separatist interpretation of the law. Ruth (as now edited)[49] demonstrates the permissibility of marriage with Moabites (contrast Deuteronomy 23.4).[50] Jonah demonstrates that Yahweh cares for all peoples, sends prophets to them, and will pardon them if they repent. Also the ridicule of the prophet in the Book of Jonah – he is represented as a petty, malevolent person, who has no human feeling and is also unwilling to obey Yahweh – may be due to its upper-class origin. The aristocrats probably had no love for the prophets of Yahweh, and this satirical portrait of a segregationist shows how they pictured them. By contrast Ruth is blessed by the prayer that she may be 'like Rachel and like Leah who both of them built up the house of Israel' (4.11). Rachel, here given first place, was the mother of the north Israelite tribes (whence the Samaritans) and 'both of them' is emphatic. Her husband, Boaz, is blessed by the prayer that his house may be like that 'of Perez whom Tamar [a Canaanite!] bore' to the patriarch Judah as the result of an irregular connection (so the Judaeans were in no position to throw stones at their northern neighbours).[51] Nevertheless, by these very arguments the author shows that he is familiar with the national legend. He appeals to its authority. For him, Yahweh is 'the god of Israel' (2.12). Similarly, the author of Jonah – *if* the psalm in chapter 2 is part of the original book[52] – is concerned for the glory of the temple at Jerusalem and opposes the worship of idols (2.5, 8f.).

With Judith, the process of Judaization has gone much further: Judith keeps the pure food laws even when dining *tête-à-tête* with Holofernes (12.19); the author goes out of his way to tell the national legend, with unquestionably Deuteronomic traits;[53] he can make his heroine declare that there is no longer in Israel anyone who worships idols or alien gods (8.18ff.). But the declaration is probably intended to assure the separatists that the Samaritans have now accepted the basic Yahweh-alone demand, for he also includes Samaria among the cities of post-exilic Israel (3.4). In 5.16 he is careful to maintain the Israelite ancestry of the Shechemites: 'Our ancestors drove out' the original Shechemites, and Israelites came and dwelt in their place, so the Shechemites of Judith's day were children of Israel. Finally, the sub-plot of his book has for its hero an Ammonite and for its climax this Ammonite's conversion, circumcision, and admission to 'the house of Israel' – an admission prohibited by Deuteronomy 23.4.[54]

Tobit is also an apology for north Israelites – originally for Samaritans and Ammonites, as Milik has brilliantly shown.[55] It explains that they were always scrupulously faithful to the Jewish legal tradition.[56] The author evidently accepts the tradition, but accepts the north Israelites, too. This concern for north Israelites and Ammonities in these two works is in striking contrast to their attitude toward Gentiles in general, and shows that some members of the gentry had, by this time, accepted the separatist attitude toward the Gentile world at large, but were still anxious to justify the inclusion in Israel, or admission to it, of those neighbouring groups with which they had personal connections.

All these works must come from that wing of the gentry which was most sympathetic to Judaism – the resolutely hostile wing which provided many of the Hellenizers under Antiochus Epiphanes presumably produced works the Jewish tradition did not care to preserve. Yet even the preserved works show the gentry holding tenaciously to their alliance with the neighbouring peoples. Moreover, by the fact that the works were preserved, they show also how far the other Jews were willing to go in tolerating that alliance. We have seen that the gentry slowly accommodated themselves to the religion; apparently they also accommodated the religion to themselves.

When we turn from the gentry to the levites, who were the backbone of the separatist party, we find an entirely different sort of literary tradition. From the gentry, as we saw, came a series of original works of Greek fashion, approximately datable and (except when interpolated) expressing consistently the opinions of individual authors.[57] From the levites we have Chronicles-Ezra-

Nehemiah and Psalms – huge compilations of old and new material, edited and re-edited over long periods of time,[58] and always with some addition and alteration and suppression. To attempt here a detailed analysis of these patchwork quilts is out of the question; we can only indicate some of the relations between the characteristics of this tradition and the levites' role in fourth- and third-century Judaism.

Nehemiah, as we saw, found the levites in poverty scattered throughout Judaea. He concentrated them in Jerusalem, supported them by a 10% tax on all grain, oil and wine produced in Judaea (13.10ff.), drove out the assimilationists among them (13.29) and established them in the temple as guards to enforce the observance of his party's purity law (13.30). He also used them as special police in the city to enforce observance of the Sabbath and doubtless for other purposes.[59] These facts explain the well-known problem as to the Old Testament's account of the levites – the problem of their function in the temple. In the P material they do practically nothing save guard the purity of the tent-temple from the approach of non-levites, and carry this tent and its utensils around the wilderness.[60] Accordingly the 'liturgical' levites in Chronicles have really no certain liturgy to perform,[61] and subsequently disappear without explanation.[62] The explanation is that Nehemiah introduced the levites into the temple not to perform any specific services but to enforce on the priests and the people his purity rules. Therefore their essential function was 'to mount the guard'[63] – just as P says – and no other was required. This accounts for the fact that their undescribed work is referred to as military service,[64] and that they are described as having a sort of police power over the temple, and supervision of its utensils and purity rules.[65] When they lost this police power their primary function disappeared and their special status almost disappeared with it.

But they were also given by legend another function: that of carrying the tent-temple and its vessels. This has been thought to go back to the time of the judges, in which the levites are supposed to have been a class of holy men, one or more groups of whom carried about with them an 'ark' – some sort of sacred box.[66] Whatever the facts may have been in pre-Solomonic times, it does seem likely that such a box was used in the Jerusalem temple and was carried in procession there, by the levitical priests,[67] until

Josiah (reportedly) prohibited the practice (II Chronicles 35.3).[68] No doubt the custom was preserved in the syncretistic cult of Yahweh, for processions of similar boxes or baetyls, thought to be dwellings of the deity, were a regular feature of the religion of the neighbouring countries;[69] this probably explains Josiah's (or the Chronicler's source's) prohibition, which clearly contrasts the carrying of the ark with the proper didactic and liturgical service of Yahweh and his people Israel. But in spite of these objections the rite won its way back into 'orthodox' circles and was perpetuated in synagogue services, the box containing the sacred law (the 'Torah') being used as the ark.[70] When this synagogue usage began is unknown. Deuteronomy 10.1–5 represents the ark as a portable Torah shrine (and therefore is probably a very late addition).[71] That it was such a shrine and that the levites continued to carry it in synagogue services is indicated by the great concern of the later strata of Chronicles for the ark.[72] This concern presumably reflects some religious ceremony of the Chronicler's time. Von Rad has shown that the passages in which this concern appears are mostly secondary; that the original work of the levites, in the earliest stratum of Chronicles, was 'guarding the tent'.[73] He has also shown, however, that the priests of Jerusalem (who claimed to be levites) had originally an ark tradition over which their concern for the tent-temple later prevailed.[74]

Therefore we can reconstruct the development as follows. The stories which represent the levites primarily as guards reflect the position given them by Nehemiah as a guard to enforce his rules in the temple and the city. Possessed of this position, they began to cut a figure in synagogue worship, and introduced into it practices drawn from their cult tradition, especially the processional carrying of a sacred box, now Judaized as the Torah shrine. Concern for their exclusive right to carry this box therefore appears chiefly in the later strata of their biblical writings, though the actual carrying of it had been one of their earliest functions and is therefore found also in the tradition of the priests, since many of them, too, had been, or claimed to have been, originally levites.

Nehemiah changed not only the social position of the levites but also, by winning them over to his party, their theology. We have seen[75] that there had been levitic elements in the Yahweh-alone party, and that the Deuteronomic code had shown much concern for the levites.[76] This concern was now implemented by Nehemiah, whose establishment of the levites in the temple without giving them priestly functions may be seen as a compromise between the ruling of the code – that they might serve in the temple (Deuteronomy 18.6ff.) – and the objections of the Jerusalem clergy (II Kings 23.9). In return the levites held to the Deuteronomic tradition. Chronicles-Ezra-Nehemiah have closer ties with Deuteronomy than with any other book.[77] So does Psalms, which shares with Deuteronomy as with no other book its constant concern for the poor. This concern reflects not only the prior poverty of the levites themselves but also the policy of their patron, Nehemiah, and the fact that after Nehemiah's demise the power of the separatist party must have depended on the support of the Jerusalem *plebs*.

The levites' adoption of the Deuteronomic tradition, together with their activity in synagogue services, accounts for the traces of Deuteronomic preaching which recur frequently in Chronicles,[78] and for the representation of the levites as mission teachers in II Chronicles 17. The prayers in post-exilic Old Testament works are predominantly Deuteronomic in language and the predominance of the Deuteronomic tradition in prayer may be due to the revival of that tradition by the levites. The story of Ezra's reading of the law, in Nehemiah 8, was made over by the editor into a typical synagogue service;[79] most prominent of his additions was that of levites to translate (?) and explain the law after it had been read. With explanation went the preaching and teaching already referred to. This liturgical and, especially, homiletic work of the levites may have been of great importance in winning over the peasantry, first of Judaea and then of northern Palestine (II Chronicles 17.7ff.). Accordingly, it is plausible to suppose that the levites played a leading part in the liturgical revolution which did most to separate Palestinian Judaism from the syncretistic forms of the cult of Yahweh – the substitution of synagogue worship for sacrifice.[80] This substitution was in accord with the philosophic thought of the hellenistic world, where criticism of sacrifice and the insistence that worship should be spiritual were increasing.[81]

Besides extending their influence through the synagogues and through preaching missions to the peasantry, the levites also attempted to improve their position in the temple. They seem to have tried, perhaps on the strength of Deuteronomy 18.6ff. and of their former standing as priests, to perform some priestly functions.[82] This the priesthood succeeded in preventing, a victory celebrated (along with earlier ones) by the legend in Numbers 16.[83] Here the arch-villain is the levite, Korah, whose 'descendants' included one of the guilds of singers most often mentioned in the Psalms; they also figured largely in the levitical genealogies in Chronicles and (less largely) in those in the Priestly history.[84] We shall return to the priests' victory later.[85] One of its consequences seems to have been that the levites lost their special police functions (at least with respect to surveillance of the priests) and consequently their special status. We may guess that in consequence they now turned to the lower classes of the temple personnel, especially the singers and doorkeepers, and not only won their support but succeeded in fusing with them and assuming their functions, and this so successfully that by the end of the fourth century 'the singers' stand in Antiochus III's list of temple personnel where 'the levites' had stood in Nehemiah 3[86] – an indication that the 'liturgical levites' had practically disappeared. Fusion with the singers presumably accounts for the importance of hymnody in Chronicles and of 'levitic' singers in the Psalms; it was probably through the levites that temple psalms began to play a large part in synagogue services.

The levites may also have tried to include prophecy in their liturgical functions. II Chronicles 20.14 shows a levite prophesying in the midst of a temple service, but this is slight evidence.[87] Chronicles does show, however, that the levites set much store by prophecies, and both preserved and manufactured them. Many of the late interpolations in the prophetic books are of homilectic material which might well have come from the levites, and many are prophecies against Egypt.[88] It is probable that the levites, following Nehemiah, were mainly pro-Persian.[89]

Other elements of the levites' tradition are the literary reflections of their rivalry with the priests. Accordingly, we find them laying claim to judicial authority; that they ever possessed it is dubious.[90] They also are represented as teaching the law.[91] This they probably did. They certainly developed a historical tradition, preserved in Chronicles, to which their patron, Nehemiah, owes the preservation of his memory.[92] Significantly, that section of the holy history which the Chroniclers chose to relate in detail began with David, who fore-ordained the temple service of the levites, and ended with Nehemiah, who re-established them in the temple. Since Chronicles certainly knew Samuel-Kings and often deliberately contradicted it, we must suppose it intended as a counter account to 'correct' the 'official' history, that is, that preserved by the priests.

In spite of the opposition to which the two histories testify, Chronicles shows also the approximation of the levites to the priestly tradition. This appears not only from its constant representation of the levites as the friends and helpers of the priests – no doubt an expression of prudence – but also from the fact that its style and content have been deeply influenced by P.[93] Thence have come, for example, much technical vocabulary, the religious concern for history combined with indifference to historical fact, and the habit of fabricating genealogies.[94] In this, however, these authors were not alone. The Greek historian Hecataeus of Miletus, about 500 BC, had written a book called 'Genealogies' which must have been rather like Chronicles.[95] Bickerman has argued that 'the Chronicler' is like Herodotus and other Greek historiographers of the fifth and fourth centuries (but unlike oriental 'historians') in that: (*a*) He does not simply transcribe his sources, but corrects them according to his own standards. (*b*) His purpose is not to give a mere chronicle, but an explanation of the history. (*c*) His finds this explanation in the divine disposition, which works particularly in retribution. (*d*) He drives home his point by introducing speeches from foreboders of doom and counsellors of wisdom. (*e*) His account becomes fuller as it approaches his own time, but does not come down to his own *floruit*. (*f*) He gives a large place to the reproduction of official records.[96] Along with these parallels to Greek historiography, Chronicles shows equally striking parallels to the third-century Egyptian 'Demotic Chronicle', which (although in prophetic, not historical, guise) explains history in the same fashion – every success or misfortune is referred to the merit or guilt of the ruler, and this is measured solely by the degree of his conformity to the divine law.[97]

Evidently Judaism itself, in spite of its policy of segregation, was moving in the same direction as the surrounding world. Indeed, even the policy of segregation was a typically Hellenistic move. Such resistance to syncretism and such efforts to preserve a small, limited society were well known in Greek tradition: for example, Pericles' legislation against inter-marriage, the segregationist ideal of Plato as expressed in the *Republic*, and the widespread admiration of conservative Greeks for the self-segregation of the Spartans.[98]

The works produced by the gentry and the compilations of the levites show fairly clear-cut traditions with well-marked and persistent characteristics. By contrast, the material preserved in the great priestly anthology of legends and laws, the Pentateuch,[99] is surprisingly self-contradictory.[100] Unfortunately, attempts to disentangle and date the strands of Priestly tradition and edition have resulted in wide disagreement among competent specialists.[101] Therefore we cannot here attempt a detailed analysis, but must do what we can to explain the contradictions from the make-up and history of the priesthood.

The priests of the Jerusalem temple had been instrumental in introducing the Deuteronomic reform under Josiah which prohibited sacrifice outside Jerusalem,[102] but they had refused to implement the Deuteronomic law that levites from other holy places might serve in the Jerusalem temple.[103] They had co-operated in syncretistic worship of Yahweh with the rulers before and after Josiah, but they had also, during or after the exile, claimed that only they, the *soi-disant* descendants of Zadok, had remained faithful to Yahweh alone, and that, in consequence, only they should be permitted to serve at the altar of the restored temple.[104] However, when the Jerusalem temple was restored a number of non-Zadokite families seem to have been accepted in the priesthood[105] (perhaps to get help for the restoration?) and the genealogies of priestly families continued to be revised down to Maccabaean times to make room for newcomers – most of them, like the Maccabees, probably of levitic stock.[106] In matters of theology the record was equally mixed. The high priest Joshua, in the time of Zerubbabel, had been attacked by the separatist party as unclean, but had come to terms with them to get their recognition of the powers claimed by the priesthood and their support for the building of the temple.[107] Ezra had been a priest, but there had been priests among the assimilationists in his time.[108] This record makes it probable that the priesthood was a divided group in Nehemiah's day when many of its members went into exile in Samaria, but many (presumably) stayed in Jerusalem to benefit from Nehemiah's measures on behalf of the temple.[109] (It will be recalled that not even the levites were completely united by

Nehemiah; some of them had married aliens and may therefore have sided with the assimilationists.)[110]

By driving into exile one contendent for the high priesthood, Nehemiah effectively worked on behalf of another. We may assume that the man he helped was one who would follow the separatist party line, and would be maintained in power, on this condition, after Nehemiah's governorship, by the levites and the bulk of the populace, devoted to Nehemiah's memory. Accordingly, it is not surprising that in 411–410, when the Judaeans of Elephantine wrote to Jerusalem for help toward the rebuilding of their syncretistic temple of Yahweh, Anath and Bethel, they got no answer from the high priest Jehohanan and had to turn to the Yahwists of Samaria (who did help them).[111] The two or three decades after Nehemiah's governorship were probably the high point of the power of the levites. They had the popular support Nehemiah had won; the priesthood was divided and the high priest was dependent on them for his security; many leaders of the assimilationists had been driven into exile; the new governor, who was a Persian,[112] would at first be cautious and neutral. Accordingly, it is here that we should date the levites' attempt to take over priestly functions in the temple.[113]

Perhaps the failure of this attempt is to be connected with the Persian governor's decision to replace Jehohanan by his brother, most likely the brother who had married Sanballat's daughter and so had the support of the Samaritans as well as of the assimilationist party in Jerusalem.[114] The governor was a friend of the Samaritans[115] and presumably wanted peace in his province. The priestly group of the separatist party were particularly savage in their opposition to Gentiles.[116] This trait can hardly have recommended them to a Persian governor. If it were compounded with troubles caused by an attempt to give the levites priestly functions (so as to counterbalance, or even oust, the assimilationist majority of the priesthood?) the governor's decision to get rid of a high priest who was the creature of such troublemakers would be understandable. When his move was forestalled by the murder of his candidate, he revenged himself by a heavy tax on every lamb offered in the daily sacrifices. The murderer was soon succeeded by his son.[117] Even if the new high priest was of his father's party, this scandal and the consequent limitation of the temple worship must have done much to damage the separatist party's prestige, and probably resulted in its fall. A further factor in the situation was probably the Persian loss of Egypt in 401, which must have damaged Persian prestige in Palestine and so diminished the influence exercised there by the Yahweh-alone party, from its stronghold in the Persian central administration. (It cannot be supposed that Ezra and Nehemiah had left no friends behind them.)

At all events, the assimilationists almost certainly came back to power in Jerusalem early in the fourth century. But things were different now from the days of Eliashib. The separatists still had strong support from a large body of the population, and they had set an example of government on behalf of the poor and, through the levites, of popular teaching and preaching, which must have communicated to all but their most determined opponents something of their ideals of ethnic purity and – within the ethnos – of fraternal assistance.[118] Whether for these reasons, or for others lost to us, the new authorities behaved with moderation. The levites remained subordinates in the temple, but they remained, and some families, who had forced their way into the priesthood, were even permitted to remain there (with appropriate adjustment of their genealogies).[119] However, the levites now lost their police powers over the priesthood and their special status; their fusion with the lower groups of singers and doorkeepers began. The settlement was evidently a compromise. That it was successful is proved by the emphasis in Chronicles on the cooperation of the levites with the priests, and by the friendly references to the priests in Psalms. The great document of this compromise, however, is the Pentateuch,[120] a new, official edition of sacred laws and attached legends, including material from both parties which had to live together in the temple. (No compromise, of course, reconciles all members of both parties. In this instance the irreconcilable separatists, led by a few priests and more levites, made a new covenant of their own and put at the head of its articles the battle cry of the separatist party. No intermarriage with Gentiles! The piety of the levites has preserved the document and attributed it to Nehemiah [Neh. 10]. It is interesting as the first example of Jewish sectarianism,[121] but in its day it must have been insignificant by comparison with the moderate and inclusive legal compilation sponsored by the assimilationist priesthood.)

Prerequisite for such inclusiveness must have been the development of an oral exegesis which reconciled for practical purposes the contradictory requirements of the various laws included.[122] Among these laws it is customary to distinguish the 'Covenant Code' (Exodus 21–23), the Deuteronomic code and its editorial developments, the 'Holiness Code' (Leviticus 17–26), and a large body of miscellaneous Priestly material (P) closely cognate to the Holiness Code and often spoken of as including it. Of these laws, the Covenant Code was already part of the national legend; the Deuteronomic code was the inheritance of Nehemiah; the Holiness Code seems to be the product of some special Priestly tradition; while the rest of the various elements in the Priestly material were probably derived from equally various elements in the gamut of the priestly families, and ranged from pre-exilic traditions to *ad hoc* legislation and genealogical and other inventions produced at the time of this edition.[123] To what extent these bodies of legal material (and the national legend) had been combined before this time, it is impossible to say. Presumably there had been an earlier collection (or collections), since the Priestly material, even when it appears as editorial expansion of earlier passages, is itself not uniform, but sometimes shows an earlier, separatist stratum 'corrected' by assimilationist revision.[124] But of the many attempts to distinguish such editorial strata, none has secured general acceptance. We must therefore resign ourselves to take both the assimilationist collection (substantially the present Pentateuch) and the Priestly material in it as they stand, and so try to determine their general characteristics.

This Priestly material is distinguished by uniformity of ideas (in spite of contradictory rulings)[125] and, especially, uniformity of language. It has a peculiar vocabulary of technical terms, because the authors were a professional caste: when they wrote of professional matters they wrote in professional jargon. The first certainly datable work in which their jargon (with minor variations) predominates is that of the priest Ezekiel.[126] This professional caste was evidently an aristocracy. Its members were immensely interested in genealogies – a fashionable topic of their times. They even invented a family tree of nations, to make Israel the head of the family.[127] On the practical level, no element of their tradition later than the Holiness Code (commonly dated in the sixth century)[128] shows any concern for the relief of the poor. (The provision that poor men may bring cheaper offerings at least enables them to bring something; one may question whether it was primarily intended to aid the poor or the priesthood.)[129] As well-to-do professional 'religious', these priests were indifferent to the eschatological speculation and the vivid angelology which were becoming popular in their time, and they cared little for the enthusiastic side of worship, the side of music and festivity.[130] Both as priests and as authors of material for professionals, they were indifferent to homiletic and rhetorical effects;[131] the work of the priests was not preaching, but offering the sacrifices.

Their interests were those of their position: first of all, the cult, their principal occupation. Sacrifices and festivals were much developed and were regulated in detail.[132] Greatest of all festivals is now the Sabbath, the goal and completion of creation, the cause of the commandments, the sign of the eternal covenant between God and Israel.[133] They were much interested in those aspects of the cult from which they derived their income – the perquisites of the priests, the payment or redemption of vows, taxes for the support of the clergy, these also were substantially increased.[134] Next come questions of ritual purity on which they were the authorities. (Note the absence of civil and criminal law, which was not in the jurisdiction of priestly courts.)[135] After cult and purity laws comes the sacred tradition, conceived as a collection of precedents for ritual rules.[136] One development deserves special notice. Earlier story referred to a tent which housed the ark and (another tent?) where Moses went to talk with Yahweh.[137] The P tradition made this tent the archetype of the Jerusalem temple, and accordingly retrojected, into the wilderness of national legend, not only the equipment, services, ordination ceremonies and administrative disputes of the fourth century,[138] but also their own notions of what would have been fitting in the past, their dreams of what should be in the future, and their visions of what existed in the eternal present of the heavenly world.[139] The resultant tangle is notorious.[140]

It is chiefly in the stories and rules connected with this tent-temple that the peculiarities of the Priestly theology appear. These priests were especially concerned about atonement, usually effected by their sprinkling or pouring the blood of sacrifices on or near an altar, and by their eating the sacrifices so that the iniquity would be transferred to them.[141] Further, they were concerned about the temple as the dwelling place of Yahweh, where Yahweh manifested himself and where the high priest met him. Hence the high priest was a mediator between Yahweh and men, a means of revelation,[142] as conceded by the Yahweh-alone party in the time of Zerubbabel.[143] The concern for holiness' – not only ritual purity, but also moral likeness to Yahweh – which distinguishes the Holiness Code does not appear consistently in the P material, but the P tradition preserved the code. The concern for ritual cleanliness is probably not a theological peculiarity, but merely the professional preoccupation of this group.

Besides these general characteristics the different strata of the priestly material show special attitudes and concerns.[144] Often the late material is datable by its reflection of the increased power and pretensions to royalty of the high priest[145] (pretensions which can hardly have been possible until the breakdown of Persian provincial administration in the fourth century, culminating in the satraps' revolt and, for Jerusalem, the alliance with the Egyptians against Persia).[146] Often this later material shows the irenic concern of the assimilationist editors. Various scholars have remarked different results of this concern: Morgenstern noted the greater lenience toward old popular rites.[147] Baudissin supposed the purification for the levites was added to give them greater dignity.[148] Von Rad found a great number of 'doublets', for instance:

Genesis 17.15–22/Genesis 17.1–8 (assimilationist expansion)

Genesis 17.15–22/Genesis 17.23–27 (extension of God's blessing to Ishmael, the ancestor of the Arabs)

Genesis 27.46; 28.1, 2, 6, 7/Genesis 28.3–5, 8f. (apology for Edomites)[149]

Besides such indications in the text, evidences of assimilationist control in Jerusalem are to be found in the historical events and archaeological remains of the period. If we have been correct in supposing that the separatist party was pro-Persian, then the alliance with the Egyptians and the Spartans against Persia is evidence that the assimilationists were in power. (Perhaps at this time occurred the first contacts which led to the friendship of the Jews and the Spartans.)[150] At this time, too, is dated the famous coin bearing the inscription YHD (i.e., *Judaea*) and showing a deity, perhaps Yahweh, in the guise of a Greek god, seated on a winged throne and confronting a Dionysiac mask.[151] This coin shows that the authorities in Judaea (perhaps, now, the Jerusalem priesthood)[152] were adopting Greek ways and had probably explained Exodus 20.4 ('Thou shalt not make any image') as prohibiting only statues made for the purpose of worship. How far they were willing to go toward satisfying the surviving syncretist element in the Judaean peasantry is shown by Leviticus 16, which prescribes that once each year a goat is to be sent from the Jerusalem temple into the wilderness for 'Azazel', presumably one of the 'satyrs' whose cult had long ago been attacked by the Yahweh-alone party.[153]

Among the most important steps taken by the assimilationist legislators was the creation of a new legal status, that of the 'proselyte', the alien who has accepted the Jewish law, is subject to all its requirements, and enjoys all the rights it confers. For such an individual they used the term *ger*, of which the history shows the stages which led to this concept.[154]

Ger at first meant 'resident alien',[155] a meaning it never lost.[156] The number of such aliens seems to have increased in the last days of the monarchy, partly from refugees fleeing the Assyrians, partly from the influx of semi-nomadic groups who came as migratory agricultural workers.[157] Accordingly, they were an important part of the poor for whom the Deuteronomic code was concerned, and the code made many provisions on their behalf.[158] It did not, however, subject them to the laws it made for Israelites; in fact, it provides, as a charitable measure, that 'unclean' food which an Israelite may not eat is to be given to a *ger*.[159] However, when the authors of the Holiness Code legislated for the holy people which was to be, their concern to protect the people from contact with unclean things led them to subject the *ger* to the prohibitions and cleanliness rules of the Israelite code.[160] They also ruled explicitly that he should be subject to the same civil laws as were Israelites, and they urged that he should be treated as kindly as if he were a native,[161] but they did not extend to him the religious privileges of the law, let alone consider him a fellow Israelite,[162] and they made no provision by which a *ger* might, if he wished, obtain the privileges of the law. Deuteronomy 23.7f. had provided that a third-generation descendant from an Edomite or an Egyptian (but not an Ammonite or a Moabite!' might be considered, legally, an Israelite, Ezekiel 47.22 had foreseen that in the coming 'End' *gerim* who had begotten children in the holy land should be as natives and share in the Israelites' inheritance.[163] But meanwhile there was nothing to do.

The question became important as a result of its connection with purity law. The sixth century had seen an abnormal development of the concern for purity (e.g., Ezekiel's fixation on the subject, and the epidemic of Orphic purifications in Greece).[164] In Palestine this concern survived into the following centuries. We have already remarked that the struggle between the Yahweh-alone party and the Jerusalem priesthood, from Zerubbabel down to Nehemiah, turned on the question of purity, which therefore became the basis of the difference between the separatist and assimilationist parties. It was also the basis of the attack on mixed marriages, for ritual purification is a legal privilege. A Gentile cannot be purified. Accordingly, Ezra attacked mixed marriages as communicating to the married the impurity of the Gentiles, and divorce was recommended as 'the immersion pool for Israel'.[165]

Another factor in this position was the notion of the cult law as a complete and indivisible rule of life, a notion which appears in the Yahweh-alone party with the Deuteronomic code. This notion was an important cause of the dispute over the admission of Gentiles to the temple. No doubt Yahweh had always made certain purity requirements of those who wished to visit him; many gods of the ancient world did so.[166] But these requirements usually could be satisfied by a few days' observance of certain taboos and performance of some ritual lustrations. Thus they made possible what may be called 'occasional conformity'. For Ezra, by contrast, what Yahweh required of those who would worship him was observance of his Law – a lifelong commitment, and a commitment possible only to Judaeans.

That the aliens involved in the mixed marriages might become proselytes – that is, might accept the obligations of the law and also receive its benefits, including purification – was something Ezra never considered.[167] Nor was it considered in Nehemiah's time,[168] not, at least, by Nehemiah. But the idea was apparently introduced during Nehemiah's governorship, by the author Isaiah 56.1–7, who announced it as a new revelation.[169] He attempted to moderate between the parties. He recognized Nehemiah's achievement in rebuilding the walls and repairing the temple (v. 5); he agreed with him as to the importance of the Sabbath; but he opposed his treatment of aliens. He was so unkind as to console him publicly for being a eunuch,[170] and he added insult to charity by bracketing eunuchs with Gentiles (whom Nehemiah was driving out, v. 3) and by assuring the members of both groups that their devotion to Yahweh and their worship at the temple were welcome and would be rewarded. At the same time, however, he required of the Gentiles that they should 'be joined to Yahweh to serve him and to love the name of Yahweh, to be slaves to him', to keep the Sabbath without profaning it, and to hold fast to his covenant (v. 6).

The prophecy of Isaiah 56 was fulfilled by the legislation of the priestly authors of Exodus 12.43–50; Numbers 9.14; 15.1–31; 19.10 and 35.15; Deuteronomy 29.10; and Joshua 20.9. The passage in Exodus provided that a *ger* who wishes to do so may be circumcised and offer the Passover, 'and so he shall become as a native of the land' (12.48), that is, privileged not only to use the same Passover law (12.49; Numbers 9.14) but also, as a native Israelite, to follow all the prescriptions of the indivisible, holy Law. Exodus 12 probably represents a slightly earlier form of this legislation than does Numbers 9: it still uses *ger* to refer to the as yet uncircumcised resident alien,[171] whereas Numbers takes for granted that the *ger* has already been circumcised; it thinks of the *ger* as the alien who has already accepted the law, and it merely rules that in celebration of the Passover (as in all other respects) he is to follow the same rules as the native Israelite.[172] So, too, Numbers 15 presupposes that the *ger* is a member of 'the congregation of the children of Israel'; atonement made 'for the congregation' results in pardon for 'all the congregation of the children of Israel including the *ger* among them, because all the nation acted in ignorance' (15.25f.). Here the *ger* is one of 'the nation'. The verses following specify that the legal provisions for expiation of sins are available to the *ger* as to the native; again they are to follow the same law. Similarly the legal means of purification are made available to *gerim* in Numbers 19.10 and in 35.15 and Joshua 20.9 both they and the *toshabim* (see below) are granted the protection of the cities of refuge.[173] Finally, the very late author of Deuteronomy 29 included the *gerim* as part of 'the people' in Israel's covenant with Yahweh.[174] The authors of these laws must have been among the latest editors of the Pentateuch: they presupposed the Holiness Code, which had subjected the *ger* to the prohibitions of the law, therefore they said almost nothing of these prohibitions. As a consequence of the new technical meaning which they gave to the word *ger*, a new word was needed for 'resident alien' (*ger*'s former significance), so the word *toshab* was used for this purpose in the latest strata of the Priestly laws.[175]

By thus developing the concept 'proselyte', the assimilationist priesthood proposed to settle by compromise the problem of mixed marriages: the separatists' concern for purity and observance of the law would be satisfied, but the marriages could be tolerated. Ultimately, though not without opposition,[176] the compromise prevailed.

But individual proselytism was not sufficient to undo the damage which the separatist party had done in cutting Judaea off from Samaria and so separating the two largest Palestinian groups of the worshippers of Yahweh. To heal this breach an agreement had to be reached directly between the Jerusalem priesthood and the rulers of Samaria. This was probably facilitated by the family relationships between the two and was eventually reached (or celebrated) by further family alliances (which helped Josephus confuse the situation under Artaxerxes I with that under Artaxerxes III).[177] Another facilitating factor was the relationship of the populations (and their awareness of it). We have seen that the Assyrian conquest left a considerable Israelite population in the country.[178] Although Ezra, Nehemiah, and their disciples tried to appropriate the name 'Israel' for the Judaeans,[179] yet Zechariah still prophesied to 'the house of Israel' as well as to 'the house of Judah' (8.13), and even the authors and editors of Chronicles (when they were not writing polemic) referred to the northern Palestinians as Israelites.[180] Nehemiah did not know the word 'Samaritan' as a gentilic term which he could apply abusively to Sanballat (as he applied 'Ammonite' to Tobias); he did the best he could with 'Horonite', which probably referred to Sanballat's birthplace (or principal residence?), Beth Horon.[181]

Since the Judaeans and the north Israelites continued to worship Yahweh, and since we are told that the cult in the north was sacrificial,[182] the problem which had to be overcome on the Judaean side was that of explaining away the passages in Deuteronomy which prohibited sacrifice outside Jerusalem. This problem the assimilationist priests had already met when they combined the Deuteronomic and Holiness Codes in a single collection, since the Holiness Code anticipated (and seems framed to necessitate) sacrifices in every village.[183] Perhaps their harmonistic exegesis simply interpreted Deuteronomy's references to sacrifice at 'the' place which Yahweh would choose as meaning 'any' such place, that is, any established shrine ('the' often has the meaning of 'any' in Priestly legal texts).[184] Whatever the explanation, it was judged sufficient by the authorities (who had produced it), and – what mattered – it did suffice to satisfy both the Samaritans and the moderate elements in Jerusalem. Of course the extreme separatists were furious. But the essentials of the law were not affected, so the moderates consented to go along. II Chronicles 33.17 palliates sacrifice at the high places, provided it is offered to the Lord.

The Samaritans were probably less concerned with textual interpretation than with practical politics. Their alliance with Jerusalem would constitute the most important group in Palestine, a centre of power important in the disintegrating empire of Artaxerxes II. Because of the separatist party in Jerusalem, this alliance could not be secure unless Samaria accepted the Jerusalem law. Formerly that had been impossible, but now the assimilationists had gained control of the Jerusalem priesthood and had produced this new edition and interpretation of the law which was not incompatible with continuance of the established cult in Samaria. It would therefore be accepted. Policy dictated its acceptance, so that was that. The arrangement was made between the authorities on either side; it was almost a family matter.

No doubt enforcement in Samaria was at first extremely lax and acceptance by the Samaritan populace came slowly. There must have been islets of determined resistance. Syncretist names, at least, continue in the Samaritan papyri down to the time of Alexander.[185] But the process of acceptance was probably facilitated by the fact that most of the provisions in the Pentateuch reflected the immemorial usage of local courts or customs. It was not so much a new or alien law which the Samaritans accepted as a new collection of works embodying their own laws and traditions. Its acceptance revived some ancient customs, like the observance of the Sabbath, which had almost disappeared from common use (Nehemiah 13.15ff.),[186] and helped to kill out others, like sacrificial worship at local shrines, which were going out of fashion, anyhow. As to consequences in terms of practice during the next century, there is very little evidence. For this purpose the stories retailed by Josephus are practically worthless.[187] They project on to earlier periods the hostilities of his own day.

Finally, two points deserve special notice. In the first place, sacrifice was rapidly going out of fashion as an element of private religion. In the priestly material private sacrifices have been reduced to works of supererogation and are consistently slighted.[188] The spread of the village synagogues probably killed off the village high places in northern Palestine as it did in Judaea.[189] Prayer and praise were cheaper than sacrifice, as Strabo's source remarked (*Geography* VI.2.36). Only the official cults at Jerusalem and Samaria and perhaps a few holy places in the north, most likely Mt Gerizim, required reconciliation. The interpretation necessary to reconcile them was not more difficult than that which later was required to justify the temple at Leontopolis, the Maccabaean high priesthood, the theology of Paul, and the perpetuation of rabbinic Judaism without any sacrificial cult whatever. In the second place, the chief legal point at issue was the approval of sacrificial worship. What Deuteronomy had forbidden outside Jerusalem was *sacrifice*. The building (or rebuilding?) of *a temple* on Mt Gerizim, whenever it took place, made no essential difference.[190] The 'Samaritan schism' is not to be dated from the erection of this temple but from the breakdown of relationships between Jerusalemites and Samaritans, which led to reversal of each group's legal opinion as to the permissibility of the cult carried on at the other's sanctuary.

In Jerusalem, the rule of the assimilationists was interrupted, after their alliance with Egypt, by the capture of Jerusalem by Artaxerxes III (Ochus) probably in the 350s.[191] Not only did Ochus exile many of the previous, pro-Egyptian government, and install a government drawn from pro-Persian, separatist circles, but also his punishment of the city must have produced a reaction against the previous policy. This accounts for many of the prophecies warning against alliances with Egypt[192] – our present collection of prophetic books was probably being put together about this time.[193] The change of parties in Jerusalem may have produced a temporary crisis in relations with the Samaritans, and may have contributed to Josephus' erroneous location of the 'Samaritan schism' in the period immediately following.[194]

Alexander's defeat of Darius in 333 probably brought the assimilationist party back into power. There they seem to have remained during most of the following century, in which we hear of Ptolemy Euergetes coming to sacrifice at Jerusalem[195] and of the adventures of Joseph the tax collector, whose mother was a sister of the high priest of Jerusalem and whose father was a descendant of Tobias the Ammonite (*Antiquities* XII.160ff.).[196] Joseph was able to borrow enough money from his friends in Samaria (probably the district)[197] to bribe his way into the good graces of the Ptolemaic court, and get the post of tax-gatherer for Syria, Phoenicia and Samaria. This he held for twenty-two years, in which he made a fortune (224). His son Hyrcanus[198] was in equally good favour with the Ptolemies, and for the same reason. Driven from Jerusalem by an alliance headed by his own brothers and the high priest Simon the Just, he settled in Transjordan, where he built a stronghold decorated with great carvings of animals, and a similarly decorated temple.[199]

Simon, for his part, seems to have been all things to all men. We have just seen him as an ally of the Tobiads. The Pharisaic tradition claimed to derive from him.[200] He was praised by Ben Sira, who was a Hellenized opponent of Greek teachers and towards whom the Pharisees were at best ambivalent.[201] He was extremely successful in his dealings with Antiochus III, in which he seems to have relied upon the thoroughly Hellenized members of his court.[202] In this ability to deal with all parties he was a typical representative of the Jerusalem priesthood, as it had been shaped not only by its domestic history but also by the military and administrative history of Palestine and by the development of the diaspora during the preceding century.

From the viewpoint of the history of religion, the principal achievement of the Jerusalem priesthood during this century and a half (330–180) of assimilationist control was to establish their corpus of religious law – the Pentateuch – so firmly as the law of Yahweh and the law of the land that its preservation could become the battle-cry of the Maccabees, and its interpretation the central concern of later sectarian Judaism. The unique prestige of 'the Law', like 'the Law' itself, was the work of the priesthood.

As veneration increased, understanding diminished. The Greek language was one aspect of Greek civilization which Alexander's conquest made much more important in Jerusalem than it had been before. It became immediately the language of the civil government, and probably soon thereafter the language of most literature and upper-class conversation. This must have hit

Hebrew hard, since it had been living – apart from its liturgical use – chiefly as an upper-class, quasi-literary language; among the lower classes it had been widely replaced by Aramaic.[203] Accordingly, the third century BC, the century of Ptolemaic domination, probably saw the last major corruption of the Hebrew texts of most books of the Old Testament. These books have passed through a period when their copyists and glossators were amazingly ignorant of Hebrew. This period must have been posterior to the fourth century BC, of which we have seen the rich and various Hebrew literature, and prior to the first century BC, since the Dead Sea manuscripts have shown that the consonantal basis of the common ('masoretic') biblical text was already in the main established at the beginning of that century,[204] though other text types were also in circulation. Further, Lieberman has proved that this basis resulted from the use of Hellenistic methods of textual scholarship.[205] Since Alexandrian textual criticism, which began with Zenodotus (fl. 285), reached full development only with Aristophanes (born c. 257), its influence in Palestine cannot be dated much before 200, and the reform of the text was probably accomplished in the peaceful generation from 198 to 173 (which saw also the humane Hebraism of Ben Sira), not in the troubled Maccabaean times.[206] Therefore the period of most serious corruption, which presented later scribes with the errors they so faithfully preserved, must be located in the century from 300 to 200. This is not to say that ignorance was then universal. Even the errors in the text are proof that it continued to be copied. And linguistic change is never consistent: groups which held out against the assimilationist tendency may also have preserved their linguistic purity.

During or shortly after Alexander's reign, the city of Samaria was destroyed and resettled with Macedonians.[207] Thereafter (if not before) the principal centre of the cult of Yahweh in northern Palestine became Mt Gerizim, where a temple either had been or soon was built. Josephus knew nothing of Samaria's resettlement. Therefore when he talks of 'Samaritans' in the Ptolemaic and Seleucid periods, it is necessary to decide whether he refers to pagan inhabitants of the city of Samaria or to the Yahwist inhabitants of the district of Samaria.[208] These latter we may call 'Shechemites', since Shechem, beside Mt Gerizim, was their principal town. (The archaeological evidence indicates that it was built all at once, as a new city, in the late fourth century, presumably by the people who were driven out of Samaria.)[209] It is the Shechemites to whom *Antiquities* XII.10 refers[210] and the reference shows that in the early Ptolemaic period the Jews and Shechemites in Egypt formed a single community – they quarrelled as to the expenditure of their community funds, because some wanted to send their sacrifices to Jerusalem, others to Mt Gerizim.

Since the city of Samaria was several times destroyed in the late third and early second centuries, and since the local population was doubtless drawn on to repopulate it, the sharp difference between the Macedonian settlers and the people of the neighbourhood was probably soon blurred. Shechem, too, seems to have been destroyed, at least in 198.[211] However, it was soon rebuilt, and Ben Sira (50.26) still distinguished Samaritans, Philistines and Shechemites, and disliked them all.[212] More significant than his dislike – which may represent only personal or party opinion – is the fact that he has no name for the Shechemites, because they were called and called themselves 'Israelites',[213] 'Hebrews',[214] and even 'Jews'.[215] A poet named Theodotus wrote, probably during this period, a work celebrating the 'holy city' of Shechem; it is entitled 'Concerning Jews'.[216] Now 'Israelites' they were – the Israelite strain in the stock must have been at least as strong as any other – and their adoption of the Pentateuch presumably led to their adoption of the term 'Hebrews', but the use of the word 'Jews', that is, 'Judaeans', to designate them is surprising. Presumably the city of Samaria remained largely pagan and the Yahweh cult – at least, that form of it which accepted the Pentateuch – remained, in the north, confined chiefly to the rural districts, where its members were given the name of the larger and more prosperous group to the south. Thus also in Egypt: there was a town in the Fayyum called 'Samaria' – unquestionably by the people settled there, to commemorate the city they had lost – but the inhabitants are referred to in the papyri as 'Jews'.[217]

At all events, Antiochus Epiphanes evidently considered the Shechemites and the Jews to be one religious group, and this opinion was shared by Jason of Cyrene, who wrote that Antiochus 'left governors to vex *the* [one] race, in Jerusalem, Philip . . . and in Gerizim, Andronicus. . . . And after no great time the king sent out Geron, an Athenian, to compel the Jews to depart from their ancestral laws . . . and to pollute the temple in Jerusalem and call it by the name of Zeus Olympios and that on Gerizim, of Zeus Xenios.'[218] Josephus gives what purports to be a transcript of a request in which 'the Sidonians in Shechem' declare that they had formerly been following Jewish customs in sacrificing and in observing the Sabbath, and had therefore been thought by the royal agents to be Jews, and are now being made to suffer for it. They protest that they are Sidonians by ancestry and differ from the Jews in their customs, and they ask permission to dedicate their temple to Zeus Hellenios.[219] To take this protest at its face value and suppose the community in Shechem actually the result of Sidonian settlement would be naïve. The document is an attempt to deny a generally accepted identification; to support the denial it has produced a typical Hellenistic fiction. For historical purposes it proves that the Shechemites had hitherto been considered Jews (though it suggests that there may have been a considerable Sidonian influx into the community[220] and that this was expected to give colour to the claim that it had originally been Sidonian). Josephus does not report the petition which the Hellenizing party of the Jerusalem priesthood submitted to Antiochus Epiphanes when they requested permission to dedicate the temple on Zion to Zeus Olympios. It probably followed much the same line as the Samaritan one. At all events it was granted and the dedication was put through in Jerusalem as (probably) in Samaria.[221]

These passages show that down to the beginning of the Maccabaean period there was no 'Samaritan schism'. This, too, was the evidence of the upper-class Judaean works – especially Judith and Tobit – studied earlier in the chapter. The same conclusion would seem to follow from Waltke's observation that the Samaritan Pentateuch was influenced by the proto-Masoretic text, but later went through a period of corruption[222] – probably a reflection of the two periods, first 198–173, when the Masoretic text was being formed and the upper classes of Jerusalem and Shechem were on good terms (above, n.205), then the Maccabaean period, when Shechem at first was in the hands of Hellenizers, later was at war with the Maccabees, and finally was destroyed about 107.[223] Further, no schism is proved by the fact that the Samaritans do not accept the prophets.[224] The only evidence for the canonicity of the books of the prophets before the Hasmonaean period is Ben Sira's knowledge of the collection and reverence for the men (49.10).[225] Here again, it is not safe to base a judgment as to official status on what is almost certainly an expression of personal opinion. As to Ben Sira's dislike of Shechemites: no doubt the separatist party in Jerusalem always thought the Samaritans transgressors of the law, and presumably there was an anti-Jerusalem party in Shechem, but there is no evidence that either of these parties was dominant for any length of time. Within their communities they formed 'factions' (*staseis*) – one of the most characteristic elements of Hellenistic community life. From the Samaritan acceptance of the law to the Maccabaean revolt there is no reliable sign of any lasting and official breach. Shechemites and Judaeans formed a single religious community in Ptolemaic Egypt and were treated as a single religious community by the Seleucids until the Hellenizing party in Shechem protested. Their protest may have been no more representative of Shechemite opinion than the contemporary acts of the Hellenizers in Jerusalem were of Judaean opinion, but representative or not, it began an official separation which was confirmed by the Shechemites' non-participation in the Maccabaean revolt. (The 'Samaritans' who helped the Seleucids probably came from pagan Samaria.) From this time on there were two religious communities. Both Shechemites and Jerusalemites presently revised their text of the Pentateuch to justify their practices, so from that time on there were two official texts of the Law.

With this emergence of two texts of the Law we may terminate the present study of the Palestinian parties and politics that shaped the Old Testament. The next stage of the history – the break-up of the priestly control of Jerusalem, the resultant party conflict, the ultimate triumph of the Maccabaean party, and the establishment of its leaders as a new line of priest-kings – would require another book. That book, moreover, would have to extend its survey beyond the boundaries of Palestine to the Israelite diaspora, where party politics were already, in the Ptolemaic period, shaping the development of the Greek Old Testament, and were soon to become of major importance for the transmission of Maccabaean history. Consequently it has seemed best to limit the present book to the comparatively simple and unilinear history which has been recounted and which suffices to demonstrate the close relationship of most books of the Old Testament to the party politics of Palestine.

Alt's Account of the Samaritans

The preceding text has generally avoided reference to Alt's theories concerning the Samaritans, for it contradicts them in so many points, and they are so interdependent, that they can best be discussed all at once in this appendix.

Alt begins with the following hypotheses. *Perhaps* the groups imported by the Assyrians into northern Palestine formed an upper class intended to hold down the native population. *Perhaps* this upper class depended for its foreign support on its distinction from the native population and therefore did not assimilate. *Perhaps* it was able to hold out in Samaria, when Josiah conquered the rest of the country (as Alt thinks he did), and *perhaps* it was restored to its privileges by the Babylonians and *perhaps* it was maintained by the Persians and *perhaps* through the Babylonian and early Persian periods it voluntarily continued its policy of self-segregation.[1] Therefore *perhaps* the Israelite population of the country remained substantially free from foreign admixture until the time of Christ.[2]

The evidence for these hypotheses is Ezra 4.9f., which identifies the officials of the Persian regime in Palestine as men of Erech, Babylonians, etc., settled there by 'Osnappar'. Now 4.9f. is generally recognized as a gloss on the accompanying letter.[3] The only question is whether it reliably reports the content of the original letter (as Rudolph thinks, arguing chiefly from the Persian titles) or whether it is an invention of an interpolator who wished to show 'what a mixed rabble the Samaritans really were' (so Torrey,[4] arguing from the accord of purpose with such obviously polemic passages as II Kings 17.24–41). Most likely it is both. The Persian titles of the officials probably do come from the original letter, the list of dubious gentilics and what follows it is probably polemic (4.14 suggests that the writers were salaried officials, not gentilic groups). Apart from 4.9f. and 4.2, which reflects the same polemic purpose, Alt has no substantial evidence for the existence of a consciously Mesopotamian upper class in Samaria during the days of Nehemiah. (The Aramaic ostraca to which he refers[5] prove nothing for this point. Of course there were foreign officials there in the Persian period, but such a permanent local upper class as his theory requires is quite a different thing from a handful of officials. Moreover, Mesopotamian names are no proof of Mesopotamian ancestry, witness Zerubbabel and Sheshbazzar.) The upper class which was there in the days of Nehemiah was certainly not exclusive,[6] and was not Mesopotamian according to Ezra 9.1, which describes its members as 'Canaanites, Hittites, Perizzites', etc. This description, of course, demonstrates only the author's imposition of ancient traditions on the peoples of his own day, but Ezra 4.9b–10, Alt's proof text, is another example of this same technique and not a bit more trustworthy than 9.1. Indeed, it is less trustworthy, for nothing except 4.2 – which comes from the same hand – confirms it,[7] whereas 9.1 is independently confirmed by Nehemiah 13.23, which reports intermarriage with 'women of Ashdod', that is, the descendants of the Canaanite-Philistine stock, and says nothing of Mesopotamians.

Moreover, it is far from certain that the groups imported by the Assyrians ever formed an upper class. The importees may have been settled in Palestine as punishment for rebellion somewhere else. No evidence that these were a privileged class is to be found in Ezra 4.4, which says that the opposition to the returned Jews came from 'the people of the land', for we have seen that this refers to the native population of Judaea.[8] Nor can their privileged status be proved by appeal to political necessity: the subjection of the country might be ensured simply by the introduction of an alien minority which would have difficulties with the native population; the central government would then be committed to neither and could play one against the other. It is also presumable that many Israelites were pro-Assyrian at the time of the conquest and that the Assyrians rewarded them with permission to remain in the land and take over some properties of the exiles. (As for the notion that the Israelite population remained free from foreign admixture, we have dealt with that above in Chapter 4.)

Next Alt goes on to hypothecate: *perhaps* Judaea was part of the province of Samaria until Nehemiah's time,[9] and *perhaps* in the period before Nehemiah the temple at Jerusalem was the only 'privileged' (i.e., government authorized and supported?) centre of worship in the whole province, and *perhaps* in this period it regained the allegiance of the supposedly pure Israelite lower class of the whole province.[10] *Perhaps*, therefore, Ezra was sent out to enforce his law on the whole province, and *perhaps* this accounts for the adoption of the Pentateuch by the native, uncontaminated Israelite stock of Samaria.[11]

The opinion that Judaea was part of the province of Samaria prior to Nehemiah's time is based on the fact that no Judaean governor is mentioned in the stories of the investigation of the building of the temple, the interference with the wall building, the visit of Ezra, and the arrival of Nehemiah.[12] But the silence of these stories is not probative, especially since, in the case of Nehemiah, at least, the explanation cannot be that there was no prior governor, for Nehemiah 5.15 shows that he had predecessors of his own rank – otherwise the point is lost.[13] Again, Alt has no reason except the needs of his theory to doubt that the regular title of Zerubbabel meant what it is regularly supposed to mean, 'Governor of Judah'.[14] Therefore the silence is reduced to that of the local officials who investigated the building of the temple, in Zerubbabel's time, and that of the Ezra story with the related story of the wall building. But both these stories concern peculiar moments, at which it may have been that there was no governor of Judah for the nonce. The investigation seems to have followed Zerubbabel's disappearance, as well it might, and it might equally well have preceded the appointment of a successor. It may be that the elders of Jerusalem got permission to go on with the temple because they persuaded the investigating officials that Zerubbabel had been put out of the way on account of his incipient disloyalty. That a successor was appointed is indicated by Malachi 1.8, which is normally understood to refer to the governor of Judah (and here again Alt has no reason save the needs of his theory to doubt this interpretation). It may be that Ezra was sent out as a special commissioner, instead of a normal governor, because of the legal change the court contemplated at that time. That *he* undertook the rebuilding of the walls would explain why the neighbouring authorities had to be sent to stop it. These arguments were sufficiently strong when they were first written in the 1950s. Since then the question has been settled by discovery of the seals of the governors whose existence Alt denied; see N. Avigad, *Bullae and*

Seals from a Post Exilic Judean Archive, Jerusalem, 1976 (*Qedem* V), 33f.

Thus the administrative union of Judaea and Samaria never took place. Therefore no one need be surprised that it is never mentioned by the preserved literature and there is no indication that it had any effect on the religious life of the province. That in this period the Jerusalem temple was the only centre of Yahweh worship in the whole province is a hypothesis unsupported by any evidence. Consequently, it is unlikely that Ezra was sent to enforce his law on the whole province of Samaria. For this latter hypothesis Alt's evidence is Ezra 7.25f.,[15] which does not refer to Samaria but to the whole satrapy of 'Beyond the River', that is, everything west of the Euphrates, north of Egypt, and south of Turkey – a reference which already marks it as unhistorical. This proof passage seems, by structural relation to its context, a late addition, and, by content, an improbable piece of wishful thinking.[16] There is no report of any attempt to carry out its orders; Ezra's reforms extended only to Jerusalem and even in Jerusalem they probably raised such a storm that he was recalled within, at most, two years, so his enforcement of the law on Samaria could not have amounted to much, at best.

However, any enforcement of any law code of the Deuteronomic tradition, as interpreted by a man of Ezra's spirit, would have required the suppression of the native Yahwist cult in Samaria. (To suppose that the north Israelites remained worshippers of Yahweh from 722 to 458, but had no sacrificial cult of their deity, is absurd.) Suppression of their native and long-established cult would have been contrary to what is generally reported of the Persian administration's protection of local religious groups; it would have required a military occupation to make it effective; and it would have exasperated the population of an area danger-ously close to Egypt, which was in revolt at both of the times usually proposed for Ezra's visit (458 and 398 BC). Therefore the Persians would never have tried it. If they had tried it, the separatists in Judaea would have celebrated the action with whoops of joy which would certainly have come down to us. But we hear nothing of any attempted suppression of the northern cult. Therefore it was never attempted. But even if it had been attempted and if the law had been successfully imposed, by force, in 458, on the whole district of Samaria-plus-Judaea, the imposition on

Samaria would hardly have continued after Judaea was separated
(as it was by Alt's account) in 444, and the Samaritans would
hardly have continued to accept a law which had to be forced on
them in the first place only fourteen years before. Therefore the
problem of acceptance is not alleviated by this hypothesis of
Persian imposition. Nor could the imposition of a law in the time
of Ezra account for the acceptance of the present Pentateuch,
which, as Alt admits, did not take shape till after Nehemiah's
time.[17] Finally there is, in fact, clear evidence that the north
Israelites were not won to Judaism in the time of Ezra, nor long
after: II Chronicles 30.10f. reflects Jewish missionary enterprise
in Samaria and Galilee at the time of the Chronicler.

Neglecting these difficulties, Alt goes on to hypothecate: *perhaps*
the uncontaminated Israelites in the south of the Samaritan district
remained loyal to the law and to the Jerusalem temple after the
political separation from Judaea had led the alien upper class to
establish a temple of their own on Mt Gerizim. *Perhaps* this loyalty
enabled the Maccabees to plead to the Seleucid government that
those who were devoted to the Jerusalem temple should be under
the civil jurisdiction of its high priest, and *perhaps* Demetrius II's
transfer, in 145, to the Maccabees, of three districts of southern
Samaria is to be explained by the fact that 'the Seleucid government
of Palestine . . . now accepted this argument'.[18] Evidence for this
is 1. that the transfer was previously offered by Demetrius I (I
Maccabees 10.26–45); 2. that this offer was so worded as to suggest
that the districts to be transferred were in some sense subject to
the high priest already; and 3. that the final transfer limits its
benefits 'to those who sacrifice in Jerusalem.'[19] Since this chain of
hypotheses, resting on these three arguments, is the only evidence
Alt has for the existence of an uncontaminated Israelite lower class
in the southern part of Samaria, it is worth while to examine first
the arguments and then the hypotheses. Arguments 1. and 2. can
quickly be disposed of: I Maccabees 10.26–45 does not offer the
transfer, it speaks of it as already made. Therefore it never bothers
to name the districts transferred. This anachronism is one of the
many traces of an unusually clumsy forger, who may have had
some genuine text to expand, but who expanded it with palpable
absurdities (vv. 34f., 39, 44f.). Argument 3. depends on inference
from a text manifestly corrupt and probably to be corrected[20]
according to the résumé in Josephus, *Antiquities* XIII.128.

According to that, the reference to 'those who sacrifice in Jerusalem' has nothing to do with the transfer of the territories. It belongs to a grant of certain tax exemptions to those who sacrifice at the specified shrine, that is, either to the priests who actually perform the sacrifices, or to the donors who give the objects sacrificed. The common notion that these donors would be only 'orthodox Jews'[21] is certainly wrong; many non-Jews brought sacrifices to Jerusalem.[22]

It is ludicrous to suppose that the gang of Cretan mercenaries who ruled through Demetrius II[23] were motivated by statesmanlike concern for the religious liberties of their subject populations. On the contrary, they were motivated by statesmanlike concern for all they could get. They probably guessed that their time would be short. Consequently they sold Jonathan a legal claim to the territory in return for some handsome bribes in hand (I Maccabees 11.24) and a promise (perhaps no better than the claim) of 300 talents quick cash. Jonathan wanted the territory as a step toward the port of Jaffa.

Granting that there were numerous Jews in these territories and that this may have been a factor in the Maccabaean acquisition of them, it by no means follows that these Jews were pure remains of the original Israelite stock. Conversion was frequent in the Maccabaean period, and in the 300 years between Nehemiah and Jonathan the population of Judaea may have overflowed its bounds.[24] Certainly it is more plausible to suppose the Jews outside Judaea either converts or émigrés than to accept Alt's account of their origin.

Least likely of all, however, is Alt's account of Samaritanism as the result of adherence, by an unassimilated Israelite lower class, to a temple built in the last years before Alexander's conquest by an alien aristocracy, concentrated in Samaria, which had maintained its exclusiveness and, presumably, its hostility to said Israelite lower class for the past four hundred years.[25] A temple established by such an aristocracy would scarcely attract at once the loyalty of their victims. But within a few years after Alexander's conquest, Samaria was resettled with Macedonians. Alt's former upper class, concentrated there, would have been utterly ruined. Thereafter the support for the temple on Mt Gerizim was principally rural. It was also amazingly obstinate; even the Jewish conquest of the whole territory and the destruction of its temple

failed to shake it; whereas, according to Alt, the Israelite population, which had so long been loyal to Jerusalem, should have
seized the first opportunity to go back to Judaism.

In sum, neither Alt's alien aristocracy nor his uncontaminated
Israelite lower class is to be found in the evidence, or is even
reconcilable with the course of events which the evidence does
reveal.

ABBREVIATIONS

A and P	R. Charles (ed.), *The Apocrypha and Pseudepigrapha of the Old Testament*, 2 vols., Oxford 1913.
AAJR	American Academy for Jewish Research
AIPHOS	*Annuaire de l'Institut de Philologie et d'Histoire Orientales et Slaves*, University of Brussels
AJA	*American Journal of Archaeology*
ANEP	J. Pritchard, *The Ancient Near East in Pictures*, Princeton 1954
ANES	*Journal of the Ancient Near Eastern Society of Columbia University*
ANET	J. Pritchard (ed.), *Ancient Near Eastern Texts*, Princeton ²1955
AfO	Archiv für Orientforschung
ARW	Archiv für Religionswissenschaft
ASOR	American Schools of Oriental Research
ASTI	*Annual of the Swedish Theological Institute*
ATD	Das Alte Testament Deutsch
ATR	*Anglican Theological Review*
B	Babylonian Talmud
BA	*Biblical Archaeologist*
BAH	Haut-Commissariat de la Republique Française en Syrie et au Liban, Service des Antiquités, Bibliothèque archéologique et historique
BASOR	Bulletin of the American Schools of Oriental Research
BBB	Bonner Biblische Beiträge
BCH	*Bulletin de correspondence hellénique*
BEHE	Bibliothèque de l'Ecole des hautes Etudes
BEIFAO	Bibliothèque d'étude ... de l'Institut Français d'Archéologie Orientale
BIES	*Bulletin of the Israel Exploration Society*
BJRL	*Bulletin of the John Rylands Library*
BKAT	Biblischer Kommentar zum Alten Testament
BO	Bibliotheca Orientalis
BWANT	Beiträge zur Wissenschaft vom Alten und Neuen Testaments
CAH	Cambridge Ancient History
CAT	Commentaire de l'Ancien Testament

CBQ	*Catholic Biblical Quarterly*
CNI	*Christian News from Israel*
CPJ	*Corpus Papyrorum Judaicarum*, ed. V. Tcherikover, A. Fuks *et al.*, 3 vols., Cambridge, Mass. 1957–64
CRAI	*Comptes Rendues de l'Académie d'Inscriptions et Belles Lettres*
CSSH	Comparative Studies in Society and History
EM	*'Enzyqlopediyah Miqra'it*, Jerusalem, 1955–
ERE	*Encyclopedia of Religion and Ethics*, ed. J. Hastings
FGrHist	*Die Fragmente der Griechischen Historiker*, ed. F. Jacoby. Berlin and Leiden 1923–
FHG	*Fragmenta Historicorum Graecorum*, ed. C. and T. Müller, 5 vols., Paris 1928
FRLANT	Forschungen zur Religion und Literatur des Alten and Neuen Testaments
FV	H. Diels, *Die Fragmente der Vorsokratiker*, 3 vols., Berlin ^{7}1954
FWCJS	Fourth World Congress of Jewish Studies
GHKAT	Göttinger Handkommentar zum Alten Testament
GRBS	Greek, Roman, and Byzantine Studies
HBAT	Handbuch zum Alten Testament
HDB	*Hastings' Dictionary of the Bible*
HdKzAT	Handkommentar zum Alten Testament
HSM	Harvard Semitic Monographs
HTR	*Harvard Theological Review*
HUCA	*Hebrew Union College Annual*
ICC	International Critical Commentary
IDB	*Interpreter's Dictionary of the Bible*
IEJ	*Israel Exploration Journal*
IG	*Inscriptiones Graecae*, Berlin Academy ed., Berlin 1873–
JAOS	*Journal of the American Oriental Society*
JBL	*Journal of Biblical Literature*
JCS	*Journal of Cuneiform Studies*
JE	*Jewish Encyclopedia*
Jer	Jerusalem Talmud
JNES	*Journal of Near Eastern Studies*
JnlSS	*Journal of Semitic Studies*
JQR	*Jewish Quarterly Review*
JRS	*Journal of Roman Studies*
JSS	*Jewish Social Studies*
JTS	*Journal of Theological Studies*
KAT	Kommentar zum Alten Testament
Kittel^2	*Biblia Hebraica*, ed. R. Kittel, corrected, Stuttgart ^{2}1925
Kittel and Kahle	*Biblia Hebraica*, ed. R. Kittel and P. Kahle, completed

	by A. Alt and O. Eissfeldt, Stuttgart ³1937
KS	A. Alt, *Kleine Schriften zur Geschichte des Volkes Israel*, 3 vols., Munich, 1953–59
LXX	Septuagint
MGWJ	*Monatsschrift für Geschichte und Wissenschaft des Judentums*
NTS	*New Testament Studies*
OCD	*Oxford Classical Dictionary*
OtS	Oudtestamentische Studiën
OTWSA	*Die Ou Testamentiese Werkgemeenskap in Suid-Afrika*
PEQ	*Palestine Exploration Fund, Quarterly Statement*
PGM	*Papyri graecae magicae*, ed. K. Preisendanz, 2 vols., Leipzig, 1928–31
PJB	*Palästinajahrbuch*
POxy	*Oxyrhynchus Papyri*, ed. B. Grenfell, A. Hunt, *et al.*, London, 1898–
P-W	*Paulys Real-Encyclopädie . . .*, ed. G. Wissowa *et al.*, Stuttgart ²1894–
RA	*Revue d'Assyriologie et d'Archéologie Orientale*
RB	*Revue Biblique*
RBI	*Rivista Biblica Italiana*
REG	*Revue des Etudes Grecques*
REJ	*Revue des Etudes Juives*
RH	*Revue Historique*
RHPR	*Revue d'Histoire et de Phiosophie religieuses*
RHR	*Revue de l'Histoire des Religions*
RIDA	*Revue Internationale des Droits de l'Antiquité*
RSI	*Rivista Storica Italiana*
RSO	*Rivista degli Studi Orientali*
RSV	Revised Standard Version
RTP	*Revue de Théologie et de Philosophie*
Schmid-Stählin	Wilhelm von Christ's *Geschichte der griechischen Literatur*, ed. W. Schmid and O. Stählin, 2 Teil, 1 Hälfte, Munich ⁶1920
SGU	*Sammelbuch Griechischer Urkunden aus Ägypten*, ed. F. Preisigke *et al.*, Strassburg 1915–
SKGG	Schriften der Königsberger Gelehrten Gesellschaft, Geisteswissenschaftliche Klasse
SNVA	Skrifter utgitt av Det Norske Videnskaps-Akademi i Oslo
T	Tosephta
ThLZ	*Theologische Literaturzeitung*
ThR	*Theologische Rundschau*
UPZ	*Urkunden der Ptolemäerzeit*, ed. U. Wilcken, 2 vols., Berlin 1927–56
VT	*Vetus Testamentum*

WMANT	Wissenschaftliche Monographien zum Alten und Neuen Testament
YHI	*Yediʿot haḥ ebrah haʿibrit leḥ aqirat ʾerez Yisraʾel*
ZAW	*Zeitschrift für die Alttestamentliche Wissenschaft*
ZDPV	*Zeitschrift des Deutschen Palästina-Vereins*
ZNW	*Zeitschrift für die Neutestamentliche Wissenschaft*
ZRG	*Zeitschrift für Religions- und Geistesgeschichte*
ZTK	*Zeitschrift für Theologie und Kirche*

NOTES

1. The Old Testament and its Interpretation

All references to the Old Testament are to the Kittel and Kahle text (unless otherwise specified)

1. Mishnah Yadayim 3.
2. Josephus, *Ant.* XIII.297; Acts 23.8.
3. Cross, 'Fragment'; Sanders, 'Scroll'.
4. Eissfeldt, *Introduction*, 707f. (also 684 and 696).
5. See especially Bickerman, 'Notes', and now J. Tigay, *The History of the Gilagamesh Epic*, Philadelphia 1982.
6. So Freedman, 'Purpose', 436ff.
7. Eissfeldt, *Introduction*, 531–5; Bickerman, *Ezra*, 21ff.
8. See Cook, *Age*, 19.
9. So Cassuto, *Questione*, 93–178.
10. Notably by Engnell, *Gamla Testamentet*.
11. *ANET*, 320.
12. This appears from comparison of major introductions in English, French and German: Pfeiffer, *Introduction*, [2]1953; Lods, *Histoire*, 1950; Eissfeldt, *Introduction*, [3]1965. The following list in the text is based on these three works.
13. Eissfeldt, *Introduction*, 177–82, 188 (on the Pentateuch); 372ff. (on Ezekiel); 518 (comments *à propos* of theories about Daniel). An example of the practical application of these conclusions is de Vaux's *Ancient Israel*.
14. Eissfeldt, *Introduction*, 9–127.
15. See Haldar, *Associations*, and Johnson, *Cultic Prophet*; contra, de Vaux, *Ancient Israel*, 384ff.
16. This has been shown by the attempts to prove the contrary. See the works cited in the previous note.
17. Noth, *History*, 90ff.
18. Mowinckel, *Neujahr*, also *Psalmenstudien* II; cf. de Vaux, *Ancient Israel*, 504ff.
19. For the amphictyony this is recognized by Noth himself, *History*, 91. On the covenant renewal cf. ibid., 92, and de Vaux, *Ancient Israel*, 137. The wishful legislation of Deut. 31.10ff. for a *septennial* ceremony (an echo of the innovation reported in Neh. 8?) suggests that no annual one was known to the author.
20. Eissfeldt, *Introduction*, 684f., and the opening chapters of Lieberman, *Hellenism*. Though there were scribes before there were Pharisees, the

'corrections of the scribes' are probably often corrections of the Pharisaic scribes; cf. Mark 2.16.

21. The priesthood had the support of the Seleucid government and used government troops, therefore the author of I Macc. represents the action as initiated by the Seleucids (I Macc. 1.56). He was concerned to represent his heroes as rebels not against the priesthood of the Jerusalem temple but against an alien civil government. So Bickerman, *Gott*; cf. Heinemann, 'Glaubenszwang'.

22. II Macc. 2.14.

23. Eissfeldt, *Introduction*, 451 and 526ff.; Pfeiffer, *Introduction*, 637.

24. II Macc. 2.13. The last phrase is explained by the chronicle of the temple of Athena in Lindus (Blinkenberg, *Tempelchronik*).

25. A good summary of the arguments for recognizing P material in Joshua is given by Vink, 'Date', 64ff.

26. Abot 1.

27. E.g., Ex. 20.24 and Deut. 12.4ff.; Lev. 17.3ff. and Deut. 12.20ff.; Ex. 21.7 and Deut. 15.12; Num. 18.21 and Deut. 14.22; Ex. 12.9 and Deut. 16.7; Deut. 14.22–29 and Num. 18.21–24; Lev. 10.13 and Deut. 18.3.

28. Hagiga 13a. Occasional preservation of material inconsistent with an editor's theories is merely evidence of the difficulty of editing a scroll thoroughly. Such inconsistencies are frequent in undoubtedly edited works, e.g. Chronicles, and Marcion's edition of Luke (Bauer, *Leben Jesu*, 494). Cf. Ben Hayyim, *'Ivrit*, 8.

29. Such harmonistic exegesis has occasionally been added to the written laws: e.g., Deut. 12.8ff. shows how the difference of Deut. 12.4ff. from Ex. 20.24 was 'explained'.

30. Contrast Noth, *Überlieferungsgeschichtliche Studien* and *Laws*. Much better is von Rad, 'Sermon'.

31. See Noth, *History*, 45, on the importance of realizing what is *not* said by the texts of the Old Testament. For examples of deliberate suppression, de Vaux, *Ancient Israel*, 290 and 292 (stories indicating the cultic importance of Shechem and Mamre).

2. Religious Parties among the Israelites before 587

1. A likely guess at the god's personal name, in English translations usually replaced by 'the Lord', or 'Jehovah'.

2. Ecclesiastes does so only thanks to its glossators: 8.12f.; 12.13.

3. On the importance of defining 'Israel', see Noth, *History*, 1ff., 137, 184.

4. The name is of the same type as the names of many Bedouin tribes, de Vaux, *Ancient Israel*, 4f.

5. Mixed multitude, Ex. 12.38; Midianites, Num. 10.29ff.; Moabites, Num. 25.1–5; Gibeonites, Josh. 9; II Sam. 21; Jebusites, Josh. 15.63;

Judg. 1.21; Zech. 9.7; Jerahmeëlites, I Sam. 27.10; 30.29; Kenites, Judg. 1.16; 4.11, I Sam. 27.10; 30.29; Hebrews, I Sam. 14.21; cf. 13.7.

6. Judg. 1, 2, 10, etc.

7. Noth, *History*, 141ff., 192ff. The disappearance of Simeon may have been due to assimilation, de Vaux, *Ancient Israel*, 6. On Issachar see Gen. 49.14f.

8. For instance, I Kings 11.1ff. Note the deletions of the Septuagint (hereafter abbreviated LXX).

9. Noth, *History*, 191ff.

10. Ibid., 191; cf. Ezek. 16.3.

11. Greenfield, 'Cherethites'; Noth, *History*, 198. A special troop of 600 Philistines from Gath was evidently less important than the main body of Philistines and Cretans: II Sam. 15.17ff.; cf. I Kings 1.44, etc. Queens: I Kings 11.8; the religious personnel could be numerous, cf. I Kings 18.19 (450, a fiction supposed credible). Artisans and traders: I Kings 5.16ff., 32; 7.13f.; de Vaux, *Ancient Israel*, 78f., 312.

12. II Sam. 11.3, 27. Her father's parents had worshipped 'Am, but may have been Israelites.

13. I Chron. 2.17.

14. Hosea 5.7 (probably metaphorical) need not refer to exogamy; Wellhausen, *Kleinen Propheten*, translated 'Bastarde'.

15. Ex. 34.16 and Josh. 23.12 seem echoes of Deut. 7.3 (see McNeile, *Exodus*; Driver, *Deuteronomy*; Beer-Galling, *Exodus*). Judges 3.6 is part of the framework of the Deuteronomic editor. In I Kings 11.2ff., Montgomery, *Kings*, recognises that the attack on foreign wives is a deuteronomic expansion. The attacks on Jezebel (I Kings 16.31; 18.4, 19; 21.1–29; 22.53; II Kings 9.7, 22, 34ff.) are on her policy, never on her provenance. Gen. 26.34f.; 27.46; 28.1, 6–8 are probably P (so Gunkel, *Genesis*, 315 and 384ff.). The strongest evidence that such hostility did exist in earlier times is therefore Gen. 24.3, Judg. 14.3 and Num. 25.1–5. Of these, Gen. 24.3 is probably an invention to connect Abraham with the traditions of immigrations from Mesopotamia (it does not amount to a prohibition of intermarriage with non-Israelites, see Gunkel's notes pp. 384f.). The hostility to the Philistines of Judges 14.3 is understandable. Num. 25.1–5 (JE) may be the source of the Deuteronomic theory (vv. 6–19 are probably P, as are 31.15ff.; see Gray, *Numbers*).

16. So Peisker, *Beziehungen*, 82–89. See Dt. 7.3ff. and the Deuteronomic interpolations indicated in the preceding note.

17. Deut. 21.10ff.

18. But note the differences of dialect, Judg. 12.5f.; 18.3. I Kings 22.32f. suggests that even the Aramaeans could tell a Judaean from a (north) Israelite as soon as he opened his mouth.

19. Gen. 9.8ff.; 12.1ff.; 15; 17; 22.15ff.; 26.1–5; 28.20ff.; 35.1–15; Ex. 12; 13; 24; 34; Lev. 26; Num. 25.12; Josh. 8.30ff.; 24; II Kings 11.17; 23.3, etc.

20. As the text stands, the terms of the agreement are contained in chs. 20–23.

21. For the date see Freedman, 'Babylonian Chronicle'. 586 is defended by Vogt, 'Bemerkungen', *Biblica* 1975, 223ff.

22. E.g., II Kings 17.7–18; 21.1–15.

23. E.g., de Vaux, *Ancient Israel*, 274ff.

24. Calf, Ex. 32, etc. Amos (5.25), for instance, projected on to the desert period his own contempt for sacrifice. Similar idealization in Jer. 2.1ff. For further examples, de Vaux, *Ancient Israel*, 13f.

25. De Vaux, *Ancient Israel*, 262.

26. Bickerman, review of Bright; Noth, *History*, 54.

27. With the following cf. von Rad, *Theology*, I.20–25 and 29; the historical observations on these pages contradict his dogmas on pp. 26f. and 30. On Gen. 35.1–5 see below, n. 112.

28. Cf. de Vaux, *Ancient Israel*, 294, 310; Herbert, 'Exclusivism'; Albright, *Biblical Period*, 18; Eissfeldt, 'Ba'alšamēm', 2 n. 4. Also possibly Tseba'ot, de Vaux, *Ancient Israel*, 304.

29. Some Yahwists later rejected the implied identification. Jer. 48.13 puts Kemosh, the god of Moab, and Bethel, the god of the north Israelites, on the same footing. For Bethel see E. Kraeling, *Brooklyn . . . Papyri*, 89.

30. Cf. Josh. 24.25; Judg. 9.4.

31. Noth, *History*, 99; de Vaux, *Ancient Israel*, 271f., 284–8.

32. De Vaux, *Ancient Israel*, 491, 494, 500; other borrowings also, Noth, *History*, 100ff.

33. De Vaux, *Ancient Israel*, 384.

34. Noth, *History*, 208; de Vaux, *Ancient Israel*, II, 312ff.

35. Eissfeldt, *Introduction*, 28f.

36. Bottero, 'Divinités', 27ff. In early Mesopotamia names are the most important evidence for popular religion as opposed to that of the priests and the literary tradition. Almost the same could be said of the religion of Israel before the Yahwist reforms of the ninth century.

37. Contrast Albright, 'Reform', 82 n. 2; his 'archaic hypocoristicon' is an apologetic invention.

38. Therefore the name *was* used in the earlier period. The prohibition of its use 'in vain' (Ex. 20.7) probably refers to its use in false oaths (so *Mekilta de R. Ishmaël, ad loc.*).

39. On divine names see Gray, *Studies*, and Noth, *Personennamen*. Also Noth, *History* (Asher); Herbert, 'Exclusivism' (Shalem and Tsedek); Albright, *Biblical Period*, 18 (Tsur). Yet other deities appear on early Hebrew archaeological material, Yadin, *Art of Warfare*, 352f.

40. Note the substitutions for Baal of *boshet*, *'el*, etc. Dhorme, 'Baal', 59, similarly the vocalization Ashtoreh, from *boshet*, and the like.

41. I Chron. 8.33f. Cf. Gideon's family, on which de Vaux, *Ancient Israel*, 306; Albright, *Biblical Period*, 42.

42. His life was saved by his teraphim (I Sam. 19.11ff.) – images of

household deities (Gen. 31.19, 30ff.) thought to give oracular responses (Zech. 10.2f.). He seems to have attributed one of his major victories to Baal (II Sam. 5.20; the evidence of the place name is more reliable than that of the surrounding – Yahwist – text).

43. Or 'between', or possibly, 'dwells in'. Cf. Lev. 16.2; Ezek. 1; Ex. 37.9; Num. 7.89, etc.

44. II Sam. 6.2.

45. II Sam. 6.17.

46. I Kings 2.28f.

47. II Sam. 24.18ff. Note that the Jebusites retained ownership of land.

48. I Kings 3.4.

49. Gen. 14.18.

50. The tent and ark were taken into the temple (I Kings 8.4ff.) and thereafter disappeared. When the north Israelites took Jerusalem about 790 they did not think it worth while to carry off the ark (II Kings 14.13f.). Therefore it is improbable that the ark was an important centre of devotion or loyalty for all Israel.

51. Gray, *Studies*, 259ff.

52. I Kings 11.5ff.; II Kings 23.13. Soggin, 'Synkretismus', has even suggested that David and Solomon took the lead in introducing syncretism, to unite their people, and that Solomon's temple was built as a centre for the new syncretistic cult. For this there is little evidence and there probably was no need.

53. So I Kings 12.28ff., explicitly, also 19.18, and Hosea 8.5f.; cf. 10.5 and 13.2; Ex. 32.4f. The identification with Yahweh is indicated by the claim that these are the gods who brought Israel out of Egypt. Cf. Num. 23.22, 'El brought them out of Egypt; he has horns like those of a wild ox.' In Deut. 33.17 the horns are transferred to Joseph, qua first-born of Yahweh, 'his bull'. Like father, like son. The bull cults of Egypt may have had influence here. Solomon's chief queen was an Egyptian (I Kings 3.1; 9.16, 24); Jeroboam had been an exile in Egypt (I Kings 11.40); Egypt overran Palestine in the fifth year of Jeroboam's rule (I Kings 14.25); and Egyptian amulets, including bulls, are frequent in Palestinian sites of the period (Pal. Arch. Museum, *Gallery Book, Iron Age*, 47f.). Per contra, there is no trustworthy evidence of important political connections with northern Syria, still less Anatolia, to which appeal is usually made in support of the apologetic claim that the bulls did not represent the deity, but merely carried him.

54. I Kings 14.23f.

55. I Kings 15.11ff. On the position of the dowager queen, de Vaux, *Ancient Israel*, 117–19.

56. I Kings 18.40; 19.1–3.

57. II Kings 10.

58. II Kings 11.

59. Eissfeldt, 'Ba'alšamēm', 16ff., did not succeed in eliminating the

plurality; no more does Mulder, 'Ba'al'. And the preserved evidence cannot reflect more than a small fraction of the ancient practice. Cf. Östborn, *Yahweh*, and Dhorme, 'Baal'.

60. Eissfeldt, *Introduction*, 424 on Zeph. 1.4f.

61. Jer. 2.8; 23.13.

62. Jer. 12.16. Prof. G. Cohen called my attention to Hosea 2.18 as evidence of this practice; Prof. Bickerman, to the Deuteronomists' concern to prevent swearing by other gods, Deut. 6.13; 10.20; Josh. 23.7; cf. Zeph. 1.5.

63. Jer. 11.13.

64. *Ibid.* and Jer. 7.9; 32.29. On 7.1–8.3 see Eissfeldt, *Introduction*, 352.

65. Jer. 2.28; 11.17.

66. II Kings 23.5. If this verse be an addition (so Montgomery, *Kings*), it is an early addition, substantiated by the rest of the account (vv. 8, 11ff.) and references in the prophets (Jer. 7.18; 10.2; 19.13, etc.).

67. See below, n. 90, and cf. Lev. 17.7, etc.

68. It is convenient to use the traditional nomenclature. (So, too, for Milkom, on whom see Dhorme, 'Baal', 59ff.).

69. Archaeological evidence of the destruction has been found, Yeivin, *Activities*, 15; Amirah. 'Tumuli'.

70. II Kings 23.7. On these see the plausible conjecture of Beek, *Geschichte*, 92. Apologetic interpretations are numerous.

71. Ibid. On Asherah see Patai, 'Asherah', where the popularity and persistence of her cult is fully demonstrated.

72. II Kings 23.32 and Jer. 11.1ff., esp. 8f., on which Eissfeldt, *Introduction*, 360; de Vaux, *Ancient Israel*, 265.

73. See also Eissfeldt, *Introduction*, 232, and my article 'The Veracity of Ezekiel', *ZAW* 87, 1975, 11–16.

74. Against Pritchard, *Palestinian Figurines*.

75. Franken, 'Excavations at Deir 'Allah, Second Season', 369; Lapp, '1963 Excavations at Ta'anek', 28ff.

76. De Vaux, *Ancient Israel*, 45; Albright, *Biblical Period*, 70f. From Judah we now have (Ne)tatsba'al on a seventh-century ostracon; see Naveh, 'More Hebrew Inscriptions', 30.

77. Cook, *Religion*, 40–71, esp. 50f. and 56f. Moscati, *Epigrafia*, 56ff. Prof. Xella drew my attention to the new material in G. Garbini, 'I sigilli del regno di Israele', *Oriens Antiquus* 21, 1982, 163ff.

78. Application of the name Yahweh to statues is attacked by Wisdom of Solomon 14.21.

79. Avigad, 'Hotam', pl.3.

80. Ibid., cf. II Kings 25.25.

81. Yadin, 'Excavations', 206.

82. Kenyon, *Archaeology*, 252, 272.

83. Amiran, 'Tumuli'; Kenyon, *Jerusalem*, 63ff. (not a high place, but a cult centre just outside the city wall.

84. Z. Meshel, 'Did Yahweh Have a Consort?', *Biblical Archaeology Review* V, 1979, 24ff.

85. II Kings 23.

86. Hence the goddess Anathyahu, supposed by E. Kraeling, *Brooklyn . . . Papyri*, 91, to have been Yahweh's daughter. Ashtar-Kemosh on the Moabite stone is an analogous formation (*ANET* 320b). Cf. Borger, 'Anath-Bethel'. A goddess Hypsiste was associated with the cult of Yahweh Hypsistos, Nilsson, *Geschichte*, II.637 n. 4.

87. On Baal Perizim see Noth, *History*, 156. Similarly de Vaux, *Ancient Israel*, 235, on Migdal Gad: 'would be a fortified temple, like that of Baal-berith in Shechem'. Again 280 and Eising, 'Ortsnamen', 12. Contra, Eissfeldt, 'Ba'alšamēm', 16ff. Further examples for other deities in Jirku, 'Orts- und Eigennamen'.

88. Judg. 9.4; Josh. 13.7; II Kings 4.42; Song 8.11; Judg. 20.33; Josh. 19.8, etc.

89. Ezek. 8.

90. That the 'abominations' in Ezekiel's temple reflected Israelite popular religion is recognised by de Vaux, *Ancient Israel*, 323; Beek, *Geschichte*, 97. Cf. Naveh, 'Old Hebrew Inscriptions', 77, where the 'figure with a lyre' is probably a satyr. I have examined the stone; the legs seem those of a goat. See above, n. 67, on II Kings 23.8.

91. The claim in Ezek. 44.15 and 48.11 that the Zadokite priests of Jerusalem remained faithful to Yahweh when all the rest of his priests participated in idolatrous worship is to the interest of the *soi-disant* Zadokite priesthood and scarcely reconcilable with what Ezekiel saw in the temple and what Josiah took out of it. Probably Ezek. 40.46; 43.19; 44.15; and 45.11 have been glossed to identify the faithful priests as the Zadokites.

92. Hosea 4.10; Isa. 1.4 and 28; Jer. 2.13; 16.11; 17.13; 22.9, etc. The influence of the prophets appears in Deut. 29.24; I Kings 9.9; 19.10, 14, etc.

93. Hosea, 4.15; 8.2; Isa. 1.11ff.; 29.13; Jer. 3.4f.; 5.2; 6.20; 7, etc.

94. I Kings 18.22; 22.6ff.; Jer. 2.8; 14.15; 23.13, 16ff.; 27.15ff.; 29.21; Ezek. 13, etc. For additional evidence see Goff, 'Syncretism'.

95. Num. 22.18.

96. II Kings 23.13.

97. II Kings 8.7ff.

98. II Kings 1.2ff.

99. I Kings 17, esp. 17.12, '*thy* god'.

100. The two mule loads of earth (II Kings 5.17) may have been needed because the priests of Rimmon claimed to own all the land of Damascus; cf. Lev. 25.23. The claim to ownership may be implied by the title *ba'al*.

101. II Sam. 11.3ff.

102. I Sam. 26.19.

103. This I have described in 'The Common Theology of the Ancient Near East', 135ff. The general similarity of Yahweh to Baal has now been demonstrated by Östborn, *Yahweh*. If Yahweh came from the desert, much of this likeness must have resulted from his assimilation to Baal.

104. Judg. 16.23, etc.; I Kings 11.7.

105. Judg. 11.24; II Kings 18.33ff.

106. Černy, *Ancient Egyptian Religion*, 63.

107. Duchesne-Guillemin, *Zoroastre*, 114ff.

108. Herodotus I.172.

109. See the exception made in II Kings 5.18. Such exceptions were no doubt commonly made by the less scrupulous, but here we are concerned with the theory.

110. For this distinction, Nock, *Conversion*.

111. Deut. 6.4. The meaning indicated by the alternative translation, 'Yahweh, our God, is one Yahweh' (i.e., is not to be divided into many local deities), was probably not perceived as distinct by ancient Israelites and was certainly secondary. With Eichrodt, *Theology* I, 226, n. 2 cf. Pfeiffer, *Introduction*, 235. By comparison with this belief, monotheism was of little practical importance. Speculations as to a single cause of the cosmos were common in the ancient world (Jaeger, *Theology*, 20f.) and both these and the natural progress of flattery (Duchesne-Guillemin, *Zoroastre*, 94) led men to describe many gods as – each of them – 'the one god' (Peterson, *Heis Theos*), 'the creator of all', 'all powerful', and so on. See the evidence I have collected in 'The Common Theology of the Ancient Near East', 138–40. Such terms were unimportant so long as those who used them continued to worship all the deities customarily worshipped. Worship of several deities is compatible with monotheism – one only to believe, for example, that the supreme ('true') deity has created beings inferior to itself but superior to men and has ordained that men should worship them. This belief is expressed in Deut. 4.19 and 32.8 (reading 'the sons of El' instead of 'the sons of Israel').

112. Pfeiffer, *Introduction*, 404; cf. 215, 218f. (on Ex. 22.19). The subject is not mentioned in the ancient list of curses in Deut. 27.15ff. Moreover, Ex. 20.2ff. and 34.14ff. and similar passages are suspiciously Deuteronomic in phraseology. Gen. 35.1–5 is clearly E and looks like a slightly distorted reflection of the *lex sacra* of the Bethel shrine. Visitors to the shrine might elsewhere worship whatever deities they pleased, but none might be brought into the *temenos*, and the worshippers must undergo preliminary purification. Therefore, since banks were not yet, the purdent worshipper before beginning his pilgrimage would bury for safekeeping in some other holy place his statuettes of other deities and jewellery with their symbols or images. Judg. 6.25–32 is said by Moore (following Wellhausen, Stade and Budde) to be a late addition to the Gideon story (*Judges*, 175, 177); so, too, Burney, *Judges*, 178. The framework of Judges is Deuteronomic, as is I Sam. 7.3f. I Kings 11.33 is assigned by Montgomery to late

prophetic 'saga' and I Kings 14.9 is declared Deuteronomic (*Kings*, 242 and 266). The earliest passage, therefore, seems to be Num. 25.1–5 (JE ?).

113. For a recent example see Eakin, 'Yahwism'.

114. From the period of the Judges we have only Jerubbaal's destruction of the altar of Baal (Judg. 6.25–33), a late invention to explain his embarrassing name (cf. de Vaux, *Ancient Israel*, 306) and Samuel's reformation (I Sam. 7.2–17 – crude editorial invention irreconcilable with the historical material in the stories of Saul), and, of course, the Deuteronomic framework of Judges and I Samuel.

115. The prophecies of Ahijah in I Kgs. 14 are so full of the stock phraseology of the Deuteronomic editors – e.g., 14.8ff., 15 – as to be practically useless for evidence. Cf. Yahweh's (i.e., the editor's) prophecy to Solomon, I Kings 11.11ff.

116. I Kings 15.11, 14; 22.43f.; II Kings 12.3f.; 14.3f.; 15.3f.

117. I Kings 15.26, 34; 16.19, 25f., 30f.; 22.53; II Kings 3.2f.; 10.29; 13.2, 11; 14.24; 15.9, 18, 24, 28. Even Jehoram, who apparently made some concessions to the Yahweh-alone party (II Kings 3.2), does not escape condemnation (ibid.).

118. I Kings 11.34ff.; 15.4f.; etc.

119. II Kings 16.2ff.; 17.9ff.; 23.8, 13; Jer. 2.20–23; 3.6–10, etc. De Vaux, *Ancient Israel*, 284, 310.

120. I Kings 12.28ff.; 14.9; 19.18; II Kings 10.29; 17.9.

121. E.g., Omri, I Kings 16.25f.

122. Eissfeldt, *Introduction*, 535–40.

123. Ibid., 539; de Vaux, *Ancient Israel*, 228.

124. Contrast the practice of Bright, *History*, passim.

125. I Kings 15.11ff.

126. The queen mother presumably worshipped Asherah before making her cult object. The trouble seems to have resulted from the object, not the mere worship.

127. It probably appears in the suppression of witchcraft by Saul, who certainly was not devoted to Yahweh alone (he named one son 'Baal's man', I Chron. 8.33f.). Again it appears without any connection to Yahwism among the Nabataeans, Diodorus XIX.94 (to say nothing of later Moslem sects, the followers of Ali, the Wahabis, etc.).

128. I Kings 22.43ff.

129. II Kings 8.18, 26; Noth, *History*, 236 and n. 4; Gray, *I & II Kings*, ad loc., vs. Montgomery, *Kings*, ad loc.

130. I Kings 18.19, etc.

131. Athaliah's death was followed by the destruction of the temple of Baal in Jerusalem, II Kings 11.18.

132. I Kings 18.4, 13; 19.1ff., 10; II Kings 9.7. Note 'servants' as well as 'prophets'. Was Naboth a Yahwist martyr?

133. I Kings 22.26, 40, 52; II Kings 1.17; 8.26f.; 11.1ff., etc. Noth, *History*, 242 n. 2.

134. I Kings 22; cf. 20, etc.

135. I Kings 18.4, 13.

136. Need it be argued that the Elijah-Elisha stories (of raising the dead, dividing the Jordan, and so on) are legendary? It need. An anonymous reader of this text protested that they were 'reliable early tradition'.

137. II Kings 2; 4; 6, etc.

138. I Kings 19.17.

139. I Kings 18.22, 24.

140. I Kings 22.

141. I Kings 19.16.

142. Elisha's alleged emissary prophesies independently, the verse (9.4) in which the preface featuring Elisha joins the body of the text shows a corruption (*hanna'ar hanna'ar*) which looks like the result of splicing; if preface and corruption were removed we should have a complete story (9.4ff.) like those in I Kings 20 in which the actor is an unnamed prophet.

143. Eissfeldt, *Introduction*, 292. I Kings 19.15f.; II Kings 9.25f., 36; 10.10.

144. II Kings 10.18–28.

145. Noth, *History*, 242 and n. 5.

146. Had he done so, we should certainly have heard of it, given the concern of the editor of Kings, pointed out above.

147. II Kings 10.29.

148. II Kings 13.6; 21.3; cf. I Kings 16.33.

149. Hosea 1.4; Jezreel was the city where Jehu began his murders.

150. See above, pp. 17–19.

150a. N. Avigad, 'The Priest of Dor', *IEJ* 25, 1975, 101ff.; J. Teixidor, 'Bulletin d'épigraphie sémitique', *Syria* 53, 1976, 320 no. 87.

151. Jer. 35.

152. Goodenough, *Symbols*, Vol. VI. Thus the nomads of the North African desert also abstained from wine, Appian *Libyke* (*Punic Wars*) II.11.

153. Above, n. 127 and accompanying text.

154. II Kings 10.16. The unreliable story testifies at least to Jehonadab's reputation.

155. Cf. de Vaux, *Ancient Israel*, 15; Eissfeldt, *Introduction*, 198.

156. II Kings 10.11ff.

157. II Kings 11.1ff.

158. II Kings 11.4, but cf. Greenfield, 'Cherethites', end.

159. The *'am ha'arez*. Cf. de Vaux, *Ancient Israel*, 70f.; Noth, *History*, 272; contrast Alt, 'Rolle', 12, followed by Würthwein, *'amm*.

160. II Kings 11.17, perhaps corrupt.

161. De Vaux, *Ancient Israel*, 71, 375.

162. The priests of Chnum at Elephantine, who instigated the destruction of the temple of Yahweh there, were not monolatrous: Porter and Moss, *Bibliography*, V.228.

163. Lev. 25.43, 55.

164. That Amaziah's actions were on one occasion in accordance with the law of Moses does not prove that he intended them to be so, nor that he knew the law (II Kings 14.6, editorial comment).

165. II Kings 16.1.

166. II Kings 18.5.

167. II Kings 21.11.

168. II Kings 21.19.

169. II Kings 23.25.

170. II Kings 23.32, 37; 24.9, 19.

171. II Kings 17.6.

172. Drioton and Vandier, *L'Egypte*, 551–5.

173. Noth, *History*, 264, 266, 269ff.

174. II Kings 21.5; 22.4f., 11; cf. Zeph. 1.5; Jer. 7.18; 8.2, etc.; Deut. 17.3.

175. As proved by the place names Beth Shemesh (temple of the sun), Beth Yerah (temple of the moon). See also above, n. 84.

176. At least in Hezekiah's time Jerusalem had had diplomatic relations with Babylon; Hezekiah probably looked to Babylon for assistance against Assyria (II Kings 20.12–19).

177. II Kings 21.3, 7; 23.4ff., 14. Similarly in the prophets of the period, above, p. 17.

178. II Kings 16.1; 17.17; 21.6; 23.10; cf. Jer. 7.39; 19.16; 32.5; Deut. 12.31; 18.10; de Vaux, *Ancient Israel*, 444; further M. Smith, 'A Note on Burning Babies', *JAOS* 95, 1975, 477ff. My regard for Prof. Weinfeld prohibits me from citing his reply.

179. II Kings 18.4; 23.8, 13, 19; de Vaux, *Ancient Israel*, II; Albright, *Biblical Period*, 76f. These facts make it impossible to represent Josiah's reforms merely as a declaration of independence from Assyria, essentially independent of the discovery of the deuteronomic law (vs. Noth, 'Laws', 41–8). The list of reforms in II Kings 23 shows no concern with Assyria and very little with cults which might be attributed to Assyrian influence. Further, ancient near eastern vassal treaties do not commonly provide that the vassal shall introduce in his territory the cult of the suzerain's gods. The only possible exception known to me is the vassal treaty of Esarhaddon (as restored by Wiseman), lines 393 and 409, which *might* be read as requiring introduction of the cult of Ashur. But Prof. Moshe Held tells me that this interpretation of it is unlikely (see also M. Cogan, *Imperialism and Religion*, Missoula 1974, 49–60), and I observe that Ashur is conspicuously absent from the list of Josiah's reforms.

180. II Kings 21.16; 24.3.

181. II Kings 23.20.

182. II Kings 18.1ff.

183. II Kings 18 and 20.

184. Eissfeldt, *Introduction*, 328.

185. Ibid., 643; Proverbs 25.1.

186. II Kings 21.10, 16.

187. II Kings 21.23f.; Noth, *History*, 272.

188. II Kings 22. The addition of *haggadol* to Hilkiah's title (vv. 4, 8) is anachronistic, de Vaux, *Ancient Israel*, 378. On the 'royal secretary', ibid., 378.

189. II Kings 23.

190. Noth, *History*, 253ff.

191. Cf. von Rad, *Studies*.

192. Prophecies like 3.14 and 7.9 foretell the destruction of shrines of Yahweh, and this as part of the general ruin of the land. In 8.14 those who swear by Ashimah (?) of Samaria and those who swear by Yahweh of Dan (?) are to be involved in a single ruin because of their common social (not religious) guilt. 2.4f. refers to the idolatrous worship of Yahweh, not other gods (and is probably an interpolation). 5.26f., *if* it refers to Assyrian cults, is almost certainly an interpolation. See W. Harper, *Amos*, and Sellin, *Zwölf-prophetenbuch*, on these verses.

193. De Vaux, *Ancient Israel*, 330ff.

194. Hosea 2.18 (English 16). The attempt to get rid of the term *ba'al* shows that it was understood as a reference to the god as well as his function. In the preserved text of Hosea the relationship is to both the people and the land (2.5, 16f.); this may be original.

195. Hosea 2.7, 14ff.; cf. 7.14ff., though the authorship of Hosea 4ff. is dubious (Ginsberg, 'Studies').

196. The influence of the Baal cult in many elements of Hosea and of other Old Testament books has been demonstrated by Worden, 'Influence'.

197. Hosea 1.2.

198. Cf. Nilsson, *Geschichte*, I.110–12. Hosea, of course, would not have recognised the relationship; cf. 4.14, etc. (if Hosea).

199. Hosea 2.21; 3.1; (14.5); 2.17ff.

200. Hosea 2.4–15; (9.15, etc.).

201. Hosea 2.5ff., 12; (9.14f.).

202. Chs. 1–3 (cf. 4.10, 12; 5.3–4, 7; 6.10, etc.).

203. The Israelites were aware of the relationship between prophecy and insanity; see Gesenius-Buhl, s.v. *shaga'*, and esp. II Kings 9.11; Jer. 29.26; Hos. 9.7.

204. Micah 1.7; Isa. 1.21; Jer. 3.2 and often; Ezek. 6.9 and often; Deut. 31.16 and other Deuteronomistic passages, e.g. Ex. 34.15f.

205. *Othello*, IV.ii; *Winter's Tale*, I.ii.

206. The apologetic efforts of Brongers, 'Eifer', may be read for amusement.

207. Notably Östborn, *Yahweh*, 82ff., esp. 84, has no comparable material for Baal. A closer parallel is Juno's jealousy in the *Aeneid* I.4 and 25ff., which, like Yahweh's, is a major factor in world history. Juno was

a goddess who acted. The theme also appears in the Attis legend, Firmicus maternus, *de errore* III, who also echoes Virgil, *Aen*.I.27, *spretaeque injuria formae*.

208. Ex. 20.5; Deut. 5.9; justification secondary. The context here – prohibition of the worship of other gods – requires the translation by 'jealous', not 'deeply concerned' nor any of the other meanings the word may have in other contexts; cf. Deut. 4.24; 6.15; Josh. 24.19; Nahum 1.2.

209. Deut. 32.16, 21; Zeph. 1.18; Ezek. 5.13; 16.42; 23.25; 35.6; 38.19; Pss. 78.58; 79.5. The jealousy which leads to restoration is primarily of the reputation of other gods, hence, concern for what people will think: Isa. 37.9–32; II Kings 19.9–31; Ezek. 39.25; Isa. 59.16–19; Zeph. 3.8ff.

210. Ex. 34.14.

211. I Kings 19.10, 14.

212. II Kings 10.16.

213. Num. 25.7–13 (P).

214. Pss. 69.10; 73.3; 119.139.

215. Ecclus. 45.23f.; 48.2.

216. I Macc. 2.24, 26, 54, 58; IV Macc. 18.12.

217. On the relation of the zealots to the Maccabees see Farmer, *Maccabees*, and my article 'Zealots'. Hengel's attempt to reply to this article, in the second edition of his *Zeloten*, has failed to demonstrate 1. any reference by Josephus to a Zealot organization prior to AD 68; 2. any substantial evidence for any central organization behind most of the anti-Roman disturbances in Palestine prior to the invasion of Cestius.

218. I Macc. 2.24f., 44ff.; 3.4, 8, etc. Josephus *War* IV.135ff., esp. 160f.; Sanhedrin 9.6, etc.

219. Amos 7.14.

220. Jer. 1.18; 2.8; 4.9; 5.31; 6.13, etc.; Zeph. 3.4. The attacks on prophets in earlier prophetic books (e.g., Micah 3.5, 11; Isa. 9.15) are of dubious authenticity.

221. Jer. 1.1; 29.24ff.; 26.8ff.

222. Isa. 8.2f., 16 (if genuine), 18 (unless it refer to the physical children mentioned earlier).

223. Jer. 32.12; 26.16ff.; 36.4, 19, 25; 38.7. On *sarim* see de Vaux, *Ancient Israel*, 69.

224. Jer. 26.24; 29.3; 36.12, 25.

225. II Kings 22.4ff.

226. II Kings 22.12ff.

227. II Kings 22.12ff.; Jer. 36.12, 19, 25.

228. Jer. 39.14; 40.5.

229. Perhaps there are also traces of a continuing opposition; cf. Jer. 20.1ff. (Pashur ben Immer) and 38.1ff. (Gedaliah ben Pashur).

230. Jer. 1.18; 15.15ff.; 20.10.

231. See above, n. 221, and add Jer. 14.14ff.; 23.11ff.; 26.8; 27.16; 28;

29. The cliché references to 'Yahweh's servants, the prophets' (25.4; 35.15, etc.) may be glosses.

232. Ex. 4, esp. v. 14; Deut. 32.48–52, etc.

233. See the material collected in my 'Common Theology'.

234. De Vaux, *Ancient Israel*, 387, etc.; Noth, *History*, 342, n. 1; Eissfeldt, *Introduction*, 207.

235. That Ezekiel's background was in the pro-Egyptian party is suggested by the fact that he was one of those whom the Babylonians chose to carry off in the first captivity. Experience may have sharpened his prophetic vision and led him to change sides. On the date, milieu and authenticity of most of Ezekiel see Rowley, *The Book of Ezekiel*, and now B. Lang, *Ezechiel, Der Prophet und das Buch*, Darmstadt 1981.

236. Jer. 35.

237. Lods, *Histoire*, 356, 371ff. See above all Weinfeld, 'Present State', and *Deuteronomy and the Deuteronomic School*, Oxford 1971.

238. 20.23ff. is probably from another source. The heading of the Code is clear in 21.1.

239. Typically Deuteronomic phraseology appears in Ex. 20.2, 4, 5, 6, 10, 12; 22.20, 22f., 26, etc. And the covenant code has probably suffered more from excision than from interpolation (so did the laws of Draco).

240. E.g., de Vaux, *Ancient Israel*, 338; von Rad, *Studies*, passim.

241. The arguments of Frankena, 'Vassal Treaties', and of Weinfeld, 'Traces', make it seem most likely that the essential structure of Deut. was composed by reaction against an Assyrian vassal treaty imposed on Manasseh. Some elements in the structure will have been older.

242. Against Noth, 'Laws', 41–8, see above n. 179. His thesis requires the supposition that both the nature and the effects of the Deuteronomic code were fundamentally misunderstood by the Deuteronomic school.

243. Deut. 12; 14.22f.; 15.20; 16; 17.8–11; 18.1–8; 26.1f. That Jerusalem is not named results from the intention of passing off the work as composed by Moses. For the same reason it does not name the cities of refuge (19).

244. Deut. 12.2f.; 13; 17.2ff.; 18.20; 20.16. For Josiah's conquests see Alt, 'Judas Gaue'.

245. Driver, *Deuteronomy*, xxiv. Prof. Mendelsohn pointed out to me that these are a traditional element of royal reforms in the ancient Near East. No doubt considerations of tradition as well as of interest prompted their inclusion in Deuteronomy.

246. This is part of Deuteronomy's standard equation, 'the priests, i.e., the levites'.

247. G. Wright, 'Levites', has been refuted by Emerton, 'Priests'; cf. de Vaux, *Ancient Israel*, 363f. Deut. 18.6f. shows that the author considered any Levite 'from any of your gates' as potentially an officiant at Jerusalem. On Gunneweg, *Leviten*, see the review by de Vaux, *RB* 73, 1966, 446f.; the final sentence is a model of restraint.

248. Deut. 18.6–8. It is probably from these levites – the priests of the

shrines of Yahweh outside Jerusalem – that we derive the material in the Holiness Code insisting that all domestic animals killed for food must be sacrificed at a shrine. This ruling would make impossible the Deuteronomic centralization of the cult in Jerusalem, since persons living at a distance could not bring their animals to Jerusalem every time they wanted to eat meat. The Deuteronomic editor had foreseen the difficulty and provided that domestic animals might be killed for food without being sacrificed. This the Holiness Code explicitly forbids, and it emphatically puts the prohibition first of all its rulings, in deliberate contradiction to the Deuteronomic provision (Lev. 17.1ff.; cf. Deut. 12.13ff., 21). It would seem that the Yahweh-alone levites from shrines outside Jerusalem were opposed to the Deuteronomic reform because it closed their shrines, but in other respects followed the party line and formed a considerable element in the party. During the exile their traditions were collected and developed in the Holiness Code, and this was later added to the legal corpus of the Jerusalem priesthood, probably as a result of the entrance to that priesthood, after the exile, of some priestly families from other centres. (See below, ch. 7, n. 105.)

249. II Kings 23.9. This may be a gloss, but even if a gloss it may – and probably does – truly report what happened.

250. This motif occurs in the reports of earlier royal reforms (I Kings 15.12; 22.47) and may have been due to recurrent pressure on the government from semi-nomadic groups in the population. Infiltration from the desert continued throughout the monarchic period. Noth, *History*, 13; Cook, 'Zerubbabel', 25ff.; id., 'Inauguration', 185.

251. A likely translation of *ger*. See below, ch. 7.

252. Bright, *History*, 298; this encouraged forgery.

253. Deut. 18.10ff.

254. Deut. 18.15.

255. Deut. 18.19–22.

256. II Kings 22.14.

257. Deut. 14.22ff.

258. So de Vaux, *Ancient Israel*, 337.

259. II Kings 22.11, 19. It seems likely that the laws concerning the king were not in the text read to Josiah (so Pfeiffer, *Introduction*, 238).

260. This was apparent even to the Chronicler, II Chron. 35.22.

261. Contrast the usual theory (Pfeiffer, *Introduction*; Lods, *Histoire*; Eissfeld, *Introduction*) with that of Noth, *Überlieferungsgeschichtliche Studien*, and see Noth's arguments against Rudolph, ibid., 48–51. A good account of recent theories is given by Jenni, 'Forschung', 97ff. (Das deuteronomische Geschichtswerk).

262. The dependence of Deut. on Hosea is remarked by Driver, *Deuteronomy*, xxvii f.

263. E.g., Josh. 23–24.

264. II Kings 17.7–23.

265. II Kings 23.26; 24.3f. Jeremiah, to the last moment, knew nothing of this irrevocable decision, 38.17ff.; contrast 15.4, a Deuteronomic addition.

266. Syncretistic apologetics are reflected by Jer. 44.17f. which may treat the reform of Josiah, twenty years past, as the immediate cause of the disaster, but more likely referred to the interruption of all non-Yahwistic cults during the siege of 587. See M. Smith, 'The Veracity of Ezekiel', *ZAW* 85, 1975, 11–16.

267. Maisler, 'Historiography', 84.

268. Ezra 9.6–15; Neh. 9.5–10.1; Dan. 9.4–19; Baruch 1.15–2.35; cf. Ps. 78.

269. Gen. 9.8ff.; 12.1ff.; 15; 17; 22 (15ff.); 26.1–5; 28.20ff.; 35.1–15; Ex. 12; 13; 24; 34; Lev. 26; Num. 25.12f.; Josh. 8.30ff.; 24, etc. cf. Judg. 9.46. From these it appears that such stories were associated with the Palestinian shrines as well as with the nomadic tradition.

270. Noth, *History*, 128f.

271. Deut. 5 and 28. For formulae and parallels, see Bickerman, 'Couper une alliance'. Contrast Eichrodt, *Theology* I, 36–69. The question of Yahweh's non-performance did not become common in the believers' thought until AD 70.

272. Deut. 6.4f., 12f.; 10.12ff.; 11; 26.

273. Deut. 14.2, 21, 23; 15.5f., etc.

274. Deut. 12; 13; 17.2ff., etc.

275. Deut. 7. See above, n. 15.

276. Deut. 12.29ff.; 14.1f.; 18.9–13; 20.18, etc. A similar connection of elaborate purity laws with xenophobia is observable in Egypt at the same period, Kienitz, *Geschichte*, 50.

277. Deut. 14.2f., 21; 17.7b, 12b; 18.12; 19.10, 13, 19b; 21.9, 23; 23.4ff., 10–15, etc.

278. Deut. 16.1–12; 26.1–11.

279. So von Rad, *Studies*, 15.

280. Deut. 6.6–9, 20–25; 11.18ff.

281. But does not prove, cf. *ANET* 72b; Aelian *Varia Historia* II.39.

282. Deut. 4.6, 8.

283. This account of the origin of synagogue worship is, since the work of Bacher (e.g., 'Synagogue'), the common one and is plausible, but pure speculation. For other speculations, see de Vaux, *Ancient Israel*, 343–5.

284. Israel is the people of the tradition, not the people of the book. The Old Testament was not a book before the appearance of the codex, and even thereafter the devotion has been to the Law, not to the codex. 'People of the book' is a Moslem legal term (Sale, *Koran*, 152 note y), misunderstood by analogy with Protestant bibliolatry.

3. 'Hellenization'

1. Albright, *Archaeology of Palestine*, 99f.

2. *Iliad*, 23.743, etc. D. Auscher, 'Relations', 8ff., but cf. Weinberg, *Post-Exilic Palestine*, 11ff.

3. Dothan, 'Azor, 1960', 173ff.; Biran, 'Archaeological Activities, 1968', 50; Waldman, 'Tombs', 335ff.

4. Cook, *Religion*, 180–86; G. Hill, *Some Cults*, 427.

5. Cook, *Religion*, II Sam. 8.18; 15.18; 20.7, 23; I Kings 1.38, 44. Greenfield, 'Cherethites'. (I am indebted to Prof. M. Greenberg for the information that the Greek in *ANET* 286f. – at Ascalon in the time of Hezekiah – was produced by the translator's mistaking a proper name for a gentilic.)

6. II Kings 11.4f.; cf. Greenfield, 'Cherethites'.

7. Parke, *Greek Soldiers*, 4f.

8. Herodotus II.152.

9. Aharoni, 'Arad', 14; Tadmor, 'Philistia', 102, n. 59, conjectures that the plentiful East Greek pottery at Mesad Hashavyahu, from the late seventh century, may have been left there by Greek or Cretan soldiers in Josiah's employ. For seventh-century and earlier Greek and Cypriote pottery at other sites see Auscher, 'Relations', 14; Kokhavi, 'Notes', 273; Biran and Gophna, 'Tell Halif', 77; but cf. Weinberg, *Post-Exilic Palestine*, 12f.

10. Herodotus II.159.

11. Jer. 37.1–8. II Kings 24.7 is probably mistaken.

12. Bickerman, *Ezra*, 32. Tahpanhes is Daphnae, later well known as a centre of Greek mercenaries. Greek pottery there dates from the seventh century BC, Weinberg, *Post-Exilic Palestine*, 16f.

13. Alcaeus Z.27 and B.16 in Lobel and Page, *Fragmenta*; Jer. 47.5ff.; Quinn, 'Alcaeus', 48; cf., however, Auerbach, 'Wechsel'.

14. *ANET* 308f.

15. Olmstead, *Persian Empire*, 237ff., esp. 242. Greek conscripts were used by Cambyses in his attack on Egypt in 525: Herodotus II.1.

16. The date of the Persian take-over is uncertain.

17. On the Elamite version of the Behistun inscription see Kienitz, *Geschichte*, 60 n. 4; for the rest of the chronology, Drioton and Vandier, *L'Egypte*, 603–5 and notes.

18. Herodotus III.139, but Herodotus' statement seems to be contradicted by the pottery finds, cf. Weinberg, *Post-Exilic Palestine*, 15–17.

19. Thucydides I.104–10 and Gomme's notes, which cite the other sources.

20. Heichelheim, 'Ezra's Palestine', 251ff.; see, however, the discussion by Jacoby, *FGrHist*, notes on no. 342 F 1.

21. Drioton and Vandier, *L'Egypte*, 605.

22. Following Hall, 'Egypt',; Tarn, 'Persia'. The trouble in 414–408 is

known from the Elephantine papyri, as is the continuance of Persian rule until 401. E. Kraeling, *Brooklyn . . . Papyri*, 112.

23. Noth, *History*, 318, 345.

24. Galling, 'Denkmäler', 79, which refers to many other Persian remains in the vicinity.

25. Arrian *Anabasis* II.25.4ff.

26. Compare Hall, 'Egypt', 152, with Tarn, 'Persia', 21ff.; Olmstead, *Persian Empire*, thinks attacks were made on both dates.

27. Tarn, 'Persia', 3. Xenophon *Cyropaedia* VIII.8.26 (probably propaganda, but not wholly baseless).

28. So Nepos *Iphicrates*, 2.4; Diodorus XV.41 says 20,000.

29. Jones, *Cities*, 231; Parke, *Greek Soldiers*, 106f.

30. Diodorus XV.92.2; Nepos *Chabrias* 2.3; Plutarch *Agesilaus* 36ff.

31. Reifenberg *Coins*, nos. 1–3 and pp. 8f.; cf. however, Auscher, 'Relations', 22ff., and Bickerman, review of Goodenough, 246.

32. Schürer, *Geschichte*, III.7f. Bickerman, *Ezra*, 11f. and n.8, connects the capture with that of Sidon reflected in the Babylonian docket translated in S. Smith, *Babylonian Historical Texts*, 148f. See below, Ch. 7, n. 22.

33. Diodorus XVI.44.1–4 interpreted as by Tarn, 'Persia', 22f.

34. Mesad Hashavyahu near Yahweh, an East Greek settlement begun about 640. See Naveh, 'Excavations'.

35. E.g., Tell Mahlata, SE of Arad, Kokhavi, 'Notes', 273; En Gedi, Mazar, Dothan, and Dunayersky, *En Gedi*, 30f.; cf. Weinberg, *Post-Exilic Palestine*, 12, and Stern, 'Eretz-Isreal', 118f.

36. Tell en-Nasbeh, a few kilometres NW of Jerusalem, Albright, *Archaeology of Palestine*, 143; Samaria, Reisner, *Samaria*, 62; Shechem, G. Wright, 'First Campaign', 19f., and *Shechem*, 167ff.; En Gedi, see preceding note; elsewhere, Rostovtzeff, *Hellenistic World*, 1325 n. 17.

37. *Beth Zur*, 41. Weinberg, *Post-Exilic Palestine*, 13, thinks Greek trade did not become substantial until the second half of the century.

38. *Hellenistic World*, 94, 104f., 130ff., 158f., 160 n. 33.

39. Tcherikover, *Hellenistic Civilization*, 91f.; Isaeus IV.7f.

40. Bickerman, 'Foundations', 75; Reifenberg, 'Hebrew Shekel'; Schlumberger, *Argent*, 22–24; Auscher, 'Relations', 22ff.

41. Goodenough, *Symbols*, III.668–70.

42. Rostovtzeff, *Hellenistic World*, 1338 n. 6, approving the suggestion of Sellers and Albright. Schlumberger, *Argent*, 27.

43. Palestine Archaeological Museum, *Gallery Book, Persian . . . Periods*, Nos. 759–63, 770, 728.

44. 'Discovery', 115.

45. *Gallery Book*, 685, 694, 696, 697 and 712, 703, 710–11, 713–14, 705.

46. Josephus *Ant.* XI.321ff. reflects, if anything, a meeting of Simeon the Righteous and Antiochus III; Moore, 'Simeon', 357.

47. By Perdiccas in 321, Ptolemy in 320, Antigonus in 315, Ptolemy

and again Antigonus in 312, Ptolemy in 302, perhaps the Seleucids and again the Ptolemies in the succeeding ten years, certainly Antiochus in 218, Ptolemy IV Philopator in 217, Antiochus in 201, Scopas in 199, and Antiochus in 198 (Tcherikover, *Hellenistic Civilization*, compared with Abel, *Histoire*, I.25–87, and Tarn, 'Struggle').

48. *Ant.* XII.4.

49. *Ant.* XII.133; Abel, *Histoire*, I.82f., 86.

50. II Macc. 4.27ff.

51. Josephus *Apion* II.48. Tcherikover, *Hellenistic Civilization*, 106, thinks the Decapolis was built up as a string of fortresses against the Seleucids. Rostovtzeff, *Hellenistic World*, 346ff., extends this theory to the cities of the Palestinian coast and Idumea, as secondary and tertiary lines of defence.

52. *Recherches*, 633f.

53. Rostovtzeff, *Hellenistic World*, 137; Ghirshman, *Iran*, 193.

54. *Recherches*, 642–75 and 690–700.

55. Landau, 'Greek Inscription', 61.

56. Abel, *Histoire*, I.40; Rostovtzeff, *Hellenistic World*, 130, 143ff., 262f.

57. Abrahams, *Campaigns*, is inadequate. From Abel, *Histoire*, Bouché-Leclercq, *Séleucides*, Tarn, 'Struggle', and Tcherikover, *Hellenistic Civilization*, I have compiled the following list of wars or military leaders responsible for operations in or through Palestine in (approximately) the years specified. (The Maccabees are included when they fought outside Jewish territory.) An average of at least two campaigns (one for each army) must be allowed for each year of operations. The dating of the Syrian wars differs from author to author; to those entries, therefore, I have added in parentheses the dates given by Bengtson, *Geschichte*, 571f.

321 Perdiccas	199 Scopas
320 Ptolemy	198 Antiochus III
315 Antigonus	169 Antiochus Epiphanes
312 Ptolemy	168 Antiochus Epiphanes (bis)
312 Antigonus	167 Apollonius
302 Ptolemy	166 Apollonius
301 (?) Seleucus	166 Seron
296 Demetrius	165 Ptolemy Macron
288 (?) Ptolemy	164 Lysias
280–272 First Syrian War (280–279 and 274–271)	163 Judas in Transjordan
	163 Judas in the Hauran
260–255 Second Syrian War (260–253)	163 Simon in Galilee
	162 Lysias
252–241 Third Syrian War (246–241)	161 Bacchides
	160 Nicanor
219 Antiochus III	160 Bacchides (occupied to 157)
218 Antiochus III	152 Alexander Balas
218 Ptolemy IV	150 Ptolemy VI
201 Antiochus III	

147 Apollonius
147 Jonathan in the plain
146 Ptolemy VI
145 Demetrius II
144 Jonathan in Syria
144 Simon in the plain
143 Tryphon
142 Tryphon
142 Simon in the plain
138 Antiochus Sidetes
137–135 Kendebaios
134–132 Antiochus Sidetes
128 Hyrcanus in Transjordan
128 Demetrius II
128 Cheopatra Thea (residence henceforth in Acre)
108 Hyrcanus in Samaria
107 Hyrcanus in Scythopolis, etc.
104 Aristobulus I in Galilee

104 Antigonus in Galilee
103 Jannaeus in Acre
103 Ptolemy Lathyrus
102 Ptolemy Lathyrus
102 Cleopatra III
101–93 Jannaeus in Transjordan
93–88 Jannaeus throughout Palestine
88 Demetrius III
86 Antiochus XII
84 Aretas III
83–80 Jannaeus in the plain
80–76 Jannaeus in Transjordan
74 Aristobulus II in Damascus
70 Tigranes
68–63 Aristobulus II v. Hyrcanus II and Nabateans

58. Schlatter, *Geschichte*, 383 n. 7, lists a dozen obscure places with Persian names as evidence for Persian foundation of towns in Palestine, but of these, the only one about whose settlement anything certain is known is a colony of Babylonian Jews established by Herod (Josephus *Vita* 11.54ff.; see Thackeray's note on the passage). The other places are small Jewish settlements known from Josephus or later sources and most of them are located in Galilee or northern Transjordan (where Jewish settlements would probably not have survived the anti-Maccabaean reaction, see I Macc. 5). Behind Greek colonization was the poverty and over-population of Greece. The Persians had no such motivation.

59. Contrast Tcherikover, *Hellenistic Civilization*, 90–116, with Jones, *Cities*, 227–95; see also Jones, 'Urbanization'; Schlatter, *Geschichte*, 12ff.; and Alt, 'Probleme', 6.78ff.

60. Jones, *Cities*, 250–52.

61. Jones, *Cities*, 251f., credits him with five or six Antiochs (Gerasa, Gadara, Hippos, Ptolemais [?], and Jerusalem) and three Seleucias (Abila, Gadara [*sic*], and Seleucia in the Gaulan). This last may or may not be identical with Seleucia by Lake Huleh (Tcherikover, *Hellenistic Civilization*, 101) and Antioch near Huleh (Alt, 'Probleme', 2.78). Gerasa, Gadara, Hippos and Ptolemais, at least, were probably self-governing cities before his foundation.

62. Cf. Bickerman, *Gott*, ch. III, with Tcherikover, *Hellenistic Civilization*, 188f.; Jones, *Cities*, 252; Abel, *Histoire*, I.122f., etc.

63. That Scythopolis was not entirely a new creation (in spite of its alternative name, Trikomia) is argued by the survival of the name Beth Shan (Klein, *Sepher Hayeshub*, s.v.). Cf. Jones, *Cities*, 233. Rowe,

Topography, 44, knows nothing of any interruption of settlement. Strato's Tower was probably a Sidonian settlement, Tcherikover, *Hellenistic Civilization*, 93.

64. Seleucia by Huleh, Tcherikover, *Hellenistic Civilization*, 101. Philoteria, *ibid.*, 102; Abel, *Histoire*, 1.57; cf. Alt, 'Probleme', 3.86. Atabyrion, Alt, 'Probleme', 6.81; Oehler, 'Ortschaften', 6f. Arethusa, Tcherikover, *Hellenistic Civilization*, 95; Jones, *Cities*, 259 n. 42; Schlatter, *Geschichte*, 13. Anthedon, Tcherikover, *Hellenistic Civilization*, 95, cf. Jones, *Cities*, 447 n. 16.

65. Tcherikover, *Hellenistic Civilization*, 109; Jones, *Cities*, 239; Abel, *Histoire*, I.57; C. Kraeling, *Gerasa*, 30f.

66. Tcherikover, *Hellenistic Civilization*, 95f., 103f., 105; Abel, *Histoire*, I.54; Jones, *Cities*, 238; but contrast Arrian *Anabasis* II.27, end.

67. Tcherikover, *Hellenistic Civilization*, 107–10; Jones, *Cities*, 242, 252; Abel, *Histoire*, I.122f.

68. G. Harper, *Village Administration*, 20ff. and esp. 46–57. Jones, *Cities*, 285f., tries to explain the council men as honorific; Sourdel, *Cultes*, 11 n. 1, has followed Harper; so, too, Rostovtzeff, 'Syrie', 11f.

69. Haefeli, *Samaria*, 98f., on Josephus *War* IV.420ff.

70. Homonoia on the Sea of Galilee (the name can hardly be post-Maccabaean), Oehler, 'Ortschaften', 11; Pella in Judaea (Nestle's conjecture, 'Judaea', 75, is unconvincing; a Macedonian settlement is more likely than such a scribal error); Berenike in Gaulan and Berenike in the coastal plain, Alt, 'Probleme', 4.80 n. 1; Pegai and Patras, Schlatter, *Geschichte*, 13; Arsinoe, Tcherikover, 'Palestine', 43.

71. For example, Gabara; see Thackeray's ed., Vol. I, index, s.v.

72. Compare Ta'anit 21a (a small '*ir* is one which can put 500 men in the field) with 'Erubin 60a (the minimum required for an '*ir* is three dwellings).

73. *Hellenistic World*, 348 (the inference is based on Pap. Cairo, Zen., 59006, which Edgar refers to a settlement near Gaza; compare Tcherikover, 'Palestine', 37). See further *Hellenistic World*, 346–51 and 496–502.

74. On Beth Anath see Klein, 'Notes', 139ff., who (for dubious reasons) would locate it in Transjordan on the Syrian border.

75. See the study of his correspondence by Tcherikover ('Palestine'), also Abel, *Histoire*, I.67ff., and Herz, 'Grossgrundbesitz', 107.

76. The question is complicated. Compare Abel, *Histoire*, I.60ff., Tcherikover, 'Palestine', 36ff., and Jones, *Cities*, 248f. and 274. Jones thinks this essential structure lasted through Seleucid and Maccabaean times and was taken over by Herod. Rostovtzeff, *Hellenistic World*, 348ff., comes, with reservations, to the same conclusion. See further R. Bagnall, *Administration of the Ptolemaic Possessions outside Egypt*, Columbia Studies in the Classical Tradition IV, Leiden 1976.

77. *Ant.*XII.180ff. The story must have been at least an exaggeration of recognized methods.

78. The relation of royal to local law remains one of the most obscure and important problems of this history.

79. II Macc. 5.21–6.1; cf. I Macc. 1.29.

80. Pap. Cairo, Zen., 59006.

81. 'Foundations', 93f.

82. Rostovtzeff, *Hellenistic World*, 1339 n. 8; Bengtson, *Geschichte*, 156.

83. Rostovtzeff, *Hellenistic World*, 1403 n. 149.

84. Especially 99ff. and 109ff. See also Alt, 'Probleme', 3.80ff. Alt's attempt to prove, from these estates, the prior existence of royal domain land (88) is contradicted by his own statements in 'Probleme', 5.70, and refuted by Rostovtzeff, *Hellenistic World*, 1403 n. 149.

85. Rostovtzeff, *Hellenistic World*, 351ff.; Bertram, 'Hellenismus', 270f.

86. Cumont, *Recherches*, 389. On the importance of the Phoenicians in hellenising Palestine see Stern, 'Eretz-Israel', 121.

87. Alt, 'Probleme', 2.73ff. By the late fifth or early fourth century a Phoenician trader was established in Elath, Naveh, 'Scripts', 27ff.

88. Goodenough, *Symbols*, I.65ff., and III, nos. 7–16.

89. Josephus *Ant.* XII.257–64; cf. II Macc. 6.2 (Zeus Xenios).

90. Alt, 'Probleme', 4.83, and Abel, *Histoire*, I.56, supposed a Sidonian colony existed at Shechem. Contrast Bickerman, 'Document', and 'Foundations', 87.

91. Sellers, *Beth Zur*, 69ff.; Reisner, *Samaria*, I.252f.; Rostovtzeff, *Hellenistic World*, 1324 n. 16. Kindler, 'Mint', 318ff., declares that Tyre was the major supplier of coins to Palestine through more than 400 years.

92. Cross, 'Discovery', 116f.; Kirkbride, 'Currencies', 153.

93. T. Ketubot 13 (12), end (ed. Zuckermandel, 275).

94. Tarn, 'Persia', 20ff.; Dikaios, *Guide*, 40; Galling, 'Denkmäler', 65ff.

95. Diodorus XVI.47.6; 49.1; and XLIX.7; Hall, 'Egypt', 153.

96. Phillips, *Qataban*, 277; G. Hill, *Catalogue . . . Arabia*, 45 and 47.

97. Drioton and Vandier, *L'Egypte*[4], 677.

98. By Artaxerxes III to the Caspian and Babylonia, Schürer, *Geschichte*, III.7; by Alexander to Alexandria, Josephus *Apion* II.42; by Ptolemy Lagos to Cyrenaica, ibid., II.44 (defended by Juster, *Juifs*, II.266 n. 2); by Ptolemy Lagos to Egypt, Josephus *Ant.* XII.7; cf. Deut. 28.68; by Seleucus Nicator to Antioch, Abel, *Histoire*, I.42, cf. *Ant.* XII.119. Passages predicting a new dispersion may or may not be prophecies *ex eventu*, e.g., Testament of Issachar 6.2.

99. Neh. 5.1–13; Joel 4.6ff.; Josephus *Ant.* XII.24–33 (from Aristeas 12.27); *Ant.* XII.144. Herz, 'Grossgrundbesitz', 108; Tcherikover, *Hellenistic Civilization*, 68; Rostovtzeff, *Hellenistic World*, 341ff. and 1262; Juster, *Juifs*, II.17f. and notes; Urbach, 'Halakot'; on the date of Joel, Myers, 'Considerations', makes a good case for the late sixth century, and collects much material on Greek contacts with Palestine then and before; Rudolph, 'Joel', pleads for 590, but with too many false arguments.

100. Evidence collected by Juster, *Juifs*, II.265–68 and notes; add

Josephus *Ant.* XII.119 (intended to suggest service under Seleucus Nicator). Many refs. from papyri in Launey, *Recherches*, 541–56. That even Maccabaean Jews desired such service is shown by the wishful thinking in I Macc. 10.36f.

101. II Kings 25.26 and parallels; Josephus *Ant.* XII.9; XII.119; *Apion* I.194. Not all the Graeco-Roman diaspora came direct from Palestine, *Ant.* XII.147ff.

102. Ezra 1.4–11; 2.68f., etc.; Jer. 41.4ff.

103. Cicero *pro Flacc.* 28.67; Philo *de spec. leg.* I.76f.; Josephus *Ant.* XVIII.313; Jeremias, *Jerusalem*, 76ff.; Juster, *Juifs*, I.377ff.

104. Jeremias, *Jerusalem*, 76ff., 101, 134ff.

105. *Historiarum* V.5.

106. *War* VI.335.

107. Kittel, *Probleme*, 74ff.

108. *ANET* 315b–316b; Ghirshman, *Iran*, 132f.; see my 'II Isaiah and the Persians'.

109. Probably exaggerated by Hölscher, *Palästina*, 1–4; cf. Ghirshman, *Iran*, 142ff.

110. Duchesne-Guillemin, *Zoroastre*, 128f.

111. G. Driver, *Aramaic Documents*, 15ff.

112. Ghirshman, *Iran*, figs. 60, 63, 64; plates 15 (d), 17 (a), 18; but elements of Greek style were also introduced, see Frankfort, 'Achaemenian Sculpture', and Richter, 'Greeks in Persia'. Persian readiness to appropriate alien cultural elements is remarked by Herodotus I.135.

113. Jones, *Cities*, 230, and Tcherikover, *Hellenistic Civilization*, 34f., argue that the survival of Aramaic place names proves the persistence of Semitic-speaking populations. If so, then in Gaza, Acre, Sidon and Tyre, Greek never became the exclusive language; cf. Bevan, *House of Seleucus*, I.225ff.

114. Rostovtzeff, *Hellenistic World*, 415.

115. Nock, *Conversion*, 37; Bidez, 'Ecoles', 41ff.

116. Ghirshman, *Iran*, 185ff.; Schlumberger, *Argent*, 13ff.

117. See below, Ch. 6.

118. Schlumberger, *Argent*, 17f.

119. Shown, for instance, by the history of boundaries, Alt, 'Probleme', 2; 'Judas Gaue', etc.

120. Schlumberger, *Argent*, 22.

121. Ure, *Origin*, 127ff. Further Greek borrowings: Olmstead, *Persian Empire*, 208ff.; Mazzarino, *Oriente*, ch. I.

122. The question of Hellenization as a whole, involving the West also, is a larger problem with which this study is not concerned. Compare the Greek provincialism of R. Laqueur, *Hellenismus*, and the following list of differences between 'classical' and 'Hellenistic'.

123. Rostovtzeff, *Hellenistic World*, 1101.

124. Ibid., 1134–1301.

125. Antiochus Epiphanes' playing at democracy was only an apparent exception to this rule. See Bevan, *House of Seleucus*, II.148–61.

126. Gardiner, *Athletics*, 71 and 102ff.; Plato's attacks on professional teachers of philosophy.

127. Breasted, *Development*, 293f.

128. Bickerman, 'Chaine', 46f.

129. Ferguson, 'Leading Ideas', 1f.

130. Meleager of Gadara greets the visitors to his grave in two Semitic dialects, as well as Greek. *Palatine Anthology* VII.419.

131. Nock, *Conversion*, 34.

132. G. Hill, *Catalogue . . . Phoenicia*, 156, 174, 268.

133. Harris, *Grammar*, 157ff.

134. Schürer, *Geschichte*, III.545ff.

135. Wilcken, 'Prophetie', 556ff.

136. So Rostovtzeff, equating 'Hellenistic' with 'Greek', *Hellenistic World*, 1053, 1057–73, 1098–1107, etc., though he recognizes the dangers of this equation, 1063ff., 1069, 1071ff., etc.; cf. Abel, *Histoire*, I.276.

137. *Hellenistic World*, 703ff.

138. Ibid., 848; cf. 705. These generalizations are applied specifically to Judaea, 852f.

4. The Survival of the Syncretistic Cult of Yahweh

1. Various groups of Yahweh worshippers got support from alien governments for temples or sacrificial centres, e.g. in Jerusalem, Samaria, Elephantine, Leontopolis and Sardis. Probably such support was motivated by the worshippers' influence, not by the rulers' concern for the cult.

2. On this see MacKenzie, 'City'.

3. *ANET* 284a; II Kings 17.5–23.

4. *ANET* 284b–285a; cf. Tadmor, 'Campaigns'.

5. Montgomery, *Kings*, on this verse.

6. II Kings 15.29; 17.1–6; cf. the Assyrian records, cited in n. 4. The claim of Sennacherib, Sargon's successor, to have carried off 200,150 from the smaller kingdom of Judah (which he did not wholly depopulate) cannot be accepted with confidence (*ANET* 288a). Ungnad, 'Zahl', has argued plausibly that the figure must be a corruption of 2,150; so, too, de Vaux, *Ancient Israel*, 66.

7. So Oppenheim in *ANET* 285a; cf. Tadmor, 'Campaigns', 34.

8. Lods, *Prophets*, 24ff.; Maisler, 'Golë'.

9. II Kings 17.24–28.

10. Kenyon, *Archaeology*, 251–52, 272.

11. Jer. 41.5ff.

12. Freedman, 'Babylonian Chronicle', 56f.

13. Ibid., 54–56.

14. II Kings 25.26; Jer. 43.5ff.

15. Jer. 52.30.

16. Albright, *Biblical Period*, 85ff. and n. 180.

17. II Kings 25.23; cf. the recent finds in Wadi Daliyeh, Cross, 'Discovery'.

18. II Kings 25.12; Beek, *Geschichte*, 104.

19. Ezra 9–10; Neh. 6.18; 10.31; 13.1–3, 23–30; Malachi 2.11.

20. Ezra 9.2. The offenders in Ezra 9.1 were understood by Josephus to be 'the multitude' (*Ant.* XI.140), by LXX, 'the people'. See also Ezra 10.13f. and Rudolph, *Esra*, on 10.18ff. (pp. 73f.). Contrast Alt, 'Rolle', 27.

21. This sequence will be defended in Ch. 5.

22. Neh. 13.28.

23. *Ant.* XI.312.

24. *Ant.* XII.160.

25. Diodorus XL.3, in Photius 244.

26. Rostovtzeff, *Hellenistic World*, 343.

27. Goodenough, *Symbols*, I.73.

28. *Palatine Anthology* V.160.

29. Wolfson, *Philo*, I.73ff.

30. The frequency of intermarriage in the Maccabaean period is evidenced by Test. of Levi 14.5ff.; in the Herodian period, by the material in Juster, *Juifs*, II.45 n. 5; in the Roman period, by the numerous rabbinic attacks on it (specimens in Wolfson, see the preceding note) and many direct statements, e.g., 'R. Abbahu said, "Thirteen cities became Samaritan by intermarriage in the days of the [Hadrianic] persecution"' (Jer. Yebamot 8.3 = 9d). A special form of alien admixture, which was already important in the time of Nehemiah (Kaufmann, *Golah*, 230) but must have become especially common in the Maccabaean period, was that of slaves who had become nominally Jewish in order to gain their liberty; see (Jer. Yebamot VIII.3) the statement of R. Joshua b. Levi, 'Pashhur b. Immer had 5,000 slaves and they all merged [their families] by marriage into the high priestly families.'

31. Alon, 'Moza'am', 147f. Palmyrene inscriptions show that a number of families in Palmyra contained both persons with Jewish and persons with pagan names, Cook, *Religion*, 215ff.

32. Strabo XVI.2.34.

33. Josephus *War* II.463, justly noted by Haefeli, *Samaria*, 77ff. Translate as follows: 'For, though they thought they had got rid of the Jews, yet each city regarded the Judaizers with suspicion and none was willing to kill off-hand the persons of uncertain affiliation to be found in each, and a person of mixed stock was feared as if altogether alien.' (Contrast Thackeray; I see no justification for his translation of *memigmenon* as 'neutral'.)

34. Above, n. 8.

35. Jer. 44.15ff. Cf. above, Ch. 2, n. 266.

36. Ezek. 14.1ff.; 20.31.

37. Deut. 4.28; 28.36, 64.

38. Lev. 24.15, cf. Job 2.9; Appian *Libyke* (*Punic Wars*) IX.56, 92 (examples of cursing gods).

39. Lev. 20.1–5.

40. Daiches, *Jews*, 21ff.; for the correction of 'Ninib' to 'Ninarta' see D. Hillers, *JNES* 33, 1974, 264. Sidersky, 'Onomastique', resolutely ignores the appearance of Jewish and pagan names in the same families. Similar evidence appears in the seal of Yehoyishma' daughter of Sawas [Shamash] sarusur, Avigad, 'Seals', 228.

41. E. Kraeling, *Brooklyn . . . Papyri*, 83ff., esp. 88; Borger, 'Anath-Bethel'.

42. E. Kraeling, *Brooklyn . . . Papyri*, 86ff.; further, Bresciani, 'Papiri', and Fitzmyer, 'Paduan . . . Papyri'. Cf. Noth, *History*, 295; Porten, *Archives*, 151–79 with full discussion and documentation.

43. Ezek. 33.23ff.

44. Isa. 57.1–10; cf. Pfeiffer, *Introduction*, 480f.

45. Isa. 65.1–12. That this is Israelite syncretism, not paganism, is shown by de Vaux, 'Sacrifices', 264.

46. Avigad, 'Hotam'; Cook, *Religion*, 41–83, esp. 56, 62, 70; also 82f.

47. 'The "Flying scroll" is merely a stylized abstract form of the Mesopotamian winged sun-disc.' Mazar, Dothan, and Dunayevsky, 'En Gedi', 34. An Israelite seal which belonged to a man named Saul shows the sun disc being worshipped, Avigad, 'Hotam', Plate 3.

48. Aharoni, 'Excavations', 103ff.

49. Mazar and Dunayevsky, 'En Gedi Fourth and Fifth Seasons', 139.

50. Isa. 19.19.

51. Ezra 8.17. See Rudolph's commentary and Lods, *Histoire*, 485.

52. Zech. 5.5ff. The vision of the woman (Anath?) carried off in a bushel basket by flying demons may be in deliberate contrast to Ezekiel's earlier vision of Yahweh leaving Jerusalem on his throne borne by flying beasts. Cf. the equally conjectural explanation offered by Rost, 'Erwägungen'. Further arguments for cult centres in Babylonia are given by Vink, 'Date', 73ff.

53. Reading 'to him' instead of 'not' in v. 2. These verses prove the Chronicler's belief that the cult of Yahweh had been maintained by Palestinians since Assyrian times, and this there is no reason to doubt (de Vaux, *Ancient Israel*, 334, 339, 391).

54. Aharoni, 'Trial Excavation', 157–62. Result disputed.

55. Dupont-Sommer, 'Autels', 141ff., 151–2. Restudy has discredited both Dupont-Sommer's and Albright's readings, but dedication to Yahweh remains likely. See the articles listed since 1968, almost annually, by J. Teixidor in *Syria*, in his 'Bulletin d'Épigraphie Sémitique' (see the indices under Lachish).

56. Pal.Arch.Museum, *Gallery Book, Persian . . . Periods*, nos. 720, 721.

57. De Vaux, *Ancient Israel*, 286.

58. Pritchard, 'Tell es-Sa'idiyeh', 574ff.

59. Cowley, *Aramaic Papyri*, no. 30, line 29.

60. Neh. 6.17f.

61. Cook, 'Inauguration', 169, n. 1; Cross, 'Discovery', 115 and 120f.; Zenon Papyri 59076.

62. Compare Hebron, of which de Vaux writes, 'Il reste très vraisemblable que le site a été vénéré sous la monarchie et le silence des textes bibliques pour cette époque peut s'expliquer par le désir de faire, oublier un sanctuaire où se perpétuait un culte qui n'était pas entièrement orthodoxe.' Review of Mader, 595. On Beth Shan see above, n. 10.

63. Josephus *Ant.* XI.324.

64. De Vaux, *Ancient Israel*, 280, 292; Gunkel, *Psalmen*, on Ps. 89.12f.

65. Vink, 'Date', 73ff.

66. *VT* 17, 1967, 480f.

67. Josephus *Ant.*XII.228–36.

68. By Butler, *Architecture*, 2–22, and by Lapp, 'Campaigns', 24, 29ff. However, Lapp's opinion has been questioned by E. Will, 'L'édifice dit Qasr el-Abd à Araq el-Amir', *CRAI* 1977, 69–85, and subsequent articles.

69. Josephus *Ant.* XIII.62ff. This temple was closed after 70, but occasional sacrifices may have been offered here as late as the second century, cf. Megillah 10a.

70. Contrast Noth, *History*, 317.

71. *PGM*, no. V, lines 110f.; Galatians 6.16; John 4.20–23.

72. Isa. 2.2–4; 19.21; 45.14, 22f.; 49.6; 56.3, 6f.; 59.19; 66.20, 23; Micah 4.1–3; 7.16f.; Zeph. 3.9; Zech. 2.15; 8.20ff.; 14.16; Ps. 22.28; 65.2f.; 66.4; 67.3ff.; 138.4f. It is hard to decide which of these passages refer to adhesion to the syncretistic cult of Yahweh, which to conversion to the Yahweh-alone party.

73. For example, 68, 117, 148.

74. So, in particular, 117, which may have signalled the presentation of gifts or performance of symbolic acts of reverence by Gentiles.

75. Ezra 1.2; 6.2–12; 7.11–26 (probably elaborations rather than sheer inventions, cf. Ps. 68.30ff.). Josephus *Apion* II.48; *Ant.* XII.138ff., etc.

76. 1.11. For an example of the absurdities following from neglect of the Gentiles' cult of Yahweh, see Rehm, 'Opfer'.

77. It does occur in the Letter of Aristeas, 15, but there the text attributes the thought to a Gentile, perhaps as being just what a Gentile would think. Acts 17.23b is not a parallel.

78. For example, Ptolemy Euergetes (Josephus *Apion* II.48); M. Agrippa (*Ant.* XVI.14); etc.

79. Josephus *War* II.412. This does not imply that Gentile donors were more numerous than Jews. Much of the wealth came from governmental support, which was Gentile.

80. This observation has been developed, with much evidence, by Bickerman, 'Altars'.

81. II Kings 5.15ff.

82. See Bickerman, 'Altars', and, especially, *From Ezra*, 83–86.

83. Albright, *Biblical Period*, 87; cf. Bickerman, *From Ezra*, 11.

84. De Vaux, *Ancient Israel*, 369, conjectures that some were settled there by Nabonidus.

85. Cf. the smaller estimate implied by Albright, *Biblical Period*, 87. For the Persian period cf. Stern, 'Eretz-Israel', 114f.

86. Cf. the larger estimates in Juster, *Juifs*, I.209ff., and Baron, *History*, I.168–70 and notes, p. 370 n. 7.

87. I Macc. 5.

88. Cf. Brandon, *Fall*.

89. E.g., the epistles from the Jerusalem community to the Judaeans in Egypt, urging them to observe Hanukah, II Macc. 1.1ff. Note their offer to supply books representing the party's tradition (2.14f.).

90. Josephus *Ant.* XIII.65ff.

91. For these see Diodorus I.89.5ff.

92. This information I owe to Prof. Bickerman, who bases his opinion on the letter's misuse of legal terminology.

93. Josephus *Ant.* XIV.259ff.

94. Valerius Maximus I.3.3, in Nepotianus' abridgment. It is not certain from Nepotianus' text that the altars belonged to the Judaeans, but Bickerman, 'Altars', 144ff., assumes that they did. I suppose the Jews who built them also used them. Julian *Against the Galileans* 305D–306A declares that Jews still offer sacrifices in their own houses. That the Talmuds do not mention this is not a decisive objection; the Talmuds are concerned to regulate the lives of orthodox Jews, not to describe the rituals of heretics and pagans. What do they tell us of the cult of Yahweh Hypsistos, or the sacrifice of the mass? Procopius *De aedificiis* VI.2, end, says there was a Jewish settlement at Borion in western Libya which had a temple thought to have been founded by Solomon. Justinian forced the Jews there to become Christian and changed the temple to a church.

95. Nilsson, *Geschichte*[2], II.664ff. and notes; Cook, *Religion*, 193ff.; Bickerman, 'Altars', 154ff. Kraabel, 'Hypsistos', has shown that the supposed evidence for the connection of Yahweh with Hypsistos in Lydia and Phrygia was misinterpreted, but there is no doubt of the connection in Alexandria, and little in Delos. The temple of Zeus Hypsistos founded by Hadrian on Mt Gerizim was associated with Abraham (Damascius *Vita Isidori* 141). Objects connected with the cult of Dionysus are common on Jewish archaeological material (Goodenough, *Symbols*, I.30ff. and passim), and Dionysiac elements were prominent in the syncretistic form of the cult of Yahweh introduced by the Hellenizing party in Jerusalem (II Macc. 6.7). Here also belongs the association of Yahweh with the cult of Fortune (Gad-Tyche), Isa. 65.11. Tyche, in turn, is found with Hypsistos (Nilsson, *Geschichte*[1], 637 n. 3).

96. Seyrig, 'Antiquités', 238ff. and 263ff. Cf. Bickerman, 'Altars', 156.

97. Goodenough, *Symbols*, II.153–end. The apologetic claims of Origen *Celsus* I.22 are refuted by the acquaintance with Old Testament material shown by many of the texts in which the names of the patriarchs occur as magical terms, and the subsequent sections of Origen's own treatise admit and defend the thaumaturgic use of the name of Yahweh by both Jews and Christians. Nevertheless, the 'pagan' use to which Origen testifies would be more easily understandable from a syncretistic background.

5. From Nebuchadnezzar to Nehemiah

1. For example, Lods, *Histoire*, 460ff. Against Janssen, *Juda*, see de Vaux's review; Thomas, 'Sixth Century'; and Weinberg's review of the situation in *Post-Exilic Palestine*, 3–11.

2. Ezek. 33.23ff.; Isa. 65, quoted above, p. 67f.; Zech. 10.2; 13.2f.

3. 11.18 fits the situation and the context; contra, Fohrer, *Ezechiel*, ad. loc.

4. On Ezekiel see Rowley, 'Book'; on Second Isaiah, my 'II Isaiah and the Persians'. Kuhl, 'Stand', 36ff., and Irwin, 'Problem', are less persuasive than the majority of recent scholarship which they are forced to recognise (Kuhl, 34ff., Irwin, *passim*).

5. Eissfeldt, *Introduction*, 25; Rost, *Credo*, 34f.; de Vaux, *Ancient Israel*, 146. On Joshua contrast Noth, *Überlieferungsgeschichtliche Studien*, 182–90. For a yet larger list see Auerbach, 'Aufstieg', 243f.

6. Cf. Freedman, 'Law', 251, n. 2.

7. Above, Ch. 2, n. 248. This may have resulted in the 'publication' of material which before this time did not circulate; see C. Cohen, 'Was the P Document Secret?'

8. Lev. 20.24, 26. For this dating of the Holiness Code see below, Ch. 6, n. 70.

9. See above, Ch. 1, p. 9.

10. Above, Ch. 2 end.

11. II Sam. 7.18ff.; I Kings 8.23ff.

12. It is more plausible to assign this material to the synagogue than to the levitic tradition on which the Deuteronomists drew. The priests of ancient temples generally did not preach; a preaching priesthood of the rural high places is incredible; and until the development of the synagogue there is no evidence of any institutional basis for a nonpriestly but levitic 'preaching clergy'. Cf. von Rad, *Studies*, and Gunneweg, *Leviten*.

13. Jer. 40.1ff.

14. II Kings 25.27; Albright, *Biblical Period*, 85 n. 173.

15. Jer. 29.5.

16. Ezra 1.14; cf. 6.3ff. Cyrus *might* have issued some such edicts (Bickerman, 'Edict'; de Vaux, 'Décrets'), but there are strong reasons for doubting that he *did* (Pfeiffer, *Introduction*, 821; Galling, *Studien*, 61ff.; compare Liver, 'Re'shitah', 115f.; Noth, *History*, 306).

17. Galling, *Studien*, would put the return of the main body shortly before 520.

18. For the literature see Rowley, 'Nehemiah's Mission'; for the disorder, ibid., p. 546.

19. Ezra 1.8.

20. Ezra 5.16.

21. Ezra 2.2. For the titles of Zerubbabel and Joshua, Haggai 1.1, etc.) Items 4.–13., which now follow, are here given in the order in which they occur in the text of Ezra.

22. The 'rivals' of Ezra 4.1 and the 'people of the land' of 4.4 are generally identified as Samaritans, e.g., Alt, 'Rolle', 5ff. (= *KS* II.316f.). That this identification of the former was intended by the narrator is clear from 4.4. But 'Judah and Benjamin' are here the returned exiles (cf. Ezra 1.5; 10.9; Neh. 11.4) and their actual rivals were probably the population already in Judaea. See below, pp. 86f.

23. Rudolph, *Esra*, on 4.6.

24. Haggai 2.15, cf. 18. Galling, 'Serubbabel', 69, 74ff. This disposes of J. Wright, *Building*, 16f., and Gelston, 'Foundations'.

25. Ahlemann, 'Esra-Quelle', 81ff., thinks this basically a list of those who came with Ezra; Galling, *Studien*, 89ff., supposes it was made for the Persian satrap on his visitation in 517; Mowinckel, *Studien*, I.63–109, gives reasons for thinking it part of a list of the residents of Judaea, about 400 BC.

26. Pfeiffer, *Introduction*, 821. Galling has now made this doubt very serious, see above, n. 17. On the archaeological evidence offered by Vogt, *Studie*, 15ff., see de Vaux, *RB* 73, 1966, 602ff.

27. Ezra 3.4.

28. Neh. 8.17.

29. Pfeiffer, *Introduction*, 785ff.; Eissfeldt, *Introduction*, 529ff.; Bea, 'Neuere Arbeiten'.

30. Rudolph, *Chronikbücher*, viii; Kapelrud, *Question*, 97; Galling, *Bücher*, 11f.; Kellermann, *Nehemia*, passim.

31. Both the differences and their importance are grossly exaggerated by Lemke, 'Synoptic Problem'.

32. As many had come back after 587, Jer. 40.11ff.; Torrey, *Ezra*, 297ff.; Ezek. 33.23ff.

33. Ezra 9f.; Neh. 6.18; 13.23ff., 28ff.

34. Neh. 10.32; cf. 13.15; Ezra 4.4; cf. 6.21 and Neh. 10.29; the distinction is clearly religious, not political; but they are not pagans, they have been worshipping Yahweh. Other uses of the term also survive; so Nicholson, 'Meaning', and Eybers, 'Relations'; cf. de Vaux, *Ancient Israel*, 70f, and now 'Sens'; Kessler, 'Studie', 45; Coggins, 'Interpretation', 73. The use to designate the syncretists is of course *a potiori* and does not rule out the possibility (and likelihood) that *some* of the Judaeans were adherents of the Yahweh-alone tradition. Beuken has argued that Haggai

came from this group, *Haggai-Sacharja*, 216ff. Vink, 'Date', 20, has relied on Alt's interpretation of Ezra 4.14 in rejecting Nicholson's views, but 4.14 comes from a different source; it can be used only to show the affiliations of the writers of the letter in which it occurs; we have no indication (save the Chroniclers' editorial connection, which is worthless) that these writers in the time of Artaxerxes were representatives of the group which sixty years earlier opposed Zerubbabel.

35. Ezra 4.1; 6.19f.; 8.35, etc.; without *benē*, 9.4; 10.6; Zech. 6.10.

36. Individuals of the syncretistic party may have occasionally been prominent among the returned exiles, e.g., Sheshbazzar's (or Shenazzar's) name (whatever it was) testifies to his parents' (if not his own) worship of Sin or Shamash (Albright, *Biblical Period*, 86; Galling, 'Serubbabel', 75; cf. Noth, *History*, 309 n. 1). If he was of the Davidic family and was appointed governor of Judaea by the Persians (Albright, loc. cit.; Ezra 5.14; I Chron. 3.19), he had reasons for return which most syncretists lacked. But others may also have returned; a Babylonian found at En Gedi, in remains from the Persian period, shows the worship of Marduk (Mazar and Dunayevski, 'En Gedi Fourth and Fifth Seasons', 139).

37. Ezra 10.18–24; Neh. 13.28f.

38. Haggai 1.1, 14; 2.2, 21. Against Alt's special interpretation as 'special commissioner' ('Rolle', 23f. = *KS* II.333f.), see the Appendix.

39. Haggai 1.1, 2, 12, 14, etc.

40. Consequently such reminiscences cannot be used as evidence of interpolation; cf. Beuken, *Haggai-Sacharja*, passim.

41. Such prophets still existed, Neh. 6.14; Zech. 13.2: the spirit of uncleanness which inspires the prophets is presumably that of the 'idols' (gods other than Yahweh) in whose names (as well as in that of Yahweh, v. 3) they prophesy.

42. Ezra 2.2; 3.2; 4.2, 4.

43. Haggai 2.23; Zech. 6.9ff. This may perhaps be the background of the 'Nasi' – 'people of the land' opposition studied by Gese, *Ezekiel* 40–48.

44. Cf. Eissfeldt, *Introduction*, 431f.

45. 6.11 as amended by Wellhausen (followed by Horst; Eissfeldt, *Introduction*, 430; Noth, *History*, 312; etc.). Joshua's name has been substituted in the text, but the pun still refers to Zerubbabel (*zer* = *tsemah*).

46. V. 13, reading *mimino* ('at his right hand') for the second *'al kis'o* ('on his throne'). So LXX, Wellhausen, and, with minor variations, Horst; Beuken, *Haggai-Sacharja*, 281. Was the original reading *'al yad kis'o*?

47. So Wellhausen. Crowning a man, as an honour, with a crown to be dedicated to the local god and to be hung in the god's temple, is good Greek practice, Dittenberger, *Sylloge*[4], no. 206.

48. On gold and silver crowns in temple treasures (a typical phenomenon of fifth-century Greek culture) see, e.g., the 422–421 inventory of treasures in the Parthenon, which had half a dozen, *IG* i[2].280.

49. The initial *u* in v. 15 probably means 'And *then*', sc., if this is done.

50. I suppose Zech. 6.9–15 an account of a symbolic action taken sometime prior to the issuance of the 'prophecy' reporting the visions; so Rignell, *Nachtgesichte*, 228ff. Alternatively, it could be supposed that Haggai 2.10–19 resulted from a preliminary agreement which did not settle all the differences between the parties; that, consequently, some Yahweh-alone groups continued their attacks on the priesthood; and that Zech. 3 and 6.9–15 show a further agreement and an effort to silence the criticism.

51. If Haggai 2.10–19 is a unit (so Wellhausen, Pfeiffer, *Introduction*, 602, etc.). Eissfeldt, *Introduction*, 427, Horst, on 1.15a, and Elliger, *ATD* 25.II.89, think 2.15–19 the lost prophecy which should follow 1.15a, and 2.10–14 a separate oracle. In any event the impure people are the Judaeans, not the Samaritans. The object of the prophecy is to persuade the people that the previous cult was inadequate and *therefore* the building of the temple, now begun (v. 18), must be carried through. The danger is that they will think the old cult was good enough. A cult in Samaria would not have occasioned this danger; it would not have seemed to any Jerusalemite an adequate substitute for worship in Jerusalem. (Contra Horst and Elliger, ad loc.; Beuken, *Haggai-Sacharja*, 67.) To talk of 'Bekehrung' and 'göttlichen Verheissungen' is to miss the point. This is a legal question. Purity can be regained only by the proper *ceremonies* and for those the temple is necessary.

52. On Zech. 3.2: continued attacks on the High Priest would be bad for the peace of the city, therefore Yahweh's concern for the city explains his anger against the attackers. The *ifs* of v. 7 show that the high priest is being promised a reward for an obedience (to the Law), which he might not otherwise give.

53. 3.2; cf. Amos 4.11. Whether the burning be the exile, or the assimilation going on in Palestine, or both, is uncertain.

54. A claim perhaps justified by the former history of the priesthood (Johnson, *Cultic Prophet*, 8ff.), certainly exemplified in the production of the Pentateuch, and evidently exemplified in the production of the Pentateuch, and evidently kept up (Diodorus XL.3.5), taken over by the Maccabees (Josephus *War* I.68f.; *Ant.* XIII.299f.), and attributed even to the Herodian appointees (John 11.51). Cf. Bammel, 'Archiereys'.

55. This ruling survived (with modifications) in rabbinic law, Mishnah 'Abodah Zarah 3.6.

56. Haggai 2.14; Zech. 3.3, contrast Kaufmann, 'Toledot', 241f. Bentzen, 'Priesterschaft', 282, follows another strand of the problem, but reaches similar conclusions.

57. Ezra 6.21; Neh. 10.29; contrast Kaufmann, 'Toledot', 180ff. From now on the basic differentia of Jewish sects are usually legal; see my article 'The Dead Sea Sect'.

58. Haggai 2.11 and Wellhausen's comment.

59. Ezra 2.63; 4.23; 5.8f., etc.; Josephus *Ant.* XI.297ff.; Cowley, *Aramaic Papyri*, no. 21; Posener, *Domination*, 15f.

60. Haggai 2.4, contrast Ezra 4.1–4. It is no help to argue that 'all the people of the land' in Haggai 2.4 is used in its pre-exilic sense (= the citizens) – so Beuken, *Haggai-Sacharja*, 220. The difficulty lies in the 'all', for among the land-owning citizens of Judaea at this time there were certainly many syncretists (above, 75f.). But Zechariah also prophesies to 'all' the people of the land (7.5).

61. Ezra's dating of the repulsed offer is worthless, see above. Batten argues (*Ezra*, 157) that this use of the singular ('people' not 'peoples') is unique in Ezra-Nehemiah and should therefore be emended, with I Esdras 5.69, to the plural. This diminishes the terminological difficulty but not the underlying historical problem.

62. E.g., Alt, 'Rolle', 5f. (= *KS* II.316f.); Rudolph and Galling, ad loc.; etc.

63. Ezra 3.13–41.

64. Above, pp. 81f.

65. On Alt's attempt to explain the Samaritan opposition, see the Appendix.

66. Against the theory that Nehemiah's work was added to Ezra by a later editor (so Galling, *Bücher*, 218, etc.; Mowinckel, *Studien*, I.29–50, etc.), see Kellermann, *Nehemia*, 89ff. The question is not essential here, since any editor who could have inserted the story of Nehemiah could also have changed the phraseology of Ezra.

67. Ezra 6.3–13.

68. So Holmes and Parsons' codices 62 and 147 of LXX, accepted by Nowack in Kittel[2]. In this event Yahweh's killing of three shepherds in one month and subsequent annulment of his covenant with the Gentiles (breaking of his staff of 'good pleasure', *no'am*, vv. 8–10) might refer to some events during Darius' struggle for the throne (when at least a dozen claimants were killed within the year Sept. 522–Sept. 521, Olmstead, *Empire*, 108ff.). The covenant broken would be that made with Cyrus in whim Yahweh had been well pleased (Isa. 42.1; 45.1). This accords with Olmstead's evidence that Darius was widely considered a usurper. The reasons for dating most of Zech. 9–14 at this time are well summarized by Lamarche, *Zacharie*, 148, but it is hard to believe that the chapters are all by one hand. See the critique of Lamarche in Otzen, *Studien*, 213–28. Otzen himself, p. 172, admits dissatisfaction with his own exegesis of chs. 12–13.

69. 12.2b, reading *'am* for *'al*.

70. 12.4, reading *le* for *'al* and *'eno* for *'enai* as Procksch proposes (in his notes to Kittel and Kahle,[3] ad loc.).

71. 12.5 according to the Syriac.

72. 12.6c (mistranslated in RSV).

73. *Kleinen Propheten*, ad loc. A second reference to the same hostility,

Zech. 14.14, is probably a reminiscence of this chapter. The B text of I Esdras 4.45 says 'the Judaeans' burned the temple, but the original reading was probably 'the Idumaeans', cf. v. 50.

74. I Chron. 3.19. That Nehemiah was of the house of David is incredible. Had he been so he would certainly have told his readers, with all his winning modesty.

75. Zech. 12.10, reading with Aquila and Theodotion *'elaw* for *'elai*, as implied by the second half of the verse. With the following explanation cf. Waterman, 'Camouflaged Purge'.

76. Contrast Ezra 6.6f.

77. Ezra 4.3.

78. Evidently the prophecy in Zech. 4.9 proved false, like the prophecies of Zerubbabel's messianic future.

79. Ezra 4.12, 15, 19 presumably referred originally to Zerubbabel's plan to revolt, since the revolts against the Babylonians, a hundred and forty years earlier, would hardly have figured in Persian records. Ezra 4.15d and 20 are editorial expansions to change the reference. This report cannot be supposed the first. Galling's argument in 'Serubbabel', 94f., is built on 1. the silence of a skimpy tradition, 2. the corrupt text of Ezra 4.6, 3. the false supposition that Zerubbabel's opponents were Samaritans.

80. If there was a local revolt in the borderland between Judaea and Samaria (so Stern, 'Eretz-Israel', 123) it has left no trace in the biblical material.

81. Above, pp. 89f. The problem as to the identity of the author (now raised by Maas, 'Tritojesaja') is not essential to the present question.

82. For the meaning of *kena'ani* here, cf. Elliger, ATD 25.II.186; though he translates 'merchant' he recognizes that the question is one of purity, not trade. That the verse may be a gloss does not affect the argument here, since the glossator would presumably have approved of the preceding verses which he transcribed and commented.

83. An early date for Malachi is proposed because: 1. its legal reminiscences are predominantly of Deut. (Pfeiffer, *Introduction*, 614); 2. it knows the Arab conquest of Edom as recent and not yet complete (1.2–5, contrast Nehemiah's time, Alt, 'Nachbarn', 73f. = *KS* II.344f.); 3. it still identifies the levites as priests and therefore refers to the priests as one of the lowest social classes (2.9), whereas by the time of Ezra and Nehemiah the distinction between priests and levites was evidently complete and the priests were an upper class. Further arguments for the same date in Eissfeldt, *Introduction*, 442f. (who thinks the attack on mixed marriages an interpolation – 442). Contrast Finkelstein, *Pharisees*, 557f.; Treves, 'Conjectures'; Vink, 'Date', 59ff.; etc.

84. Joel may well belong with Jonah. Cf. Treves, 'Date of Joel'; Wolff, *Joel*, 2–4; and Rudolph, 'Wann wirkte Joel?'

85. Neh. 3.8 and 31f.

86. Lods, *Histoire*, 535; cf. the *hammanim* and the incense altars at Lachish, above, Ch. 4, notes 54–57. Aharoni, 'Trial Excavation', 163f.

87. Neh. 2.19; 6.1ff.; 13.28.

88. Cook, 'Age', 25ff., 32f.; I Esdras 4.45, 50; Pfeiffer, *Introduction*, 159–67; Noth, *History*.

89. Ezra 9–10; Neh. 6.18; 13.23–29.

90. Diodorus XL.3 in Photius 244.

91. Reifenberg, 'Shekel', 101f. If Schlumberger, *Argent*, is right in dating the coin later, it could be referred to the period before Nehemiah's governorship (c. 456–445) when the assimilationists were evidently back in power (Neh. 13.4ff.). The importance of such coins as evidence of assimilationist control of the city is remarked by Kanael, 'Kawwim', 109f.; see further his 'Altjüdische Munzen', 164 and 221f.

92. *B Sanhedrin* 64a, *B Yoma* 69b.

93. Reviews of the controversy are available in Rowley, 'Order'; Snaith, 'Date'; Cazelles, 'Mission'; and Kellermann, 'Erwägungen'. Michaeli and Myers, here as elsewhere, add nothing of importance.

94. Eissfeld, *Introduction*, 543ff.; Rudolph, *Esra*, 71ff.; Mowinckel, *Studien*, III; against Torrey; Noth, *Überlieferungsgeschichtliche Studien*, 146; and now Kellermann, *Nehemia*, 56ff. For the considerations on either side, see above, pp. 79ff. For the variety of opinions as to the Ezra story's exact limits, Pfeiffer, *Introduction*, 830f.; Ahlemann, 'Esra-Quelle'; Rudolph, *Esra*, 99ff., 156f., 163ff., 172f.; Cazelles, 'Mission', 117. Nehemiah 9 and 10 are matters of dispute. I think 9 editorial and 10 the product of a sectarian group, probably of the early fourth century, see below. The suggestion of Liebreich, 'Impact', that 9 was in the pre-Maccabaean liturgy is plausible.

95. Rudolph, *Esra*, locc. citt.; Lods, *Histoire*, 632; Rowley, 'Mission', 534 n. 4; Mowinckel, *Studien*, III. The arguments of Vink, 'Date', 30ff., to prove Ezra 7–10 a Maccabaean (!) invention are not substantial. It is not surprising that the terminology of Ezra 9 and 10 is close to that of Qumran, since the Qumran sect was fond of Chronicles-Ezra-Nehemiah. Talk about 'the proud and triumphal feelings of the Persian period' neglects Neh. 1.3 and the behaviour of Bagoses. The distinction between levites and singers is not 'post-' but early 'Chronistic' (see below pp. 127ff.). Ezra 9.1 is less severe than Deut. 7.1–4 (which commands extermination) and does not directly contradict Deut. 23.8–9. The philological phenomena alleged are trivial.

96. Noth, *History*, 332. Cazelles, 'Mission', 118f., 123–26. Oudjahor-resne was sent by Darius to Egypt to restore the colleges of temple scribes, Posener, *Domination*, 22. On the *pr-'nh* see Volten, *Traumdeutung*, 17ff. Additional evidence in de Vaux, 'Décrets', 87ff.; Kellermann, 'Erwägungen', 81ff.; Porten, *Archives*, 23.

97. Ahlemann, 'Esra-Quelle', 77; Rowley, 'Order', 154f.; 'Mission',

550f.; Cazelles, 'Mission', 117; Kellermann, 'Erwägungen', 62; cf. Snaith, 'Nehemiah XII.36' (literary convention mistaken for historical evidence).

98. Rowley, 'Sanballat', 166–80. The papyri from Wadi Daliyeh have now shown that the name 'Sanballat' recurred in that of the Jerusalem high priests; still, it is somewhat unlikely that they should have recurred together and in the reign of an Artaxerxes. A further consideration is that a 'Gashmu', presumably Nehemiah's 'Geshem', flourished in NW Arabia about 450–425, Eybers, 'Relations', 77; but see the just reservations of Kellermann, 'Erwägungen', 173. Schiemann, *Sanballats*, is incredible.

99. Neh. 1.1; 2.1; 5.14; 13.6. On the uncertainty of the dates see de Vaux, *Ancient Israel*, 192; Mowinckel, *Studien*, II.16, 35ff.; Kellermann, *Nehemia*, 74f., 48f. The date given in 2.1 is perhaps a year too early. The words 'in the thirty-second year of Artaxerxes, King of *Babylon*', in 13.6, give Artaxerxes a title he probably never bore and are therefore most likely a late gloss based on 5.14, which probably gives the approximate date at which Nehemiah wrote, i.e., 432. When this gloss is removed there is no reason to doubt anything in the context. It is intrinsically probable that in the course of twelve years Nehemiah should at some time have gone back to consult with the king. Josephus *Ant.* XI.168 is contradicted by Neh. 5.14 as well as by 1.1 and 2.1.

100. Eissfeldt, *Introduction*, 553; Kellermann, 'Erwägungen', 75ff.; Bright, 'Date', has been refuted by Emerton, 'Ezra'.

101. Ezra 9–10.

102. Neh. 13.6; see above, n. 99.

103. Neh. 13.23ff.

104. Above, pp. 78ff.

105. Rudolph, *Esra*, 165ff.

106. Ecclus. 49.11–13; II Macc. 1.18; 2.13ff. The Jewish tradition led Englander, 'Ezra', 327f., to explain these omissions by supposing the authors did not think Ezra's work deserved special mention. This disposes of Bright's contention that it is 'unbelievable' that Ezra should have failed, because 'the whole course of Judaism was shaped by his work' (*History*, 378). For the latter proposition there is no substantial evidence.

107. Kellermann, 'Erwägungen', 70.

108. Rowley, 'Order', 139, 143f., 148f., on which see J. Wright, *Date*; Cazelles, 'Mission', 116; Rudolph, *Esra*, 69f.; see the refutation by Jepsen, 'Nehemia', 101ff.

109. This conclusion has now been reached independently and on somewhat different grounds by Kellermann, 'Erwägungen'. His thorough discussion of the minor arguments makes it unnecessary to treat them here. I add only two general observations. 1. Arguments from personal names (of which Rowley makes much) are generally worthless because of the frequency of papponomy at this period, and the frequency of most of the names concerned. 2. Legal actions alone do not suffice to prove the actor's (or the author's) knowledge of those documents of the Pentateuch

in which the corresponding laws are now found. Much of the P material may have circulated orally and in various documents for a long time before it was given its present form. In particular, Cazelles's contention that Nehemiah was dependent on Deut. but ignorant of P is unlikely. His statement that the tithe of Nehemiah is 'précisément' that of Deut. ('Mission', 120) is false; they differ widely. Moreover, Nehemiah sharply distinguishes the levites from the priests. So does P. Contrast Deut.

110. With the genealogy of Ezra (from Aaron) in 7.1ff. cf. that of Leonidas in Herodotus VII.204 (from Heracles). Identical in form and in reliability, they are two products of a single type of mentality. See further Ch. 7, n. 95.

111. For Ezra's official status, Schaeder, *Esra*, 40–51. The appointment is to be attributed to party support (in spite of Ezra 7.6 and 28) because the plan proposed by Ezra was a group project (7.13).

112. Ezra 7.14, defended by Cazelles, 'Mission', 125f. (25–26) remain incredible as vocalised, but might be defended if one accepted H. L. Ginsberg's proposal to read '*ammeh* for '*ammah*, i.e. his people – the people of Ezra's god – in 7.25 (and also in 7.13). But even with this emendation the wording of 7.25 remains peculiar and suspect. Mowinckel, *Studien*, III.121–36, is refuted by Vink, 'Date', 38ff.

113. Ezra 7.12. Yahweh is equated for the Persians with Baalshamen; cf. Andrews, 'Yahweh'.

114. See Thucydides I.104 and 109–10, with Gomme's commentary ad loc. which cites the other sources and discusses the number of the ships.

115. See above, Ch. 3 n. 20, and cf. Tarn, 'Persia', 2; Kellermann, 'Erwägungen', 71f. and 74.

116. This refutes the theory of Alt, *Geschichte*, 104f. (= *KS* II.355f., followed by Cazelles, 'Mission', 131) that Ezra was sent to enforce on the whole of Judaea *and Samaria* the entire pentateuchal law (including the prohibition of sacrifice outside Jerusalem!). This theory, invented to explain the acceptance of the Pentateuch by the Samaritans, would have required forcible suppression of the cult of Yahweh maintained by the people of the land (Ezra 4.2). We hear nothing of such suppression, nor of the Persian army which would have had to do it. It is incredible that the Persian government should, at this time, have authorized a reform so obviously certain to create widespread disaffection in a province threatened by the Athenians.

117. Ezra 7.8f. For the conversions here and in the following dates see Parker and Dubberstein, *Chronology*; local errors in ancient calendaric calculation make these conversions slightly inaccurate.

118. Neh. 8.2, 13ff.; 9.1. De Vaux, *Ancient Israel*, 500; Auerbach, 'Versöhnungfest', 342. Cf. Noth, *History*, 335, for further arguments to the same conclusion. Homiletic attempts to escape it, most recently by Vink, 'Date', 29f., are at best amusing.

119. Neh. 8.2, 9.

120. Neh. 8.13ff. On the novelty see de Vaux, *Ancient Israel*, 500.

121. Ezra 9.1ff.

122. Cf. Plato *Apology* 34bff.; Plutarch *Antonius* 14.

123. Ezra 10.9.

124. Ezra 10.16f. The sequence of events indicated by these dates is a strong argument against Mowinckel's rearrangement of the material (*Studien*, III.8ff.), which not only makes the events of December immediately follow those of August, but also supposes Ezra went through his first New Year and Sukkot in Jerusalem without taking any special action. Not Ezra!

125. Ezra. 4.7–23.

126. Schaeder (*Esra*, 27) attempts to explain the present position of Ezra 4.8–23 as quotation of an earlier document in a larger appeal for rebuilding the walls, 4.8–6.15. But the necessary explanation and conclusion of the supposed appeal are not to be found in the text. Moreover, it is incredible that an appeal for rebuilding the *walls* should begin by citing a recent refusal as justified by confirmed (!) reports that Jerusalem was a centre of rebellion, and then jump back three-quarters of a century to a permit for building the *temple*. Actually the position of 4.8–23 is simply explicable by association. *A propos* of the opposition to Zerubbabel (4.4f.) the editor has collected a group of similar cases of opposition, to show the *continued* malice of the neighbours, and thereby justify his use of this malice to explain the imaginary interruption of the work on the temple (4.5 and 24). He needed the interruption to reconcile his connection of the rebuilding with the great name of Cyrus and his tradition that the temple was not finished until the sixth year of Darius. But interruption required malice and malice required examples, therefore he listed one report of accusations under Xerxes (4.6?) and two, under Artaxerxes (4.7 and 4.8–23). Then (4.24) he went back to his story. So Eissfeldt, *Introduction*, 55.

127. Neh. 13.28.

128. Neh. 5.6f., etc.

129. Neh. 6.7; Ezra 4.12, 15, 19; see above, n. 79.

130. The Samaritan hostility to Ezra expressed in the medieval *Liber Josuae* probably reflects knowledge of the Book of Chronicles and of the importance attributed to Ezra by late rabbinic legend, rather than recollection of events in the fifth century BC.

6. Nehemiah

1. Pfeiffer, *Introduction*, 834; Lods, *Histoire*, 550; Eissfeldt, *Introduction*, 544. The term 'memoirs' overlooks the religious and propagandistic sides of the work, but is convenient. Mowinckel, *Studien*, II.50ff. and 92ff., errs by trying to locate Nehemiah in ancient Mesopotamia. Cf. von Rad, 'Denkschrift', and Mowinckel's apologetic reply, *Studien*, II.122ff. Neither

one noticed that the first Greek memoirs were written by a contemporary of Nehemiah, Io of Chios. New forms could appear in Palestine as well as in Greece, and Nehemiah's work is novel in adapting the traditional form of commemorative religious inscription to the needs of party propaganda. The adaptation, but not the motive, was well described by von Rad, 'Denkschrift', 181.

2. Hölscher, *Palästina*, 28f., cf. Mowinckel, *Studien*, II.13ff.; Kellermann, *Nehemia*, 8ff.

3. Compare Rudolph, *Esra*, 172ff., with Jepsen, 'Nehemia', and with Mowinckel and Kellermann as in the preceding note. Even those who believe the agreement in ch. 10 to be Nehemiah's work do not usually assign the text to his memoirs. It will be discussed in the following chapter.

4. Neh. 5.19; 13.14, 22, 31.

5. Neh. 6.10–17; 3.36f.; 6.14; 13.29.

6. The similarity of Solon's legal reform to Nehemiah's will be discussed below. Another similarity worth notice is the concern of both for the dialect of their cities, Neh. 13.24, Solon Fr. 24 (Diehl) 10ff.

7. Cowley, *Aramaic Papyri*, 248ff.

8. This rules out Judith.

9. Neh. 2.1–8. On the date, see above, Ch. 5, n. 99.

10. Olmstead, *History*, 312f. Galling, *Studien*, 156, misunderstood Olmstead and thought that Megabyzus stayed in Syria, but it appears from Ctesias (*FGrHist* no. 688, F. 14, p. 467) that he did not.

11. Cross, 'Geshem'; Geshem would not have authorized, officially, such raids, but his power opened the country to such raiders.

12. Hölscher, *Palästina*, 19f.; Cook, 'Age', 33; cf. Morgenstern, 'Jerusalem'. It is incredible that the battle of Marathon (a minor mishap to a Persian expeditionary force on a far-off frontier) should have had any repercussions in Palestine.

13. Neh. 1.3.

14. Ezra 4.23.

15. Neh. 1.3; 2.13–16; 6.15. Contrast Josephus, *Ant.* XI.179; Albright, *Biblical Period*, 91. The longer period in Josephus is probably a reflection of the larger circuit of the walls in his time.

16. There is a hint that the queen (?) was somehow involved (2.6).

17. Olmstead, *History*, 312.

18. The conclusion of the Deuteronomic prayer in Neh. 1.5–11 indicates that others were associated with Nehemiah in his prayers on behalf of the holy city; this is unreliable evidence.

19. 2.12; 5.8; contrast 2.9.

20. Not to be confused with the 'Judaeans', 1.2; 2.16; 3.33f; 4.6; 5.1, 8; 6.6; 13.23f., who were probably the heads of the Judaean clans. RSV is mistaken in translating 'Jew'. Nehemiah was evidently concerned about them (1.2), but did not take them into his confidence (2.16).

21. Neh. 2.10, 19; 3.33f.

22. 6.17ff.; 13.4ff., 23ff., 28.

23. Thus the hostility is explicable without resort to Alt's conjecture ('Rolle') that Judaea had formerly been attached to the province of Samaria and was separated only when Nehemiah was appointed governor. This hypothesis is part of a structure to be dealt with in the Appendix. In so far as it concerns Nehemiah it is refuted by Neh. 5.15 (of which the point depends on there having been previous officials in the same position as Nehemiah). Local political rivalry, while not unlikely in itself, is unknown to the records, and Alt's statement ('Rolle', 6ff. = *KS* II.316ff.) that both parties seem only to be defending what they think their legal rights is exactly contrary to the facts; there is no appeal to any legal claim.

24. Neh. 2.11–18; contrast Rowley, 'Mission', 559.

25. Neh. 2.9; 4.10, 17; 5.10, 15f.; 7.2; 13.19; see Rudolph's note on 7.1–3, and Launey, *Recherches*, quoted above, p. 48.

26. *IG* ii².1657 (394–393 BC); Neh. 3.1–32. This list probably comes from the temple archives – it gives the priests first place and says nothing of Nehemiah. But in spite of this it may be in the main reliable; see Mowinckel, *Studien*, I.109ff.; Kellermann, *Nehemia*, 14ff.

27. 3.5; 4.4. Notice that the passive resisters were rural gentry.

28. Nehemiah did not neglect to point out the connection, 6.17ff.

29. Probably the release of persons enslaved for debt is not mentioned because most had been sold abroad and were out of reach of redemption, see above, Ch. 3, n. 99. Therefore 'we' in 5.8 are the (principally diasporic) Yahweh-alone party, as opposed to 'you', the assimilationist local gentry. See the following note.

30. Cf. 5.7 and 6.17.

31. 5.8, cf. Plato *Apology* 24d.

32. The combination of remission of interest and ransoming of prisoners turns up in the praises of Androtion, Athenian governor in Amorgos, 357–356 BC. Dittenberger, *Sylloge*⁴, no. 193.

33. As cupbearer with direct access to the Great King he had occupied one of the most bribeable positions in the empire.

34. 5.17; the word lacking is *horim*, cf. 5.7; 6.17, etc.

35. 6.15; 7.4 (probably the introduction to material like that in 11.1ff.).

36. On the date in 13.6, see above, Ch. 5, n. 99.

37. 6.7, on which Kellermann, *Nehemia*, 179–82. Even if Kellermann's interpretation were correct, this episode would be evidence only of the aberrations of a few fanatics. There is no evidence that Nehemiah shared their opinions. He knew the power of Persia too well to have messianic illusions; there is no evidence that he was a Davidide; his silence on the subject is almost proof that he was not; and his writing is that of a sensible, practical politician, not a visionary. Finally, the Persian court would seem to have investigated the charges of intended revolt, exculpated him, and restored him to his governorship. Accordingly, Kellermann's messianic interpretation of Nehemiah's career cannot be maintained (and, in

general, there is no evidence that messianic expectations played a major role in party divisions in Jerusalem between 515 and 201). See further my review of Kellermann, *ATR* 51, 1969, 68f.

38. On Tobias and the Tobiads see McCown, 'Araq el-Emir'; Mazar, 'Tobiads'; *CPJ* I,115ff.; Lapp, 'Second and Third Campaigns', and Will, 'L'édifice', above, Ch. 4 n. 68, Kellermann, *Nehemia*, 167ff., is fantasy.

39. Cf. the action of the Persian's agent Udjahorresne in expelling aliens from the temple of Neith in Saïs and purifying that temple; Posener, *Domination*, 15.

40. The role of Nehemiah as a religious reformer vs. the priesthood was recognized by Bentzen, 'Priesterschaft', 284.

41. Deut. 14.27, 29; 16.11, 13; 18.1ff., etc.

42. On the levites, see above, Ch. 2, notes 246–248. The distinction of 'priests' from 'levites' would seem to have been *de facto* to the time of Malachi, who still writes of the whole group as one of the lowest social classes, a description which cannot have applied to the priesthood of the restored temple and therefore must have referred *a potiori* to the whole group (Mal. 2.9, v. Morgenstern, 'Studies', 122). The terminological distinction, 'levites' v. 'priests', probably crystallised from current usage in the century between Malachi and Nehemiah (contrast Gunneweg, *Leviten*, passim). For the breakdown of their employment in the temple and their distribution about the land see Neh. 13.10 and Ezra 2.70, parallel Neh. 7.73; for their role in Nehemiah's reform vs. the priests, Bentzen, 'Priesterschaft', 284.

43. Observance was lax in Elephantine, too. Porten, *Archives*, 126.

44. Will, 'Tyrannies', 442f., on the aristocrats as both landowners and money-lenders.

45. 13.25, cf. Deut. 25.2.

46. 13.28f., 'son' and 'grandson' are alike possible; cf. Josephus *Ant.* XI. 306–12.

47. Cowley, *Aramaic Papyri*, no. 30, lines 17ff. There is no sufficient reason to connect with Nehemiah any of the Hananiahs (however spelled) of the Elephantine papyri; see below, Ch. 7, n. 13.

48. Denniston, 'Herodotus', 421.

49. Andrewes, *Tyrants*, 116f., 127, 143; Berve, *Tyrannis*, I.85ff., 91, 95, 97, 100, 102ff., 106, 115ff., etc. I.85ff. gives a good account of the Persians' tyrants in general; see also I.165 on the recurrence of the pattern in later times. Esther 9.3 (LXX) lists 'tyrants' among the governmental officials of the Persian empire. The term became standard and survived as an administrative title to Sassanid times, see the 'Narratio de beato Simeone bar Sabba'e', 38, etc. (ed. M. Kmosko, in R. Graffin, *Patrologia Syriaca* II, Paris 1907, cols. 846ff.).

50. Berve, *Tyrannis*, I.121f., 165, 176, 178, 182f., 186ff. Berve's refusal to recognize as 'tyrants' the non-Greek rulers for whom Herodotus and

other Greek writers use the term shows that his definition is considerably narrower than the ancient meaning.

51. *Rep.* 565d–566a.

52. Andrewes, *Tyrants*, 27.

53. With Andrewes, *Tyrants*, 20–28, cf. Berve, *Tyrannis*, I.3–12, and see the critique by Will, 'Tyrannies'.

54. Andrewes, *Tyrants*, 78ff., esp. 82.

55. Aristotle, *Politics*, esp. V.5.6–10 (1305a7ff.). New rich, Ure, *Origin*, passim. Mavericks, Berve, *Tyrannis*, I.46, 78, 101, 107, 160, etc. Hereditary rulers, ibid., 124ff.

56. Friends, Berve, *Tyrannis*, I.96, 107, 137, etc.; ethnic group, Andrewes, *Tyrants*, 30–41, 54–65; Berve, *Tyrannis*, 26, 29, etc.; private troops, ibid., 51, 80, 132 (?), 137, etc.; Persian government, see above, notes 49 and 50.

57. Tyrants with lower-class support, prior to 400, Berve, *Tyrannis*, I.17, 23, 27, 31, 33, 56, 78, 98, 107, 129, 130, 137, 158, 188.

58. Andrewes, *Tyrants*, 18, 43, 57, 99, etc.

59. For these variants see the contexts of the passages cited from Berve in n. 57.

60. I Kings 9.26, etc.

61. I Kings 14.25f.

62. D. Barag, 'Survey'. This refutes Neufeld, 'Emergence', who dated the economic development in the period from Saul to Solomon, without explaining why its consequences, did not appear until the time of Amos.

63. De Vaux, *Ancient Israel*, 73.

64. Amos 7.14ff.

65. Amos 2.6; 4.1; 5.7, 11f., 24; 8.4ff.

66. Hesiod *Theogony* 22ff.; *Works and Days* 213ff., 238ff.

67. So, in Sumer, the Lipit Ishtar code, in Athens the codification by Draco, in Rome the Twelve Tables.

68. Dates from Bury, *Greece*, 179, 182, 155, 195, except for Megara, for which see Meyer, 'Megara', 184f. To simplify matters I have taken instances from the history of Athens, whenever available.

69. A date of about 720 for the core of the Covenant Code (Ex. 21–23) is indicated by its social concerns. It puts first of all (Ex. 21.2–11) provisions for liberation of enslaved Israelites and good treatment of Israelite girls sold into slavery by their fathers. This reflects the development of lending and the progressive improverishment of the settled Israelite peasantry. (Why else would Israelites become slaves of Israelites? Cf. Amos, 2.6; 8.6, etc.) It is concerned with deposits, and knows 'silver' as one of the two main classes of deposited objects, the other being 'goods' (*kelim*, 22.6) – here 'silver' is evidently the common medium of exchange. It is concerned to protect debtors, and prohibits usury (22.24ff.). All of this is understandable only as reaction to the social development outlined in the text. See further, Neufeld, 'Prohibitions', refuting Cazelles, *Etudes*,

and Stein, 'Laws'. (Do not see Meislin and Cohen, 'Backgrounds', an ignorant muddle.) Neufeld's error lay in supposing that urban, commercial society developed in Palestine before the time of Solomon (see above, n. 62). As the complaints produced in Palestine by that development find their first (preserved) expression in Amos, who knows no law code to which he or the poor can appeal (2.4f. is generally recognized to be an interpolation), it is most plausible to assign the first resultant codification of laws to the half century after Amos, and to associate its preservation with that of the books of the prophets and the national legends, as part of the propaganda of the Yahweh-alone party, called forth by the development of the religious conflict in the late eighth century. Finally a date of about 720 would make it likely that the Covenant Code was the basis or product of the legal reforms of Hezekiah. The stories of those reforms in Kings and Chronicles are manifestly full of anachronisms; concerns and measures of later times have been attributed to the good king of old. Consequently we are left with little more than the fact that he did undertake legal reforms (and a few picturesque details like his suppression of the bronze serpent). Discrepancy between the stories of the reforms and the content of the Covenant Code is therefore no objection to the supposition that the code's *original* text (which is also a matter of speculation) may have been somehow connected with the *actual* reforms. See above, pp. 36f.

70. Against Reventlow, *Heiligkeitsgesetz*, and Feucht, *Untersuchungen*, see Elliot-Binns, 'Problems'; further Kilian, *Literarkritische*; Noth, *Leviticus*, 127ff.: Lods, *Histoire*, 494; Eissfeldt, *Introduction*, 238f. For the present purpose a more exact dating is not necessary.

71. Contrast Noth, *Exodus*, 187, on the peculiar life of Israel.

72. Permits it in dealing with Gentiles (from concern for trade and banking interests?).

73. Only Nehemiah and Megara compel the return of interest previously exacted.

74. Again, foreigners excepted.

75. Verses 47–55 deal especially with Israelites sold to aliens resident in Palestine.

76. Charity, not law.

77. Andrewes, *Tyrants*, 70, cf. Will, 'Histoire', 427. In both Greek (Athenian) and Israelite (priestly) law we also find the notion of 'sale on the condition that the seller has a right to redeem', as a means of securing long-term loans (with the distinction that in Greek law the 'seller' usually retained possession of the property, in priestly law, the 'purchaser' held it). Cf. Lev. 25.25ff., Finley, *Land*, 31ff. The Greek practise *may* date from the seventh century; ibid., 7 and n. 23.

78. Contrast North, *Sociology*, Ch. 7; Noth, *Laws*, 25f.

79. Ure, *Origin*, 188, etc. Head, *Historia*, 399, 365ff., 564ff. The date of the beginning of coinage has fluctuated in recent years, see M. Price and

N. Waggoner, *Ancient Greek Coinage* I, *The Asyut Hoard*, London 1975, and the ensuing discussion. In this case the argument is not based exclusively on coinage, but on the general economic development, which makes it somewhat more secure.

80. Ure tries to show this for every tyrant he discusses.

81. Andrewes, *Tyrants*, 123–7; see above, notes 49 and 50.

82. Herodotus V.106f.; Plutarch, *Moralia* 261c.

83. Andrewes, *Tyrants*, 51; Ure, *Origin*, 62f. (Pisistratus penalised idleness); 76f. and n. 5 (the building programmes); 191 (Periander prohibited idleness); Berve, *Tyrannis*, I.23, 30, 33, 56, 108, 110, 119, 130, 134, etc.

84. The history of the Alcmeonidae at Athens is a typical example, Andrewes, *Tyrants*, 101; Bury, *Greece*, 205ff. On similar 'fifth-column' activities in classical Greece see L. Losada, *The Fifth Column in the Peloponnesian War*, Mnemosyne Supplement 21, Leiden 1972.

85. Wars and rumours of war, Aristotle *Politics* 1313b; Andrewes, *Tyrants*, 140; bogus attacks, ibid., 100 (Pisistratus and Dionysius of Syracuse).

86. Andrewes, *Tyrants*, 58f., but cf. Will, 'Tyrannies'.

87. Gomme, 'Pericles', 664; Aelian, *Varia Historia* VI.10.

88. Aristotle *Politics* 1313b.

89. Andrewes, *Tyrants*, 23; Berve, *Tyrannis*, I.53, 106.

90. Ure, *Origin*, 194 (Cypselus); Aristotle *Athen. Pol.* 16.4 (Pisistratus).

91. Andrewes, *Tyrants*, 111; Berve, *Tyrannis*, I.53, 56; Ure, *Origin*, 272, 278.

92. Aristotle *Politics* 1314a.

93. Berve, *Tyrannis*, I.142f., 149.

94. Andrewes, *Tyrants*, 113; Berve, *Tyrannis*, I.23, 29, 59ff., 67, 75, 109f., 119, 130, 133f., etc.

95. Lockwood, 'Scholarship', 812.

96. Berve, *Tyrannis*, I.112 and 67.

97. Andrewes, *Tyrants*, 112f.; Aristotle *Politics* 1314b–1315a; cf. Berve, *Tyrannis*, I.59 and notes (in Vol. II).

98. Ure, *Origin*, 273f.; Andrewes, *Tyrants*, 139; Aristotle *Politics* 1315a – the liberation of slaves; Berve, *Tyrannis* I. 130, 137, 160f.

99. Aristotle *Athen. Pol.* 16.4.

100. Will, *Korinthiaka*, 481–88.

101. Aristotle *Politics*, 1311a–b.

102. Cf. Herodotus VI.7.10; VII.10.3, etc.

103. Cf. Finkelstein, *Pharisees*; the Pharisaic tradition was essentially bourgeois.

104. This development is studied in detail (for a later period) by Jeremias, *Jerusalem*, 222ff.

105. Finkelstein, *Pharisees*, 561, thinks the decline had set in already

before Nehemiah's time. Cf. Morgenstern, 'Studies', 102ff. (but his evidence is dubious).

106.. Discussed above, Ch. 4.

107. Deut. 11.19. Cf. above, pp. 41f.

108. We should of course suppose that the persons he selected to increase the population of Jerusalem were either members of his own party or at least persons he thought likely to become such.

109. This successor, the high priest Jehohanan, will be discussed in the following chapter.

7. From Nehemiah to Antiochus Epiphanes

1. E.g., by Eissfeldt, *Introduction*, 490 Song; 483 Ruth; 497 Eccl.; 597 Ecclus.; 447f. Psalms; 476 Proverbs; 470 Job; 527 Daniel; 540 Chronicles; 552 Ezra, Nehemiah; 394 Jona; 405 Joel; 338ff., 437 interpolations; 208 P. This is a somewhat reactionary list; use of either Pfeiffer or Lods would have enlarged it.

2. Cf. the survival of Phoenician in the Hellenistic period, illustrated by the inscriptions in Donner and Röllig.

3. Pointed out by Bickerman, *From Ezra*, 21f. Persian influence may also have contributed to historical writing, cf. Momigliano, 'Fattori'.

4. Eissfeldt, *Introduction*, 524f.

5. See Lieberman, *Hellenism*; Alon, 'Hahishkihu'; Haran, 'Problems'.

6. Maisler, 'Historiography', 83.

7. *Ant.* XI.297–XII.236. That he here and there has a few additional stories, e.g., *Apion* II.48, does not alter the picture.

8. The nature of the stories is clear from their content, in spite of Josephus' attempts to launder them.

9. II Macc. 2.14.

10. With the following analysis cf. Vogt, *Studie*.

11. On this list see above, Ch. 6, n. 26.

12. Neh. 4.10, 17; 7.2, etc. See above, Ch. 6, n. 25.

13. Neh. 1.2; 5.14; 7.2. Andrewes, *Tyrants*, 124; Parke, *Greek Soldiers*, 169. There is no reason to suppose that Hanani, Nehemiah's brother, was the Hananyah of Cowley, *Aramaic Papyri*, nos. 21 and 38. The equivalence of the names is insignificant. There were two Hanani-Hananyahs in Nehemiah's circle (7.2) and half a dozen in the Elephantine papyri. The sender of no. 21 was probably the same as the 'Anani of no. 38 (they had the same servant), i.e., a confidential secretary of Arsames (in no. 26 he draws up an order for the repair of a government boat). This explains how he could learn of Darius' order to Arsames and tip off his 'brethren' in advance. He *perhaps* had a real brother, *perhaps* resident in Jerusalem (nos. 30 and 31, lines 18; 'the nobles of the Jews' *may* be the subject of the following verb); but this brother's name was Ostanes, not Nehemiah. Cowley's careless note on no. 30, line 19, should not be misunderstood as locating 'Anani at Jerusalem. Contrast Tuland, 'Hanani'.

14. The 'singers' are probably glosses by the editor. So Rudolph, *Esra*, on Neh. 13.10, the only possibly genuine reference. Note their absence from the list of wall builders. The *netinim* in that list are a gloss (Rudolph on 3.26; cf. Levine, 'Netinim'). This is not to say that these groups did not exist, but only that Nehemiah and the list of wall builders found no occasion to mention them; de Vaux, *Ancient Israel*, 389.

15. 3.22; contra, Rudolph.

16. 6.7, 12, 14.

17. 2.16b; 4.8, 13. Nehemiah often uses 'Judaeans' in its ordinary sense, but the 'Judaeans' in 2.16, 5.1, 5.17, and possibly 6.6 appear to be a group with some official standing, cf. Ezra 6.7, 14. Neh. 5.1 suggests that the people could appeal to them for help against the moneylenders (so the reading *'el*, not *'al*, LXX πρός, not ἐπί).

18. 7.2 (4.10 is probably a gloss); contrast de Vaux, *Ancient Israel*, 69f.

19. 3.8, 31f.; cf. 13.20.

20. Josephus *Ant*. XII.138ff.; authenticity demonstrated by Bickerman, 'Charte'; contrast Alt, 'Antiochus III'.

21. 138 and 142.

22. The more so if, as Stern has conjectured ('Eretz-Israel', 124), there was an Egyptian conquest of the coast in the time of Nepherites and Hakoris (399–380), followed by a Persian reconquest in 380. It is perhaps likelier that coastal towns were encouraged by the Egyptian fleet to revolt, and there is nothing to indicate that Persian control of the interior was ever shaken, but the situation was certainly tense. My thanks are due to Dr M. Broshi for calling Stern's work to my attention.

23. Barag, 'Effects', 8 n. 10, oversimplifies. The reconquest may have shortly followed the Egyptians' withdrawal, or may have been connected with either of Artaxerxes III's campaigns against Egypt (351–350 and 343 – see Tarn, 'Persia', 21ff., Olmstead, *History*, 417–41). The evidence of Eusebius, Jerome, Orosius, and Syncellus is more interrelated, complex, and ambiguous than Barag represents.

24. Above, Ch. 3, n. 32.

25. No reliance can be placed on the legend in Josephus *Ant*. XI.320ff.

26. Above, Ch. 3, p. 68.

27. Bevan, 'Syria', 502; Josephus *War* I.31ff.

28. Daniel 11.14.

29. On these see my article 'The Dead Sea Sect'.

30. The following pages were written before I saw Hadas, *Hellenistic Culture*, which has many of the same observations in a somewhat different context.

31. Most of 22.17–31.31. Pfeiffer, *Introduction*, 645ff., esp. 653; cf. Eissfeldt, *Introduction*, 474f.

32. *ANET*, 427b ff.

33. *ANET*, 424 and Couroyer, 'Origine égyptienne'.

34. The controversy about Job is presumably endless. To the bibli-

ography in Eissfeldt, *Introduction*, 454ff., add Fohrer, *Buch Hiob*; Gordis, *Book*; and Pope, *Job* (with the review of de Vaux, *RB* 74), to name only major commentaries. Here and throughout the rest of this chapter it will be impossible to enter into detailed discussions of individual works, or justifications of the views advanced concerning them. Such justifications are the less needed because, for the most part, the views are familiar, and the purpose of the chapter is to show that, in accordance with these familiar critical opinions, the Old Testament material here discussed can be understood as the products of certain religious parties, and as records of the history of these parties during the two and a half centuries between Nehemiah and the Maccabees.

35. Aristotle *Poetics* 13 makes a rule of this custom.

36. Job 1.17 is probably a reminiscence from the Persian period of the bad old days when Nabonidus' forces went foraging from Taima, c. 552–544.

37. Cf. Job 18–19.22 with Aeschylus *Prometheus* 944–76. The resemblance has often been remarked, see Kallen, *Job*. Later influence of Greek drama on Jewish thought is shown by the drama of the poet Ezekiel. Imitation of Greek forms in Hebrew probably preceded the attempt to use Greek. Von Rad, *Theology*, 418f., remarks the radical difference between the speculative theodicy of Job and the traditional 'wisdom' which was 'a practical knowledge of the laws of life and of the world, based upon experience'. This new speculation presumably came from a new influence.

38. On the remains of early Greek romances, Schmid-Stählin 2.1.298ff.; Trenker, *The Greek Novella*; Braun, *History and Romance*.

39. G. Cohen, 'Song', has made a new case for the theory that the poems are a deliberate work of (Hellenistic) allegory.

40. Except by Loretz, *Qohelet*, 45–56, esp. 49 – a remarkable specimen of determined blindness.

41. Remarked by von Rad, *Theology*, 412, 433ff.

42. Prov. 25.1 is probably secondary.

43. Cf. Isa. 40–55 and the fragments of Xenophanes (for whose use of *ho theos* see *FV* III *sub voce*).

44. Job 12.9 is a gloss.

45. So are the Arab raids (Job 2.13ff.); see above, pp. 97f.

46. On Ecclesiastes, Esther, Jonah and Daniel see the brilliant studies by Bickerman, *Four Strange Books*.

47. Eccl. 5.1f.

48. 12.13a may possibly be genuine. See Pedersen, 'Scepticisme', 362. However, Pedersen overestimates the original author's piety. The author believes in a god, but he does not believe in this god's justice (9.2), which is what matters. (So, again, Epicurus.)

49. Eissfeldt, *Introduction*, 480ff.

50. Burrows, *Scrolls*, 205, thinks the 'hostility to Ammon and Moab . . .

characteristic of much of the Old Testament, especially the Books of Chronicles', was the aftermath of Nehemiah's trouble with Tobias. See further Vesco, 'Date', esp. 243 and 247. That the law on Ammonite and Moabite proselytes did not apply to women (Yoma 54a) and had, anyhow, no applicability since the Assyrian conquest (Mishnah Yadayim 4.4) are rabbinic rulings the author of Ruth did not foresee.

51. 4.12, cf. Gen. 38. The argument was noticed by the author of Mt. 1.3 and 5, who used the examples of both these ladies to excuse the irregularity in Jesus' pedigree.

52. It may be, though the case against it is well stated by Wolff, *Studien*, 60ff. But the original author may have inserted a psalm not of his own composition. The use of verse sections in a prose narrative, found in many of these works (Tobit, Judith), was introduced to the Graeco-Roman world by Menippus of Gadara in Transjordan, probably a younger contemporary of the author of Jonah (early third century BC?), Schmid-Stählin II.1.89, n. 6; Wolff, *Studien*, 66ff.

53. 5.6ff., esp. 5.16. These and the following remarks apply to the LXX text of Judith. As to the original form, they will have to be modified in the light of the evidence presented by Dubarle, *Judith*.

54. On Ammonites, see above, n. 50.

55. Milik, 'Patrie'.

56. Worship only at Jerusalem, 1.6; tithes, 1.7; pure food laws, 1.10f.; no intermarriage with Gentiles, 4.12; etc. Glasson's proposal of a Greek background ('Source') is more ingenious than convincing.

57. Proverbs is, in these respects, exceptional. Compare the problems raised by the text of Theognis.

58. That Chronicles is composite was shown by Welch, *Work*, and has since been generally recognised; see above, Ch. 5, notes 29 and 30. Evidence of editing by the levitic school has also been found in Haggai and Zechariah (Beuken, *Haggai-Sacharja*) and might, perhaps, be found elsewhere. Whether or not the traditions about the levites, mainly in the Pentateuch and the historical books, are 'levitic traditions', as Möhlenbrink assumed ('Levitischen Überlieferungen'), is another question. A thorough study of the work and history of the school is a primary need of OT criticism.

59. Neh. 13.19, 22ff.; reflected in I Chron. 23.4; 26.29.

60. Baudissin, *Geschichte*, 33ff.

61. Von Rad, *Geschichtsbild*, 91f.

62. Vogelstein, *Kampf*, 84.

63. Num. 1.53; 18.3; Baudissin, *Geschichte*, 33ff.; Gunneweg, *Leviten*, 139, 149.

64. Num. 4.3, 23, 30; 8.24, etc.

65. I Chron. 9.28ff.; 23.28ff.

66. Baudissin, *Geschichte*, 73, etc.; Hölscher, 'Levi', 2170ff.; Pfeiffer, *Introduction*, 322. On the problem of the ark cf. Haran, 'Ark and the

Cherubim', de Vaux. 'Arche' (esp. 66ff.), and von Rad, *Theology*, I.236ff., and see the fully annotated study by Maier, *Ladeheiligtum* (with Haran's review, *JBL* 85.248f. cf. Vink, 'Date', 130f.).

67. Against Gunneweg's contention (*Leviten*) that the levites, before the exile, were not priests, and vice versa, see de Vaux's review (*RB* 73.446f.). In support of de Vaux it may be remarked that if a levite was, before the Deuteronomic reform, something quite distinct from a priest, it would be hard to understand why the reformer should have chosen to make the levites priests, or why the priestly families should have claimed levitical ancestry. Ezekiel 44.12 *yesharethu . . . liphené gillulehem* clearly indicates that the levites *were* priests in the pre-exilic period (v. Gunneweg, *Leviten*, 203. Fohrer, *Ezechiel*, ad loc.). And while Gunneweg, 209, accepts Chronicles as evidence of practice but dismisses Deuteronomy as programmatic (69–81), it is likely that the sources of Chronicles were programmatic, and yet more likely that the Deuteronomic code agreed in the main with the social order of its day, since it was accepted by the king and enforced, and we hear nothing of a turnover in the Jerusalem temple from a non-levitic to a levitic priesthood.

68. Whether or not the report is true, it indicates that the practice was known to the reporter; cf. Haran, 'Disappearance'. There is no reason to emend the text; previous conjectures (e.g., Rudolph, *Chronikbücher*, ad loc., echoed by Maier, *Ladeheiligtum*, 76) are based on ignorance of the contemporary pagan practice and consequent failure to understand the order.

69. Cook, *Religion*, 164ff.; Dibelius, *Lade*, 59ff., 86ff.

70. Maier, *Ladeheiligtum*, 80; Cook, *Religion*, 214ff. and refs. there, to which add Aphraates *Demonstratio* 12.11. Goodenough, *Symbols*, indices, *s.v.* Torah shrine. The text used at first was probably the Deuteronomic code, to which the levites were devoted, see below.

71. Pfeiffer, *Introduction*, 183; so I Kings 8.9 and Montgomery, *Kings*, ad loc.

72. I.6.16f.; 22.19; 28.2, 18; II.1.4; 5; 6.11, 41; 8.11; 35.3. Von Rad, *Geschichtsbild*, 100ff., who noticed this importance, tried to explain it by supposing that the levites claimed admission to the inner area of the temple because they had carried the ark and it had got in. Since this argument is never advanced to justify the levites' entrance, the hypothesis is unlikely.

73. *Geschichtsbild*, 107ff.

74. *Priesterschrift*, 183f.

75. Above, Ch. 2, n. 248.

76. Above, pp. 49f.; cf. Bentzen, 'Geschichte', 175.

77. Von Rad, *Geschichtsbild*, with the reservations made by Eissfeldt, *Introduction*, 538ff.

78. Von Rad, 'Sermon'. On the functions of the levites compare, with the following section, Gunneweg, *Leviten*, 205–16. Gunneweg seriously

underestimates the importance of wishful thinking in the Chroniclers' 'history'.

79. Rudolph, *Esra*, notes *ad loc.*

80. Finkelstein, *Pharisees*, 562ff. and 567 no. 20.

81. The antithesis appears in Empedocles (died c. 433) and Theophrastus (d. 285), cf. Eusebius *Praeparatio evangelica* IV.10–14; Wettstein, *Novum Testamentum*, on Rom. 12.1, quotes it from Isocrates (d. 338) and many others.

82. The resultant conflict is traced by Vogelstein, *Kampf*, which must, however, be used with caution. Cf. Haran, 'Uses of Incense', which exemplifies the uses of *pilpul*.

83. Num. 16.8–10; de Vaux, *Ancient Israel*, 393; Noth, *History*, 339 n. 2, contrast Gunneweg's attempt to explain away the obvious, *Leviten*, 171–81; almost equally implausible is Liver, 'Korah'. Pfeiffer, *Introduction*, 264, finds priestly polemic running through the whole of Num. 16–18; further passages are suggested by Morgenstern, 'Studies', 122, n. 193. Chronicles throughout represents the levites as performing priestly functions. (I.9.32; 15.26; 23.29 and 31; II.23.18; 29.11 and 34; 35.11), including – and perhaps most important – teaching the law. Moreover, it deliberately slights the priests and puts them in the shadow of the levites, Rudolph, *Chronikbücher*, xvi; Pfeiffer, *Introduction*, 795–801; Welch, *Judaism*, 227ff.

84. Pss. 42 (+43)−49; 84; 85; 87; 88; I Chron. 6.7ff.; 9.19–34; 26.1–19; II Chron. 20.19; Ex. 6.21, 24; Num. 26.11, 58. The Psalms have now been discussed by Wanke, *Zionstheologie*. On the genealogical material see also Wanke, 23–31, and Gunneweg, *Leviten*, 210ff., both against Möhlenbrink, 'Levitische Überlieferungen', 212f. and 230. Gunneweg probably exaggerates the importance of the Korahites, but they do seem to have been for a while the leading clan.

85. See below, pp. 131f.

86. The stages of the fusion are traced by Hölscher, 'Levi'; the course of it is generally recognized, e.g., Gunneweg, *Leviten*, 211; von Rad, *Theology*, 352, etc. To what extent the levites also became 'the scribes of the temple' whom Antiochus lists between the priests and the singers is uncertain. II Chron. 34.13 says that some of the levites were scribes, but non-levites, too, were scribes, cf. Bickerman, *From Ezra*, 68–71.

87. For the speculations based on it see Johnson, *Cultic Prophet*.

88. Isa. 19; 20 (esp. 5f.); 30.1–5; 31.1–3; cf. 36.6, 9 = II Kings 18.21, 24; Jer. 2.18f.; 24.9; 37.7; 42; 43; 44; 46; Ezek. 17.15ff.; 29 (esp. 16); 30; 31; 32. Bentzen, 'Remarques', 502, supposes that these prophecies would have made an alliance with Egypt impossible, but the probability is that the unfortunate consequences of an alliance with Egypt produced this rash of prophecies.

89. Bickerman, *From Ezra*, 29ff., remarks on the loyalty of Chronicles to Persia. The same conclusion follows from Caquot, 'Messianisme'.

90. Vogelstein, *Kampf*, 70; Baudissin, *Geschichte*, 165.

91. II Chron. 17.7ff.; 35.3.

92. For this view of the structure of Chronicles, Rudolph, *Chronikbücher*, viii f.; contrast Freedman, 'Purpose'; Mowinckel, *Studien*, I.45ff.; against them see Kellerman, *Nehemia*, 89ff. Against Kellerman it must be said that if the Chroniclers had been hostile to Nehemiah, they would have slandered or eliminated him, as they did the kings of Israel. Moreover, the Chroniclers are representative not of the priests but of their rivals, the levites. They gave prominent place in the story of Ezra to the scandals of the priesthood, and they used Nehemiah's account of these, and his curse on the high-priestly family, as the conclusion of their entire work. Accordingly, hostility to Nehemiah cannot be used to explain the division of Nehemiah's memoirs. It seems more likely that the Chroniclers, in Ezra-Nehemiah, arranged the material roughly by subject-matter: first, stories of the return (Ezra 1–2); then, of the rebuilding of the temple and the opposition (3–6); then Ezra's coming and attempted reform; then Nehemiah's coming and restoration of the city (Neh. 1–7); then the introduction of the law, repentance, reform, settlement of the land, and celebration at the completion of the whole programme (8–12); and finally, as the grand climax, the enforcement of the law in both the city and the temple, the purification of the temple, the establishment in it of the levites, and the expulsion of the unworthy priests (Neh. 13). A secondary concern seems to have been to subordinate Ezra (the priest) to Nehemiah (the patron of the levites). In spite of Ezra's gifts and recruits the city remains defenceless and miserable (Neh. 1.3); only Nehemiah makes it safe. Ezra's attempt to stop mixed marriages comes to nothing; only Nehemiah succeeds. Ezra's reading of the law and reformation of the celebration of Sukkoth are transferred from their original place (after Ezra 8) and located in Neh. 8 as an introduction to the repentance and new covenant under Nehemiah (Neh. 9–10). In the very ceremony of reading the law Ezra is subordinated to Nehemiah (Neh. 8.9), and he plays second fiddle also in the celebration in Neh. 12.31–40.

93. Pfeiffer, *Introduction*, 787ff.; Eissfeldt, *Introduction*, 530ff.

94. Exposed by Hölscher, 'Levi', 2180ff.; cf. de Vaux, *Ancient Israel*, 13.

95. *OCD*, s.v. Hecataeus (1). He traced his own ancestry through sixteen generations back to the gods. Herodotus II.143 reports with pleasure how an Egyptian priest countered this claim by tracing *his* ancestry back for 345 generations. In Herodotus' time (c. 450) Trojan ancestry was claimed already by (or for) the Maxyans of Tunisia and the Paeonians of Thrace (IV.191 and V.17); the Spartan royalty, on the other hand, claimed descent not only from Heracles and from Perseus, but also from the Pharaohs (VI.53). Even cities imitated the style – the list of Athenian eponymous archons was compiled backwards from Solon to the end of the monarchy, sometime before 1000 BC (von Fritz and Knapp, *Aristotle's Constitution*, 21). Eponymous ancestors were everywhere: the Persians were descended from Perses (who was also Perseus, Herodotus

VII.150), the Carians, Lydians, and Mysians from Car, Lydus, and Mysus (I.171); we can be sure that complete genealogies had been produced. Moreover, this sort of invention was not limited to Greece, Egypt, and Asia Minor. Herodotus knows Persian and Phoenician pseudo-histories too: I.1ff.; VI.54, etc. The Greeks and the Hebrews, therefore, were not exceptional, but they did keep up with the style. See Forsdyke, *Greece*, 143, on Pherecydes (c. 450 BC) who 'left no gaps in the record [of ancient mythology] and was particularly concerned to supply children, parents and names to people who previously had none. He named the six sons and six daughters of Niobe. . . . [He] constructed pedigrees for his contemporaries. . . . He is cited as an authority for the descent of. . . the first Miltiades in fourteen generations from Telamonian Aias. These myth-historians and genealogists . . . complicated the stories with their imaginative relationships and ridiculous details, which were usually designed to contradict those of their predecessors. Pausanias complains . . . that "the legends of Greece differ from one another in most respects, and not least in the genealogies."' This, *mutatis mutandis*, fits the compilers of Chronicles perfectly.

96. 'Foundations', 78ff.

97. Kienitz, *Geschichte*, 139.

98. Noticed by Baer, *Yisra'el*, 48.

99. The limits of the priestly compilation are disputed. See Eissfeldt, 'Geschichtswerke', v. Noth, *Überlieferungsgeschichtliche Studien*, 54ff. Whatever the earlier forms may have been, the one produced in the fourth century was that which the Samaritans and Jews now have in common.

100. Above, Ch. 1, n. 27.

101. See, for example, Vink, 'Date', 99–108; Elliger, 'Sinn', 121ff. The date of the Priestly redaction as a whole cannot be established by the similarities between its paschal laws and those of the 'paschal papyrus' (Cowley, *Aramaic Papyri*, no. 21, 419 BC) of Elephantine – not even if one or another of the recent reconstructions (Grelot, *VT* 17.201ff.; cf. 481ff. and Porten, *Archives*, 129) be accepted as correct. For the Priestly redaction made use of many elements of different dates, and the dating of one of these elements would provide, at best, only a *terminus post quem* for the revision (and this is all Grelot, 'Problème', could extract from it; his *terminus ante quem* of 407 – p. 265 – is baseless). As to Hanani, see above, n. 13. From what little survives of Cowley's papyrus no. 21 it would seem to report a permit, not issue a command. Porten's supposition (*Archives*, 130 and 280) that Hanani came to Egypt, as Ezra to Jerusalem, with Persian authorisation to enforce 'Jewish law' is therefore unlikely, the more so in view of Hanani's attachment to the clerical staff of Arsames. It has, further, the embarassing consequence that this representative of 'Jewish law' warned the Elephantine Jews to observe the rules about leaven, but said nothing about their practice of polytheism (nor about marriage with gentiles, which was at least as frequent at Elephantine as

at Jerusalem, Porten, *Archives*, 149). Finally the theory of Vink ('Date', 47f., 55f., 117f., etc.) that Ezra came to Jerusalem in 398 bringing 'the Priestly Code' (or the complete Pentateuch?) with its provisions that there should be one law for the Judaeans (*'ezrahim*) and the Samaritans (*gerim*), and with Persian authority to enforce this on the whole land – this depends on:

1. Cazelles's misrepresentation of Nehemiah's law as purely deuteronomic, see above, Ch. 5, n. 109.

2. The dating of Ezra in 398, see ibid.

3. The supposition (supported by no evidence) that the Persians would have contemplated enforcing Judaean law on all Palestine; see Ch. 5, n. 116.

4. The supposition that Ezra, for homiletic reasons, neglected to observe Yom Kippur, in spite of the fact that 'the Priestly Code' prescribed it; see Ch. 5, n. 118.

5. The supposition that Ezra 7–9 is a Maccabaean fake and historically worthless (for if it has any worth at all, Ezra's insistence on the divorce of alien wives and his complete oblivion to proselytism rule out the possibility that his law included all the priestly material); see Ch. 5, n. 95, and note that it is practically impossible to locate in the Maccabaean period a canonically accepted document which prohibits intermarriage and ignores proselytism, since the prohibition of intermarriage was not a major issue at that time and the Maccabees not only permitted proselytism but compelled it.

In sum, Vink's theory is based on his faith that Ezra's law was or contained 'the Priestly Code', but this faith is based on no historical evidence whatever and on the rejection of the plentiful and clear evidence which contradicts it. (Vink, however, at least deserves refutation. Auerbach, 'Aharon-Problem', 60ff., does not.)

102. II Kings 22.8, 12.

103. Deut. 18.6ff., cf. II Kings 23.9.

104. See the Zadokite interpolations in the text of Ezekiel, above, Ch. 2, n. 91. On the dubious history of these 'Zadokites' cf. Bartlett, 'Zadok', and Auerbach, 'Aharon-Problem', 53ff.

105. Ezra 2.36ff.; 8.2, etc.

106. Pfeiffer, *Introduction*, 794; Welch, 'Judaism', 234. The revision of the genealogies is traced by Hölscher, 'Levi', 2180ff., cf. Baudissin, *Geschichte*, 108 n. 1. The Maccabaean family Yoyarib appears first in glosses to Neh. 12.6 and 19 (the prefixed *waws* betray addition) and does not stand at the head of the list until I Chron. 24.7; de Vaux, *Ancient Israel*, 402.

107. Above, pp. 82ff.

108. Ezra 7.1–5; 10.18ff.

109. Neh. 13.29–31; Josephus *Ant.* XI.312.

110. Ezra 10.23; Neh. 13.29(?).

111. Cowley, *Aramaic Papyri*, nos. 30 and 31.

112. Porten's supposition of two Bagois (governing Jerusalem simultaneously?!) is needless and unlikely, *Archives*, 290 and n. 24.

113. Cf. Vogelstein, *Kampf.*

114. Neh. 13.28; Josephus *Ant.* XI.297ff. For hypotheses about this family cf. Rudolph, *Ezra*, 192, on Neh. 12.10, with Morgenstern, 'Studies', 123–32.

115. Cowley, *Aramaic Papyri*, no. 30; Morgenstern, 'Studies', 127.

116. See the P material in Num. 25.6–18 and 31, and the record of Ezra.

117. Rudolph, *Esra*, on Neh. 12.10f. and 21f., which seem to date the succession of J(eh)ohanan's son, Yaddua, before the death of Darius II (405). The punishment continued (as in a fairy tale) for 'seven' years, Josephus *Ant.* XI.297–302.

118. See the frequent use of 'your brother' in the charitable legislation in Deuteronomy.

119. See above, n. 106.

120. Cf. Cook's section, 'The Pentateuch: A Compromise', 'Inauguration', 197ff.

121. On Neh. 10 see my article, 'The Dead Sea Sect'. Rudolph, *Esra*, ad loc., has shown that the document cannot have come from Ezra's reforms (Jepsen, 'Nehemia 10', notwithstanding). But it does not reflect the conditions at the end of Nehemiah's regime, either. For instance, he had put a stop to the sale of produce on the Sabbath; the covenant supposes it a current temptation (13.21f. v. 10.32). He compelled delivery of the tithe to 'the storehouses' – presumably of the temple – the covenant (as it now stands) supposes the levites will collect it in the villages, as they later did (13.12 v. 10.38). The covenant's provisions for temple upkeep (10.33–40) are much more elaborately developed than those known to Nehemiah (13.10ff., 31).

122. Above, pp. 9 and 77.

123. For various dates see Pfeiffer, *Introduction*, 250; Eissfeldt, *Introduction*, 194; Elliger, 'Sinn', 138ff.; Koch, *Priesterschrift*, 97, 99, 102; von Rad, *Theology*, 79, 232; On the dates proposed by Grelot and Vink, see above, n. 101. Against Kapelrud, 'Date', see Vink, 'Date', 57f.

124. Von Rad, *Priesterschrift*, 21–28, on which see below. Similarly Bentzen, 'Priesterschaft', 281, recognizes an earlier stratum hostile to levites, a later, friendly. See also Schmidt, *Schöpfungsgeschichte*; Gunneweg, *Leviten*, 141, 144, 152, n. 1 (on von Rad); Koch, *Priesterschrift*, 102ff.

125. E.g., Num. 4.3, the levites serve from thirty to fifty years of age; Num. 8.23, from twenty-five to fifty.

126. Ezek. 1.3. On the relation of Ezekiel to the 'Holiness Code' see T. Chary, *Les prophètes*.

127. Pfeiffer, *Introduction*, 197. See above, n. 95.

128. See above, Ch. 6, n. 70. It is often thought to be the earliest of the P material. (Cf., however, de Vaux, *Ancient Israel*, 144, 147.)

129. Cf. Koch, *Priesterschrift*, 103.

130. Von Rad, *Geschichtsbild*, 9 and 84.

131. Von Rad, *Priesterschrift*, 187; Pfeiffer, *Introduction*, 208.

132. Lev. 1–7; Num. 28–29, etc.; de Vaux, *Ancient Israel*, 415, 420, 457, 469, 473, 503; von Rad, *Theology*, 250–79, on this point and the two following.

133. Gen. 1.1–2.3; Ex. 19.11 *versus* Deut. 5.15; Eichrodt, 'Sabbat'. This development presumably reflects the new importance acquired by the Sabbath in the diaspora as a distinguishing mark.

134. Num. 18 and 30; de Vaux, *Ancient Israel*, 379f.

135. Jer. 21.12; 22.2f., etc. Ezek. 22.26; Zeph. 3.3. Cf. Elliott-Binns, 'Problems', 28. Whatever Num. 5.6 refers to, it was not a tort. Inheritance cases (Num. 28 and 36) are regularly in the domain of religious law in the Near East to this day. The law on murder (Num. 35) is primarily concerned with the right of asylum at levitical cities; the rules for the criminal cases are stated only incidentally in the conclusion (29ff.). The Holiness Code differs in this respect from the rest of the P material; like Deuteronomy it was conceived as a rule of life for a holy nation.

136. Examples collected in Pfeiffer, *Introduction*, 250ff.

137. Ex. 33.8 (E); II Sam. 6.17; I Kings 1.39; 2.28–30.

138. Ex. 25–31; 35–40; Lev. 1–10; Num. 1–10; 16–18.

139. Ex. 25.9; the tent was made by Wisdom, Ex. 35.30–35.

140. See Görg, *Zelt*, with a review of the study (1–7) and full bibliography (xi–xvi), to which add Haran, 'Priestly Image'; Levine, 'Descriptive . . . Texts'; Rabe, 'Identity'; Rabe, 'Temple'; and Vink, 'Date', 136ff., whose conclusions afford an interesting contrast to those of Görg. It must be remembered (against Levine) that invention is possible in documents of archival form (as any income tax investigator can testify) and (against Rabe) that elements of *possible* agreement with antiquity are no proof of tradition. Ancient society changed slowly and tents remained tents.

141. Lev. 17.11; 10.17; see the concordances for the verb *kapper*. De Vaux, *Ancient Israel*, 297, 429ff.; Vink, 'Date', 109ff.; Cook, 'Inauguration', 195.

142. Von Rad, *Priesterschrift*, 184ff.

143. Above, pp. 83f. and n. 54.

144. On these in general cf. Grelot, 'Problème', and Koch, *Priesterschrift*, 102ff.

145. De Vaux, *Ancient Israel*, 105, 114, 193, 375, 385, 387ff.

146. Above, p. 45. To what extent the YH(W)D stamps and coins of the fifth to third centuries were produced for high priests and temple treasurers (Avigad, 'New Class'; Albright, 'Seal Impressions') or for Persian governors (Aharoni, 'Citadel of Ramat Rahel'), is uncertain. Cross' hypothesis that the bullae refer to potters seems to be refuted by

new discoveries, see N. Avigad, *Bullae and Seals*, *Qedem* 4, Jerusalem 1976, 6f.

149. Von Rad, *Priesterschrift*, 21–28.

150. I Macc. 12.6ff. (v. Abel, ad loc.) represents Jerusalem and the Spartan court as in correspondence already in the days of Areus of Sparta (309–265). Though the letter is bogus (Bickerman, 'Question', 21) the report may not be wholly unfounded, since the High Priest Jason, driven out of Palestine in 166, chose to go to Sparta, II Macc. 5.9.

151. Goodenough, *Symbols*, III.570 and I.271; Bickerman, *From Ezra*, 16; Kanael, 'Altjüdische Münzen', 164 and 221ff. (annotated bibliography).

152. Noth, *History*, 344; cf. above, n. 146.

153. Above, Ch. 2, notes 67 and 90; de Vaux, *Ancient Israel*, 508. Kraus's supposition (*Worship*, 69), that because the goat is sent to the wilderness the ritual came from the wilderness, neglects both the actual proximity of Jerusalem to the wilderness and the fact that the rite was regularly carried out in historical times (Mishnah, Yoma).

154. The following account of the origin of proselytism is supported by the more general considerations adduced by Weinfeld, 'Universalism'. At the time of writing I had not seen Grelot, 'Dernière étape'. In the light of Grelot's work and of the passages on proselytes in Vink, 'Date' (16f., 43ff., 55f., 97f., 117f.) I think the following account needs some revision, particularly recognition in the other Pentateuchal strata of more late Priestly glosses on behalf of *gerim*. Such revision I cannot now undertake, so I publish the section as an independent, albeit imperfect, confirmation of the line of argument which Grelot and Vink have developed.

155. Gen. 23.4; Ex. 2.22; II Sam. 4.3; Deut. 10.19, etc; cf. Pedersen, *Israel*, 1.40ff.; Kaufmann, *Golah*, I.226.

156. I Chron. 29.15; Ps. 39.13.

157. De Vaux, *Ancient Israel*, 75; Cook, 'Inauguration', 185 (the infiltration probably began earlier); see above, p. 38. For *gerim* as domestic and agricultural workers, Deut. 29.10.

158. Deut. 5.14; 12.12; 14.29; 24.14ff.; 26.12ff., etc. Cf. Ex. 20.12; 22.20; 23.12.

159. Deut. 14.21, contrast Lev. 17.15. Deut. 16.11, 14, etc., provides for the *ger*'s enjoyment of the food and merrymaking of the festivals, not for his participation in the ceremonies. Contrast his absence from the Passover in Deut. 16.1ff. with the provisions of Ex. 12.48f. So, too, the deuteronomic school. Ex. 20.10 and Deut. 5.14 confer a privilege rather than impose an obligation. Of course if a *ger* became involved in a civil or criminal case he would be subject to the law of the land (Deut. 1.16). But the civil law must be distinguished from the religious law of Deuteronomy; the latter was the peculiar possession of the members of the cult of Yahweh, the god of the Israelites.

160. Lev. 16.29; 17.8, 10, 13, 15; 18.26; 20.2; 22.18; 24.16, 22; 25.47–54.

161. Lev. 24.17–22; 19.33f.; they even foresee the possibility that a *ger* may own an Israelite slave (Lev. 25.27); no doubt this was hindsight, probably post-exilic.

162. Lev. 25.39–54. *Hatoshabim hagarim 'immakem* of v. 45 perhaps do not include *gerim*, but *'ahika* of vv. 47–54 certainly does not include them. See below, n. 175. That *gerim* might bring sacrifices (Lev. 17.8; 22.18) is irrelevant; so might Gentiles, see above, pp. 70ff.

163. Cf. Isa. 14.1 (probably even later).

164. Nilsson, *Geschichte*, 659f., Ezek. 44, etc. Burials under the Agora in Athens and under the Forum in Rome ceased about 600.

165. Ezra 9.11; 10.2.

166. Sokolowski, *Lois sacrées*, 12, 14, 18, 29, etc.; cf. Bickerman, 'Warning Inscription'.

167. Neh. 10.29 and Ezra 6.21 do not refer to proselytes, but to Judaeans won to the Yahweh-alone party from the syncretistic cult of Yahweh, see above, p. 84. Cf. Kaufmann, *Golah*, 237, n. 1; on Vogt, *Studie*, 141ff., see de Vaux, *RB* 73.604.

168. That Nehemiah's opposition to mixed marriages was connected with his concern for purity appears from 13.29ff., cf. 13.9.

169. Cf. Kaufmann, *Golah*, 237; Duhm, *Jesaia*; and Volz, *Jesaia II*, ad loc. Volz's notion that Nehemiah's opponents were opposed to Yahweh overlooks the Yahwist names in the families of Tobias and Sanballat.

170. That Nehemiah was a eunuch, Albright, 'History', 11.

171. Though it thinks of him, by anticipation, as a member of 'the congregation of Israel', Ex. 12.19.

172. The alternative interpretations (that Num. 9.14 does not mention prior circumcision because it thinks it essential [!], or that it permits celebration of the Passover by the uncircumcised) are unlikely.

173. Num. 19.10 and 35.19 and Josh. 20.9 may also be somewhat earlier than Num. 15; they still distinguish *gerim* from 'the children of Israel', while giving the two groups the same legal privileges.

174. Not the Sinai covenant, which he probably did not dare touch (his law was already fixed in a sacred book, 29.19f.), but a new covenant in Moab, which he added as an appendix. That no other document in the Old Testament knows anything of this second covenant (von Rad, *Deuteronomy*, 178) is a sign of its late date. The author anticipates the technique of Jubilees. See further Pfeiffer, *Introduction*, 185f. (dependence on Second Isaiah and Proverbs 8). The *gerim* in Deut. 31.12, and Josh. 8.33 and 35, are probably redactional.

175. E.g., Ex. 12.45; de Vaux, *Ancient Israel*, 75. The *toshabim* in Lev. 25 may have been inserted by the Priestly editors to prevent the text from making a legal distinction between the *ger* and the native Israelite.

176. See the sectarian complaints in Enoch.

177. *Ant.* XI.302ff. The following section (on 'the Samaritan schism') was completed in substantially its present form in 1957 when my thesis was deposited in the Harvard University Library. I am glad to see that similar conclusions have since been reached, to all appearances independently, by Prof. Cross of Harvard ('Aspects'). Further arguments for a roughly similar date of the schism appear in Purvis, *Samaritan Pentateuch*, 98ff., and, from a widely different set of presuppositions, in Mantel, 'Secession'. On the background contrast Rowley, 'Samaritan Schism', and Eybers, 'Relations'.

178. Above, Ch. 4, p. 63.

179. Ezra 9.1; 10.2, 5; Neh. 2.10; the levitic editor in Ezra 4.3; Neh. 13.3, etc.

180. II Chron. 30.5, 25; 35.18. Polemic passages like Ezra 9.1f. and 4.9b f. and 4.2 are mutually contradictory anachronisms of historical value solely as evidence of the separatist party line. The Assyrian importees of 722 may be assumed to have disappeared by assimilation within two centuries. On 4.9 see Parrot, *Samarie*, 64ff. on II Kings 17.24.

181. Neh. 2.10, 19, etc.

182. Even though Ezra 4.2b originally referred to Judaeans (above, pp. 85f., it shows what the author thought credible of the Samaritans. *Incredible* is the notion that they had worshipped Yahweh for the past three hundred years without a sacrificial cult.

183. Morgenstern, 'Studies', 36, on Lev. 23. Cf. Lev. 17.1–7 and 26.31, and above, Ch. 2, n. 248.

184. Lev. 1.9, 12, 13, 15, etc.; Gesenius-Kautzsch, no. 126q ff. On the theological meaning of the phrase see de Vaux, 'Lieu'.

185. Cross, 'Discovery', 115.

186. For late Sabbatarian propaganda see Eichrodt, 'Sabbat'.

187. So *Ant.* XI.302–47.

188. Pfeiffer, *Introduction*, 268.

189. Finklestein, *Pharisees*, 562ff.

190. The most likely date is shortly after the destruction of Samaria, itself shortly after Alexander's conquest in 333–332. There must have been a temple and cult of Yahweh in Samaria down to that time. That temple's destruction (and the resettlement of the city with Macedonians) would certainly have made the surviving Samaritans want to build a new temple for themselves, as they built a new city for themselves. The new city was at the foot of Mt Gerizim, the new temple on the mountain just above. For destruction, resettlement, and date of the new city, see below, notes 207 and 209.

191. Above, n. 22.

192. Above, n. 88.

193. Eissfeldt, *Introduction* 383f.; Noth, *History*, 342f.

194. *Ant.* XI.320ff. The details of Josephus' story are suspiciously similar to those known from the times of Nehemiah (Sanballat and his

exiled son-in-law), but may have recurred, as did the name Sanballat (Cross, 'Discovery', and 'Aspects'). The meeting with Alexander is probably a reflection of Simon the Just's meeting with Antiochus III, see Moore, 'Simeon'. Its secondary reflection in Megillat Ta'anit (23 Kislev) is obviously worthless. The term 'Samaritan schism' is Montgomery's (*Samaritans*, 68f.); its convenience compensates for its connotations.

195. Josephus *Apion* II.48.

196. On the Tobiads see above, Ch. 6, n. 38.

197. Josephus *Ant.* XII.168; in XII.156 we have the report that the 'Samarians' at this time were looting Judaea. Since the friendly in-laws are certainly the Shechemites, the enemies are probably the pagans of the city of Samaria. (This section of Josephus is almost hopelessly confused. Besides the studies cited by Marcus on Josephus XII.154ff., and his Appendix E [Loeb ed., Vol. VII, pp. 767f.] see Bikerman [Bickerman], *Institutions*, 29f.)

198. Born to him by a niece whom a pious brother substituted for a dancing girl who took his fancy during a (kosher?) dinner at the Ptolemaic court, *Ant.* XII.187ff.

199. Favour and reason, *Ant.* XII.215–20; alliance, retreat and buildings, ibid., 228ff.; animal sculpture, D. Hll, 'Fountain'; temple and attribution to Hyrcanus, Lapp, 'Campaigns', 24ff., and 29ff.; questions about Lapp's conclusions, Will, 'Édifice', above, Ch. 4, n. 68.

200. Abot 1.2; Moore, 'Simeon', 348ff.

201. Praise of Simon, Sir. 50. For the Pharisees' attitude cf. Moore, *Judaism*, I.44; Lévi, 'Sirach', 390; Jer. San. 10.1 (28a).

202. II Macc. 4.11 attributes the actual negotiation to 'John [Jason?] the father of Eupolemus who was the [Maccabees' first] ambassador to the Romans'. This Eupolemus is identified by Freudenthal, *Studien*, II.105ff., with the historian, some fragments of whose Greek works are preserved by Alexander Polyhistor (*FGrHist* no. 723 = *FHG* III. 220, 225, 228, etc.). Bickerman, 'Charte', 4f., has shown that the economic and religious provisions of the royal grant are typical of the favours shown by Hellenistic monarchs to temples and cities of their realms. Contrast Alt, 'Antiochus III'.

203. The replacement was already beginning in Nehemiah's day (13.24).

104. Burrows, *Scrolls*, 303f.

205. *Hellenism*, 20–46.

206. See the catalogue of campaigns above, Ch. 3, n. 57. In 201 and the three following years the city evidently suffered severely (Josephus *Ant.* XII.129ff.; Noth, *History*, 350), as did Shechem (G. Wright, *Shechem*, 182), but with the help of Antiochus III (*Ant.* XII.138ff.) recovery, at least at Jerusalem, seems to have been rapid (Sir. 50.1ff.).

207. Josephus *Ant.* XI, ed. R. Marcus, Appendix C (Vol. VI, pp. 512ff.), esp. pp. 523ff.

208. See above, n. 197. Neglect of this requirement is one of the faults of Purvis' 'Ben Sira' (reprinted in his *Samaritan Pentateuch*, 119ff.).

209. G. Wright, *Shechem*, 179f.

210. It is probable that the pagan inhabitants of Samaria are referred to in *Ant.* XII.156, 168, 175.

211. G. Wright, *Shechem*, 182f. Bickerman, in a letter to me, preferred the date 200.

212. The LXX has the more difficult reading, i.e., the one more likely to be misunderstood and emended. It is therefore to be preferred to the Hebrew fragments and the Vulgate, whose reading, Se'ir, was probably produced by ignorant archaism. In Ben Sira's day the Nabateans had long since taken over Edom.

213. Judith 4.1–4; the term here is probably theological rather than racial.

214. Josephus *Ant.* XI.344.

215. *Ant.* XI.340, cf. 344; XII.257.

216. *FGrHist* no. 732 = *FHG* III.217; Freudenthal, *Studien*, I.99. The alternative title, 'The Foundation of Shechem', given by Jacoby, is more easily understandable and therefore less likely to be genuine. (Bickerman, however, remarks that 'concerning Jews' may be due to the excerpter, Alexander Polyhistor.)

217. *CPJ* 22 lines 16, 36 (201 BC); 128 lines 1–3 (218 BC); possibly 133 line 4 (153 or 142 BC. Σικεμίτης never appears in *CPJ* nor in Preisigke, *Wörterbuch*; for its rare appearance in Greek inscriptions see L. Robert, 'Bulletin Épigarphique', 1954, no. 229. Σαμαρίτης is not in Preisigke and appears in *CPJ* only in AD 586. Tcherikover's supposition (*CPJ* ad loc.) that these 'Ιουδαιοι' were not Samaritans is therefore unlikely.

218. II Macc. 5.22f. and 6.1f.

219. *Ant.* XII.258ff. Bickerman, 'Document', has demonstrated the reliability of this report; contra, Alt, 'Probleme', 4.83, n. 2 (= *KS* II.398), and Alon, 'Moza'am', 146f. and supplement.

220. This is not unlikely, see above, pp. 52f.

221. II Macc. 6, on which Bickerman, *Gott.*

222. Waltke, 'Prolegomena'.

223. For the good relations in 198–175, see above, n. 197. Destruction of Shechem, G. Wright, *Shechem*, 183f.

224. Contrast Montgomery, *Samaritans*, 73.

225. Cf. Koole, 'Bibel', 378ff. (Since Ben Sira knows of the prophets they must have been in his 'Bible'!)

Appendix: Alt's Account of the Samaritans

1. Alt, 'Rolle', 10ff. (= *KS* II.320ff.).

2. Alt, 'Stätten', 65, 68, etc. (*KS* II.448f., 451f.).

3. Rudolph, *Esra*, ad loc. Against Schaeder see Ch. 5, n. 126. For other, less likely, hypotheses, see Galling, 'Kronzeugen'.

4. *Ezra*, 182.

5. 'Rolle', 12 (*KS* II.322f.).

6. Neh. 13.28; 3.33ff.; 4.2; 6.2, 6.

7. The comments of Josephus (e.g., *Ant.* XI.302) are not evidence but polemical repetition of Old Testament polemic. Like it, they are not perfectly self-consistent, since Josephus elsewhere seems to call the Samaritans apostate Jews (*Ant.* XI.340). Similarly, the fact that rabbinic law always considers the Samaritans as basically Gentile (Alon, 'Moza'am', 146) is merely a reflection of biblical polemic, which is reflected further by the fact that they are sometimes declared Canaanites, sometimes Mesopotamian (ibid., 148ff.). Further, rabbinic law departs from the OT by recognizing in them such a large Israelite admixture as to make their status, for marital purposes, uncertain (ibid., 147f.).

8. Above, p. 85.

9. 'Rolle', 19ff. (*KS* II.329ff.).

10. 'Geschichte', 103 (*KS* II.354).

11. 'Probleme', 5.78f. (*KS* II.419ff.); 'Geschichte', 108 (*KS* II.358).

12. Alt, 'Rolle', 22ff. (*KS* II.331ff.); Ezra 5.9; 4.23; 8.32f.; Neh. 2.9.

13. Contrast Alt, 'Rolle', 24 (*KS* II.333f.).

14. Ibid., 23f. (*KS* II.332f.).

15. 'Probleme', 5.77ff. (*KS* II.418ff.).

16. The terminology is not legal. Is the law to be valid only for those who 'know' it? And how are they, or the other persons for whom it shall be valid, to be determined? If 'all the people' were, as Meyer, *Entstehung*, 67, maintained, 'klar' (!), there would have been no need to 'define' it by adding '[that is] to all those who know the laws of thy God', after which the postscript, 'and [as for] those who don't know it', is ludicrous.

17. This difficulty Alt recognized and attempted to answer by supposing that the religious union of the province lasted, in spite of the political separation of the two territories, until the north Israelites were lured away by the building of the upper-class Samaritan temple by a second Sanballat who lived in the time just before Alexander ('Geschichte', 107 = *KS* II.358). Such desperate remedies have been ruled out by Rowley, 'Sanballat', 180ff.

18. 'Geschichte', 100 (*KS* II.352).

19. I Macc. 10.30, 38; 11.34.

20. As Oesterly suggests in *A and P*, ad loc.

21. Abel, *Maccabées*, and Oesterley, in *A and P*, both ad loc.

22. See above, pp. 70f.

23. Bevan, *House*, II.223ff.

24. Cf. the Chronicler's list of Jewish settlements (Neh. 11.25–35) with the list in Neh. 3.1–32.

25. 'Geschichte', in *KS* II.356ff.

WORKS CITED

Abel, F. M., *Géographie de la Palestine*, 2 vols, Paris 1933–38
—— *Histoire de la Palestine*, 2 vols, Paris 1952
—— 'Hellénisme et orientalisme en Palestine au declin de la période Séleucide', *RB* 53, 1946, 385ff.
—— *Les Livres des Maccabées*, Paris 1949
Abrahams, I., *Campaigns in Palestine from Alexander the Great*, Schweich Lectures 1922, London 1927
Aharoni, Y., 'Arad: Its Inscriptions and Temple', *BA* 31, 1968, 2ff.
—— 'The Citadel of Ramat Rahel', in *Archaeological Discoveries in the Holy Land*, 77ff., New York 1967
—— 'Excavations at Ramath Rahel', *BA* 24, 1961, 104ff.
—— 'Trial Excavation in the "Solar Shrine" at Lachish', *IEJ* 18, 1968, 157ff.
Ahlemann, F., 'Zur Ezra-Quelle', *ZAW* NF. 18, 1942–43, 77ff.
Albright, W., *Archaeology and the Religion of Israel*, Baltimore ³1953
—— *The Archaeology of Palestine*, Harmondsworth 1949
—— *The Biblical Period from Abraham to Ezra*, New York 1963
—— 'A Brief History of Judah from the Days of Josiah to Alexander', *BA* 9, 1946, 2ff.
—— 'The Judicial Reform of Jehoshaphat', in *Alexander Marx Jubilee Volume*, New York 1950, 61ff.
—— 'An Ostracon from Calah and the North-Israelite Diaspora', *BASOR* 149, 1958, 33ff.
—— 'The Seal Impressions from Jericho and the Treasurers of the Second Temple', *BASOR* 148, 1957, 28ff.
Alon, C., 'Hahishkiha ha'umma weḥ akameha 'et haḥ ashmona'im', *Sinai* 12, 1943, 25ff.
—— 'Moza'am shel hashomronim bemassoret hahalakah', *Tarbiz* 18, 1947, 146ff.
Alt, A., 'Galiläische Probleme 1–6', *PJB* 33, 1937, 52ff.; 34, 1938, 80ff.; 35, 1939, 64ff.; 36, 1940, 78ff.
—— 'Judas Gaue unter Josia', *PJB* 21, 1925, 100ff.
—— 'Judas Nachbarn zur Zeit Nehemias', *PJB* 27, 1931, 66ff.
—— *Kleine Schriften zur Geschichte des Volkes Israel*, 3 vols., Munich 1953–59 (abbreviated KS)
—— 'Die Rolle Samarias bei der Entstehung des Judentums', in *Festschrift Otto Proksch*, Leipzig 1934, 5ff.

—— 'Die Stätte des Wirkens Jesu in Galiläa', *ZDPV* 68, 1949–51, 51ff.

—— 'Zu Antiochus III Erlass für Jerusalem', *ZAW* NF 16, 1939, 283ff.

—— 'Zur Geschichte der Grenze zwischen Judäa und Samaria', *PJB* 31, 1935, 94–111

Amiran, R., 'The Tumuli West of Jerusalem', *IEJ* 8, 1958, 205ff.

Andrewes, A., *The Greek Tyrants*, London 1956

Andrews, D., 'Yahweh the God of the Heavens', in *The Seed of Wisdom* (Meek Festschrift), Toronto 1964, 45ff.

Auerbach, E., 'Das Aharon-Problem', *Congress Volume, Rome 1968*, Supplements to *VT* 17, Leiden 1969, 37ff.

—— 'Der Aufstieg der Priesterschaft zur Macht im Alten Israel', *Congress Volume, Bonn, 1962*, Supplements to *VT* 9, Leiden 1963, 236ff.

—— 'Neujahrs- und Versöhnungsfest in den biblischen Quellen', *VT* 8, 1958, 337

—— 'Der Wechsel des Jahres-Anfangs in Juda', *VT* 9, 1959, 113ff.

Auscher, D., 'Les Relations entre la Crèce et la Palestine avant la conquête d'Alexandre', *VT* 17, 1967, 8ff.

Avigad, N., 'Hotam', *EM*, s.v.

—— 'A New Class of Yehud Stamps', *IEJ* 7, 1957, 146ff.

—— 'Seals of Exiles', *IEJ* 15, 1965, 222ff.

Bacher, W., 'Synagogue', *HDB* IV, 636ff.

Baer, I., *Yisra'el ba'ammim*, Jerusalem 1955

Bammel, E., 'Archiereys Propheteyon', *ThLZ* 79, 1954, 351ff.

Barag, D., 'The Effects of the Tennes Rebellion on Palestine', *BASOR* 183, 1966, 6ff.

—— 'Survey of Pottery Recovered from the Sea off the Coast of Israel', *IEJ* 13, 1963, 13ff.

Baron, S. A., *Social and Religious History of the Jews*, Vol. I, New York ²1952

Bartlett, J., 'Zadok and His Successors at Jerusalem', *JTS* NS 19, 1968, 1ff.

Batten, L., *A Critical and Exegetical Commentary on the Books of Ezra and Nehemiah*, ICC, Edinburgh 1913

Bauckmann, E., 'Die Proverbien und die Sprüche des Jesus Sirach', *ZAW* 72, 1960, 33ff.

Baudissin, W., *Die Geschichte des alttestamentlichen Priestertums*, Leipzig 1899

Bauer, W., *A Greek–English Lexicon of the New Testament and Other Early Christian Literature*, ed. W. F. Arnott and F. W. Gingrich, Chicago ²1979

—— *Das Leben Jesu im Zeitalter der neutestamentlichen Apokryphen*, Tübingen 1909

Bea, A., 'Neuere Arbeiten zum Problem der biblischen Chronikbücher', *Biblica* 22, 1941, 46ff.

Beek, M., *Geschichte Israels*, Stuttgart 1961

Beer, G., and K. Galling, *Exodus*, HBAT 1R.3, Tübingen 1939

Bengtson, H., *Griechische Geschichte*, Munich ²1960

Ben Ḥayyim, Z., '*Ivrit we'aramit nosah Shomron*, Academy of the Hebrew Language, Studies, I, II, III, VI, Jerusalem 1957–

Bentzen, A., 'Priesterschaft und Laien in der jüdischen Gemeinde des 5 Jahrhunderts', *AfO* 7, 1930–31, 280ff.

—— 'Quelques remarques sur le mouvement messianique', *RHPR* 10, 1930, 493ff.

—— 'Zur Geschichte der Sadokiden', *ZAW* 10, 1933, 173ff.

Bertram, G., 'Der Hellenismus in der Urheimat des Evangeliums', *ARW* 32, 1935, 265ff.

Berve, H., *Die Tyrannis bei den Griechen*, 2 vols, Munich 1967

Beuken, W., *Haggai-Sacharja 1–8*, Studia Semitica Neerlandica 10, Assen 1967

Bevan, E., *The House of Seleucus*, 2 vols, London 1902

—— 'Syria and the Jews', *CAH* 8, 495ff.

Bickerman, E., 'The Altars of Gentiles', *RIDA*, 3ᵉ Série, 5, 1958, 137ff.

—— 'La Chaine de la tradition pharisienne', *RB* 59, 1952, 44ff.

—— 'La Charte Séleucide de Jerusalem', *REJ* 100, 1935, 4ff.

—— '"Couper une Alliance"', *Archives d'Histoire du Droit Oriental* 5, 1950, 133ff.

—— 'Un document relatif à la persécution d'Antiochus IV Epiphane', *RHR* 115, 1937, 188ff.

—— 'The Edict of Cyrus in Ezra 1', *JBL* 65, 1946, 244ff.

—— *Four Strange Books of the Bible*, New York 1967

—— *From Ezra to the Last of the Maccabees*, New York 1962

—— *Der Gott der Makkabäer*, Berlin 1937

—— 'The Historical Foundations of the Postbiblical Judaism', in *The Jews*, ed. L. Finkelstein, New York 1949, I.70ff.

—— *Les Institutions des Séleucides*, BAH 26, Paris 1938

—— 'Notes on the Greek Book of Esther', *AAJR Proceedings* 20, 1951, 101ff.

—— 'Une question d'authenticité', *AIPHOS* 13, 1953, 11ff.

—— Review of J. Bright, *A History of Israel*, *JSS* 23, 1961, 49f.

—— Review of E. Goodenough, *Jewish Symbols in the Graeco-Roman Period*, I–IV, *L'Antiquité Classique* 25, 1956, 246ff.

—— 'The Warning Inscription of Herod's Temple', *JQR* NS 37, 1947, 387ff.

Bidez, J., 'Les Ecoles chaldéennes sous Alexandre', *AIPHOS* 3, 1953, 41ff.

Bieler, L., *Theios Aner*, 2 vols., Vienna 1935–36

Bikerman, *see* Bickerman

Biran, A., 'Archaeological Activities, 1968', *CNI* 20, 1969, 33ff.

Biran, A., and R. Gophna, 'Tell Halif', *RB* 74, 1967, 77

Blinkenberg, C., *Die Lindische Tempelchronik*, Kleine Texte 131, Bonn 1915

Borger, R., 'Anath-Bethel', *VT* 7, 1957, 102ff.

Bottéro, L., 'Les divinités sémitiques anciennes en Mésopotamie', in *Le antiche divinità semitiche*, ed. S. Moscati, Studii Semitici I, Rome 1958, 17ff.

Bouché-Leclercq, A., *Histoire des Séleucides*, 2 vols, Paris 1913–14

Brandon, S., *The Fall of Jerusalem and the Christian Church*, London 1957

Braude, W., *Jewish Proselyting*, Brown University Studies VI, Providence 1940

Braun, M., *History and Romance in Graeco-Oriental Literature*, Oxford 1938

Breasted, J., *Development of Religion and Thought in Ancient Egypt*, New York 1912

Bresciani, E., 'Papiri aramaici egiziani', *RSO* 35, 1960, 11f.

Bright, J., 'The Date of Ezra's Mission to Jerusalem', in *Yeḥ ezkiel Kaufmann Jubilee Volume*, Jerusalem 1960, 70ff.

—— *A History of Israel*, Philadelphia 1959 and London 1960

Brongers, H., 'Der Eifer des Herrn Zebaoth', *VT* 13, 1963, 269ff.

Büchler, A., 'Der Patriarch R. Jehuda I und die Griechischen Römischen Städte Palästinas', *JQR* 13, 1901, 683ff.

Burney, C., *The Book of Judges*, London 1918

Burrows, M., *The Dead Sea Scrolls*, New York 1955

Bury, J., *A History of Greece*, ed. R. Meiggs, London ³1956

Butler, H., *Ancient Architecture in Syria, Section A, Southern Syria, Part I, Ammanitis*, Publications of the Princeton University Archaeological Expedition to Syria, Division II, Leyden 1907

Caquot, A., 'Peut on parler de messianisme dans l'ouvrage du Chroniste', *RTP* 99, 1966, 110ff.

Cassuto, U., *La Questione della Genesi*, Florence 1934

Cazelles, H., *Etudes sur le Code d'Alliance*, Paris 1946

—— 'La Mission d'Esdras', *VT* 4, 1954, 113ff.

Černý, J., *Ancient Egyptian Religion*, London 1952

Chary, T., *Les prophètes et le culte à partir de l'exil*, Tournai 1955

Coggins, R., 'The Interpretation of Ezra IV.4', *JTS* 16, 1965, 124ff.

Cohen, C., 'Was the P Document Secret?', *ANES* 1, 1969, 39ff.

Cohen, G., 'The Song of Songs and Jewish Religious Mentality', in *The Samuel Friedland Lectures*, New York 1966

Cohen, M., *see* Meislin, B.

Cook, S., 'The Age of Zerubbabel', in *Studies in Old Testament Prophecy*, ed. H. Rowley, New York 1950

—— 'The Inauguration of Judaism', *CAH* 6, 167ff.

—— *The Religion of Ancient Palestine in the Light of Archaeology*, Schweich Lectures 1925, London 1930

Couroyer, B., 'L'origine égyptienne de la Sagesse d'Amenemopé', *RB* 70, 1963, 208ff.

Cowley, A., *Aramaic Papyri of the Fifth Century BC*, Oxford 1923

Cross, F., 'Aspects of Samaritan and Jewish History in Late Persian and Hellenistic Times', *HTR* 59, 1966, 201ff.

—— 'The Discovery of the Samaria Papyri', *BA* 26, 1963, 110ff.

—— 'Geshem the Arabian', *BA* 18, 1955, 46f.

—— 'A New Qumran Biblical Fragment', *BASOR* 132, 1953, 15ff.

Cumont, F., *Recherches sur le symbolisme funéraire des Romains*, Paris 1942

—— *Les Religions orientales dans le paganisme Romain*, Paris 1906

Daiches, S., *The Jews in Babylonia at the Time of Ezra and Nehemiah*, Jews College Publications 2, London 1910

Deissmann, A., *Die Hellenisierung des semitischen Monotheismus*, Leipzig 1903

Denniston, J., 'Herodotus', *OCD*, 421ff.

Dhorme, E., 'Le Dieu Baal et le dieu Moloch dans la tradition Biblique', *Anatolian Studies* 6, 1956, 57ff.

Dibelius, M., *Die Lade Jahves*, Göttingen 1906

Dikaios, P., *A Guide to the Cyprus Museum*, Nicosia ²1953

Dittenberger, G., *Sylloge Inscriptionum Graecarum*, 4 vols. Hildesheim ⁴1960

Donner, H., and W. Röllig, *Kanaanäische und aramäische Inschriften* I, Leipzig 1962

Dothan, M., 'Excavations at Azor, 1960', *IEJ* 11, 1961, 171ff.

Drioton, E., and J. Vandier, *L'Egypte*, Paris ³1952; ⁴1962

Driver, G., *Aramaic Documents of the Fifth Century BC*, Oxford 1954

Driver, S., *A Critical and Exegetical Commentary on Deuteronomy*, New York 1895

Dubarle, A., *Judith*, 2 vols, Rome 1966

Duchesne-Guillemin, J., *Zoroastre*, Paris 1948

Duhm, B., *Das Buch Jesaia*, GHKAT III.1, Göttingen ³1914

Dunayevsky, *see* Mazar

Dupont-Sommer, A., 'Les autels à encens de Lakish', in *Mélanges Isidore Lévy*, *AIPHOS* 13, 1953, 135ff., Brussels 1955

Eakin, F., 'Yahwism and Baalism before the Exile', *JBL* 84, 1965, 407ff.

Eichrodt, W., 'Der Sabbat bei Hesekiel', in *Lux tua Veritas* (Junker Festschrift), ed. H. Goss, Trier 1961, 65ff.

—— *Theology of the Old Testament*, 2 vols., London and Philadelphia 1961, 1967

Eising, H., 'Sprechende Ortsnamen im Alten Testament', *Das Heilige Land* 91, 1959, 9ff.

Eissfeldt, O., 'Baʿalšamēm und Jahweh', *ZAW* 57, 1939, 1ff.

—— The Old Testament. An Introduction, Oxford 1965

—— 'Die Geschichtswerke im Alten Testament', in *Kleine Schriften* III, Tübingen 1966, 19ff.

Elliger, K., *Das Buch der zwölf Kleinen Propheten*, II, ATD 25, Göttingen ³1956

—— 'Sinn und Ursprung der priesterlichen Geschichtserzählung', *ZTK* 49, 1952, 121ff.

Elliott-Binns, L., 'Some Problems of the Holiness Code', *ZAW* 67, 1955, 26ff.

Emerton, J., 'Did Ezra Go to Jerusalem in 428 BC?', *JTS* 17, 1966, 1ff.

—— 'Priests and Levites in Deuteronomy', *VT* 12, 1962, 129ff.

Englander, H., 'Ezra the Scribe', *Journal of Jewish Lore and Philosophy* 2, 1920, 319ff.

Engnell, I., *Gamla Testamentet: En traditionshistorisk inledning*, I, Stockholm 1945

Erman, A., and H. Grapow, *Wörterbuch der Aegyptischen Sprache*, 7 vols., Leipzig 1926–63

Eybers, I., 'Relations Between Jews and Samaritans in the Persian Period', in *Biblical Essays. Die Ou-Testamentiese Werkgemeenskap in Suid-Afrika, Proceedings of the Ninth Meeting*, Stellenbosch 1966

Farmer, W., *Maccabees, Zealots and Josephus*, New York 1956

Ferguson, W., 'The Leading Ideas of the New Period', *CAH* 7, 1ff.

Feucht, C., *Untersuchungen zum Heiligkeitsgesetz*, Theologische Arbeiten XX, Berlin 1964

Finkelstein, L., *The Pharisees*, 2 vols., Philadelphia 1938

Finley, M., *Studies in Land and Credit in Ancient Athens*, New Brunswick, n.d. (c. 1952)

Fitzmyer, J., 'The Paduan Aramaic Papyri Letters', *JNES* 21, 1962, 15ff.

Fohrer, G., *Das Buch Hiob*, KAT XVI, Gütersloh 1963

—— *Ezechiel*, HBAT 1R.13, Tübingen 1955

Forsdyke, J., *Greece before Homer*, London 1957

Franken, H., 'The Excavations at Deir 'Allā in Jordan, 2nd Season', *VT* 11, 1961, 362ff.

Frankena, R., 'The Vassal-Treaties of Esarhaddon and the Dating of Deuteronomy', *OtS* 14, 1965, 122ff.

Frankfort, H., 'Achaemenian Sculpture', *AJA* 50, 1946, 6ff.

—— *The Problem of Similarity in Ancient Near Eastern Religions*, Oxford 1951

Freedman, D., 'The Babylonian Chronicle', *BA* 19, 1956, 50ff.

—— 'The Chronicler's Purpose', *CBQ* 23, 1961, 436ff.

—— 'The Law and the Prophets', *Congress Volume, Bonn 1962*, Supplements to *VT* 9, Leiden 1963, 250ff.

Freudenthal, J., *Hellenistische Studien*, 2 vols., Breslau 1874–75

Fritz, K. von, and E. Knapp, *Aristotle's Constitution of Athens*, New York 1950

Galling, K., *Die Bücher der Chronik, Esra, Nehemia*, ATD 12, Göttingen 1954

—— 'Denkmäler zur Geschichte Syriens und Palästinas', *PJB* 34, 1938, 59ff.

—— 'Kronzeugen des Artaxerxes?', *ZAW* NF 22, 1952, 66ff.

—— 'Serubbabel und der Wiederaufbau des Tempels in Jerusalem', in *Verbannung und Heimkehr* (W. Rudolph Festschrift), Tübingen 1961, 67ff.

—— *Studien zur Geschichte Israels im persischen Zeitalter*, Tübingen 1964

Gardiner, E., *Athletics of the Ancient World*, Oxford 1930

Gelston, A., 'The Foundations of the Second Temple', *VT* 16, 1966, 232ff.

Gese, H., *Ezekiel 40–48*, Dissertation, Tübingen 1955

Gesenius, W., *Hebräisches und aramäisches Handwörterbuch über das Alte Testament*, ed. F. Buhl, Leipzig [17]1921

Gesenius-Kautzsch, *see* Kautzsch

Ghirshman, R., *Iran*, Harmondsworth 1954

Ginsberg, H., 'Studies in Hosea 1–8', in *Yeḥ ezkiel Kaufmann Jubilee Volume*, Jerusalem 1960, 50ff.

Glasson, T., 'The Main Source of Tobit', *ZAW* 71, 1959, 275ff.

Görg, M., *Das Zelt der Begegnung*, BBB 27, Bonn 1967

Goff, B., 'Syncretism in the Religion of Israel', *JBL* 58, 1939, 151ff.

Gomme, A., *A Historical Commentary on Thucydides*, Oxford I (second printing), 1950; II–III, 1956

—— 'Pericles', *OCD* 664

Goodenough, E., *Jewish Symbols in the Greco-Roman Period*, Bollingen Series XXXVII, 13 vols., New York 1953–68

Gophna, R., *see* Biran, A.

Gordis, R., *The Book of God and Man*, Chicago 1965

Gray, G. A., *Critical and Exegetical Commentary on Numbers*, ICC, Edinburgh and New York 1903

—— *Studies in Hebrew Proper Names*, London 1896

Gray, J., *I & II Kings*, London and Philadelphia 1963

Greenfield, J., 'Cherethites and Pelethites', *IDB* I, 557

Grelot, P., 'La dernière étape de la redaction sacerdotale', *VT* 6, 1956, 174ff.

—— 'Le papyrus pascal d'Elephantine: Essai de restauration', *VT* 17, 1967, 201ff.

—— 'Le papyrus pascal d'Elephantine et le problème du Pentateuque', *VT* 5, 1955, 250ff.

—— 'Le papyrus pascal d'Elephantine et les lettres d'Hermopolis', *VT* 17, 1967, 481ff.

Grossmann, C., *De Iudaeorum disciplina arcani*, Leipzig 1833

Gunkel, H., *Genesis*, HdKzAT, Göttingen [3]1910

Gunneweg, A., *Leviten und Priester*, FRLANT 89, Göttingen 1965

Hadas, M., *Hellenistic Culture: Fusion and Diffusion*, New York 1959

Haefeli, L., *Samaria und Peräa bei Flavius Josephus*, Biblische Studien 5, Freiburg im Breisgau 1913

Haldar, A., *Associations of Cult Prophets*, Uppsala 1945

Hall, H., 'Egypt to the Coming of Alexander', *CAH* 6, 137ff.

Haran, M., 'The Ark and the Cherubim', *IEJ* 9, 1959, 30ff.

—— 'The Disappearance of the Ark', *IEJ* 13, 1967, 46ff.

—— 'The Priestly Image of the Tabernacle', *HUCA* 36, 1965, 191ff.

—— 'Problems of the Canonization of Scripture', *Tarbiz* 25, 1955, 245ff.

—— Review of J. Maier, *Die altisraelitische Ladeheiligtum*, *JBL* 85, 1966, 248ff.

—— 'The Uses of Incense in the Ancient Ritual of Israel', *VT* 10, 1960, 113ff.

Harper, G., *Village Administration in the Roman Province of Syria*, Princeton 1928

Harper, W., *A Critical and Exegetical Commentary on Amos and Hosea*, ICC, Edinburgh and New York 1905

Harris, Z., *A Grammar of the Phoenician Language*, American Oriental Series 8, New Haven 1936

Head, B., *Historia Nummorum*, London ²1963

Heichelheim, F., 'Ezra's Palestine and Periclean Athens', *ZRG* 3, 1951, 251ff.

Heinemann, I., 'Wer veranlasste den Glaubenszwang der Makkabäerzeit', *MGWJ* NF 46, 1938, 145ff.

Herbert, A., 'Exclusivism and Assimilation', *OTWSA*, 1967, 1ff.

Herz, J., 'Grossgrundbesitz in Palästina im Zeitalter Jesu', *PJB* 24, 1928, 98ff.

Hill, D., 'The Animal Fountain of 'Araq el-Emir', *BASOR* 171, 1963, 45ff.

Hill, G., *A Catalogue of the Greek Coins of Arabia*, London 1922

—— *A Catalogue of the Greek Coins of Palestine*, London 1914

—— A Catalogue of the Greek Coins of Phoenicia, London, 1910.

—— 'Some Palestinian Cults in the Greco-Roman Age', *Proceedings of the British Academy*, 1911–12, 411ff.

Hölscher, G., 'Levi', *P-W* 12.2, 2155ff.

—— *Palästina in der persischen und hellenistischen Zeit*, Berlin 1903

Horst, F., *see* Robinson, T.

Irwin, W., 'The Problem of Ezekiel Today', in *Doron: Hebraic Studies* (I. Katsch Festschrift), ed. I. Naamani et al., Great Barrington 1965, 140ff.

Jaeger, W., *The Theology of the Early Greek Philosophers*, Oxford 1947

Janssen, E., *Juda in der Exilszeit*, FRLANT 69, Göttingen 1956

Jenni, E., 'Zwei Jahrzehnte Forschung an den Büchern Josua bis Könige', *ThR* 27, 1961, 1ff. and 97ff.

Jepsen, A., 'Nehemia 10', *ZAW* NF 25, 1954, 87ff.

Jeremias, J., *Jerusalem in the Time of Jesus*, London and Philadelphia 1967

Jirku, A., 'Zu einigen Orts- und Eigennamen Palästina-Syriens', *ZAW* 75, 1963, 86ff.

Johnson, A., *The Cultic Prophet*, Cardiff 1943

Jones, A., *The Cities of the Eastern Roman Provinces*, Oxford 1937

—— 'The Urbanization of Palestine', *JRS* 21, 1931, 78ff.

Juster, J., *Les Juifs dans l'Empire Romain*, 2 vols, Paris 1914

Kahana, A. (ed.), *Hassepharim hah̠izonim*, Tel Aviv ²1956

Kallen, H., *The Book of Job as a Greek Tragedy*, New York 1918

Kanael, B., 'Altjüdische Münzen', *Jahrbuch für Numismatik und Geldgeschichte* 17, 1967, 159ff.

—— 'Kawwim lehitpath̠ut ha'omanut hayehudit ha'atiqah', *Papers, FWCJS* I, *Hebrew section*, Jerusalem 1967, 109ff.

Kapelrud, A., 'The Date of the Priestly Code', *ASTI* 3, 1964, 58ff.

—— *The Question of Authorship in the Ezra-Narrative*, SNVA H.F.KI.1, Oslo 1944

Kaufmann, Y., *Golah wenekar*, Vol. I, Tel Aviv 1929

—— *Toledot ha'emunah hayisra'elit*, Vol. VIII, Jerusalem 1956

Kautzsch, E., *Gesenius' Hebrew Grammar . . .*, ed. E. Kautzsch, tr. A. Cowley, Oxford ²1910

Kellermann, U., 'Erwägungen zum Problem der Esradatierung', *ZAW* 80, 1968, 55ff.

—— *Nehemia, Quellen, Überlieferung und Geschichte*, *ZAW* Beihefte 102, Berlin 1967

Kenyon, K., *Archaeology in the Holy Land*, London 1960

—— *Jerusalem*, New York 1967

Kessler, W., 'Studie zur religiösen Situation im ersten nachexilischen Jahrhundert', *Wissenschaftliche Zeitschrift* (Halle) 6, 1956–57, 41ff.

Kienitz, F., *Die politische Geschichte Ägyptens vom 7. bis zum 4. Jahrhundert*, Berlin 1953

Kilian, R., *Literarkritische und formgeschichtliche Untersuchung des Heiligkeitsgesetzes*, BBB 19, Bonn 1963

Kindler, A., 'The Mint of Tyre' (in Hebrew), *E. L. Sukenik Memorial Volume*, *'Eretz Yisra'el* VIII, ed. N. Avigad et al.; Hebrew section, Jerusalem 1967, pp. 318ff.

Kirkbride, A., 'Currencies in Transjordan', *PEQ* 71, 1939, 152ff.

Kittel, G., *Die Probleme des palästinischen Spätjudentums und das Urchristentum*, Stuttgart 1926

Klein, S., 'Notes on the History of Large Estates in Palestine I–II', in BIES, Reader B, ed. E. Stern (in Hebrew), Jerusalem 1965, 138ff.

—— *Sepher hayeshub*, Vol. I, Jerusalem 1939

Knapp, E., *see* Fritz

Koch, K., *Die Priesterschrift von Exodus 25 bis Leviticus 16*, Göttingen, 1959

Kokhabi, M., 'Notes', *IEJ* 17, 1967, 273

Koole, J., 'Die Bibel des Ben-Sira', *Oudtestamentische Studie4n* 14, 1965, 375ff.

Kraabel, A., 'Hypsistos and the Synagogue at Sardis', *GRBS* 10, 1969, 81ff.

Kraeling, C. (ed.), *Gerasa*, New Haven 1938

Kraeling, E., *The Brooklyn Museum Aramaic Papyri*, New Haven 1953

Kraus, H. J., *Worship in Israel*, Oxford 1966

Krauss, S., 'Über Siedlungstypen in Palästina in talmudischer Zeit', *MGWJ* NF 46, 1938, 173ff.

Kuhl, C., 'Zum Stand der Hesekiel-Forschung', *ThR* NF 24, 1957–58, 1ff.

Lamarche, P., *Zacharie IX–XIV*, Etudes Bibliques, Paris 1961

Landau, Y., 'A Greek Inscription Found Near Hefzibah', *IEJ* 16, 1966, 54ff.

Lapp, P., 'The 1963 Excavations at Ta'anek', *BASOR* 173, 1964, 4ff.

—— 'The Second and Third Campaigns at 'Araq el-Emir', *BASOR* 171, 1963, 8ff.

Laqueur, R., *Hellenismus*, Schriften der Hessischen Hochschulen, University of Giessen, 1924.1, Giessen 1925

Launey, M., *Recherches sur les armées hellénistiques*, 2 vols, Paris 1949–50

Lemke, W., 'The Synoptic Problem in the Chronicler's History', *HTR* 58, 1965, 349ff.

Lévi, I., 'Sirach', *JE* 11, 388ff.

Levine, B., 'The Descriptive Tabernacle Texts of the Pentateuch', *JAOS* 85, 1965, 307ff.

—— 'The Netinim', *JBL* 82, 1963, 207ff.

Lévy, I., *La Légende dè Pythagore en Grèce et en Palestine*, BEHE 250, Paris 1927

Lewy, H., 'Aristotle and the Jewish Sage', *HTR* 31, 1938, 205ff.

—— 'Hekataios von Abdera *peri loudaion*', *ZNW* 31, 1932, 117ff.

Lieberman, S., *Hellenism in Jewish Palestine*, Texts and Studies of the Jewish Theological Seminary of America XVIII, New York [2]1962

Liebreich, L., 'The Impact of Nehemiah 9.5–37 on the Liturgy of the Synagogue', *HUCA* 32, 1961, 272ff.

Liver, J., 'Korah, Dathan and Abiram', in *Studies in the Bible*, Scripta Hierosolymitana VIII, Jerusalem 1961

—— 'Re'shitah shel shivat Zion', *Erez Yisra'el* 5, 1958, 114ff. and 90

Lobel, E., and D. Page, *Poetarum Lesbiorum Fragmenta*, Oxford 1955

Lockwood, J., 'Scholarship, Greek, in Antiquity', *OCD*, 812ff.

Lods, A., *Histoire de la littérature hébraique et juive*, Paris 1950

—— *The Prophets and the Rise of Judaism*, London 1937

Loretz, O., *Qohelet und der Alte Orient*, Freiburg im Breisgau 1964

Maas, F., '"Tritojesaja"'? in *Das ferne und nahe Wort* (Rost Festschrift), ed. F. Maas, *ZAW Beihefte* 105, Berlin 1967, 153ff.

Macalister, R., *The Excavation of Gezer 1902–5 and 1907–9*, 3 vols, London 1912

McCown, C., 'The Araq el-Emir and the Tobiads', *BA* 20, 1957, 63ff.

MacKenzie, R., 'The City and Israelite Religion', *CBQ* 25, 1963, 60ff.

McNeile, A., *The Book of the Exodus*, New York 1908

Maier, J., *Das altisraelitische Ladeheiligtum*, *ZAW* Beihefte 93, Berlin 1965

Maisler, B., *see* Mazar

Mantel, C., 'The Secession of the Samaritans' (in Hebrew), *Annual of the Bar-'Illan University* 7–8, 1969–70, 162ff.

Mazar, B., 'Ancient Israelite Historiography', *IEJ* 2, 1952, 82ff.

—— 'Golë Yirsra'el beGozan', *YHI* 15, 1950, 83ff.

—— 'The Tobiads', *IEJ* 7, 1957, 137ff., 229ff.

Mazar, B., T. Dothan and I. Dunayevsky, *En Gedi*, Jerusalem 1966

Mazar, B., and I. Dunayevsky, 'En Gedi Fourth and Fifth Seasons', *IEJ* 17, 1967, 133ff.

Mazar, B., and M. Stekeles, 'Beth Yerah Excavations I', BIES, Reader A, ed. E. Stern, (in Hebrew), Jerusalem 1965, 17ff.

Mazzarino, S., *Fra oriente e occidente*, Florence 1947

Meislin, B., and M. Cohen, 'Backgrounds of the Biblical Law Against Usury', *CSSH* 6, 1964, 250ff.

Meyer, E., *Die Entstehung des Judentums*, Halle 1896

—— 2 Μέγαρα, *P-W* 15.1, 152ff.

Michaeli, F., *Les livres des Chroniques, d'Esdras et de Néhémie*, CAT XVI, Neuchâtel 1967

Milik, J., 'La patrie de Tobie', *RB* 73, 1966, 522ff.

Möhlenbrink, K., 'Die levitischen Überlieferungen des Alten Testaments', *ZAW* NF 11, 1934, 184ff.

Momigliano, A., 'Fattori orientali della storiografia ebraica postesilica e della storiografia greca', *RSI* 77, 1965, 456ff.

Montgomery, J., *A Critical and Exegetical Commentary on the Books of Kings*, ICC, New York 1951

—— *The Samaritans*, Philadelphia 1907

Moore, G., *A Critical and Exegetical Commentary on Judges*, ICC, New York 1895

—— *Judaism*, 3 vols, Cambridge, Mass. 1927–30

—— 'The Rise of Normative Judaism', *HTR* 17, 1924, 397ff. and 18, 1925, 1ff.

—— 'Simeon the Righteous', in *Jewish Studies in Memory of I. Abrahams*, New York 1927, 384ff.

Morgenstern, J., 'Jerusalem – 485 BC', *HUCA* 27, 1965, 101ff. and 31, 1960, 1–24

—— 'Supplementary Studies in the Calendars of Ancient Israel', *HUCA* 10, 1935, 1ff.

Moscati, S., *L'Epigrafia ebraica antica 1935–1950*, Biblica et orientalia, No. 15, Rome 1951

Mowinckel, S., *Psalmenstudien II*, Oslo 1922

—— *Studien zu dem Buche Ezra-Nehemia*, 3 vols, SNVA H.F.Kl., NF 3, 5, 7, Oslo 1964–65

—— *Zum israelitischen Neujahr and zur Deutung der Thronbesteigungs-psalmen*, Oslo Ak. Abhdl.1952.2, Oslo 1952

Mulder, M., *Ba'al in het Oude Testament*, The Hague 1962

Myers, J., *Ezra Nehemiah*, Anchor Bible, New York 1965

—— 'Some Considerations Bearing on the Date of Joel', *ZAW* 74, 1962, 177ff.

Naveh, J., 'The Excavations at Mesad Hashavyahu', *IEJ* 12, 1962, 89ff.

—— 'More Hebrew Inscriptions from Mesad Hashavyahu', *IEJ* 12, 1962, 27ff.

—— 'Old Hebrew Inscriptions in a Burial Cave', *IEJ* 13, 1963, 74ff.

—— 'The Scripts of Two Ostraca from Elath', *BASOR* 183, 1966, 27ff.

Nestle, E., 'Judea bei Josephus', *ZDPV* 34, 1911, 65ff.

Neufeld, E., 'The Emergence of a Royal-Urban Society in Ancient Israel', *HUCA* 31, 1960, 31ff.
—— 'The Prohibitions Against Loans at Interest in Ancient Hebrew Laws', *HUCA* 26, 1955, 355ff.
Nicholson, E., 'The meaning of the Expression *'am ha'areṣ* in the Old Testament', *JnlSS* 10, 1965, 59ff.
Nilsson, M., *Geschichte der griechischen Religion*, 2 vols, Munich 1941–50, 1945–61
Nock, A., *Conversion*, London 1933
—— 'Paul and the Magus', in *The Beginnings of Christianity*, ed. K. Lake et al., I.5, London 1933, 164ff.
Norden, E., *Agnostos Theos*, Berlin ²1923
North, R., *Sociology of the Biblical Jubilee*, Analecta Biblica 4, Rome 1954
Noth, M., *Leviticus*, Old Testament Library, London and Philadelphia 1965
—— *The Laws in the Pentateuch and Other Studies*, Edinburgh 1966
—— *History of Israel*, London and Philadelphia
—— 'The Laws in the Pentateuch', in *The Laws in the Pentateuch*, 1–107
—— *Die Israelitische Personennamen*, Stuttgart 1928
—— *A History of Pentateuchal Traditions*, Garden City 1972 reissued 1981
—— *Überlieferungsgeschichtliche Studien*, SKGG 18.2, Halle 1943
—— *Exodus*, Old Testament Library, London and Philadelphia 1962
Oehler, W., 'Die Ortschaften und Grenzen Galiläas nach Josephus', *ZDPV* 28, 1905, 1ff.
Östborn, G., *Yahweh and Baal*, Lund 1956
Olmstead, A., *A History of the Persian Empire*, Chicago 1948
Otzen, B., *Studien über Deuterosacharja*, Acta Theologica Danica VI, Copenhagen 1964
Palestine Archaeological Museum, *Gallery Book, Iron Age*, Jerusalem 1961
—— *Persian, Hellenistic, Roman, Byzantine Periods*, Jerusalem 1943
Parke, H. W., *Greek Mercenary Soldiers*, Oxford 1933
Parker, R., and W. Dubberstein, *Babylonian Chronology*, Brown University Studies XIX, Providence 1956
Parrot, A., *Samaria, The Capital of the Kingdom of Israel*, Studies in Biblical Archaeology 7, London 1958
Patai, R., 'The Goddess Asherah', *JNES* 24, 1965, 37ff.
Pedersen, J., *Israel*, 2 vols, London 1926–40
—— 'Scepticisme Israelite', *RHPR* 10, 1930, 317ff.
Peisker, M., *Die Beziehungen der Nichtisraeliten zu Jahweh*, *ZAW* Beihefte 12, Giessen 1907
Peterson, E., *Heis Theos*, Göttingen 1926
Pfeiffer, R., 'Hebrews and Greeks before Alexander', *JBL* 56, 1937, 91ff.
—— *Introduction to the Old Testament*, New York 1948, ²1953
Phillips, W., *Qataban and Sheba*, New York 1955
Pope, M., *Job*, Anchor Bible, New York 1965

Porten, B., *Archives from Elephantine*, Berkeley 1968

Porter, B., and R. Moss, *Topographical Bibliography of Ancient Egyptian Hieroglyphic Texts, Reliefs and Paintings. V: Upper Egyptian Sites*, Oxford 1937

Posener, G., *La première domination perse en Egypte*, BEIFAO XI, Cairo 1936

Preisigke, F., *Wörterbuch der griechischen Papyrusurkunden*, 3 vols, Berlin 1925–31

Pritchard, J., *Palestinian Figurines*, New Haven 1943

—— 'Tell es-Sa'idiyeh', *RB* 73, 1966, 574ff.

Purvis, J., 'Ben Sira' and the Foolish People of Shechem', *JNES* 24, 1965, 88ff.

—— *The Samaritan Pentateuch and the Origin of the Samaritan Sect*, HSM 2, Cambridge, Mass. 1968

Quinn, J., 'Alcaeus 48 (B16) and the Fall of Ascalon', *BASOR* 164, 1961, 19f.

Rabe, V., 'The Identity of the Priestly Tabernacle', *JNES* 25, 1966, 132ff.

—— 'The Temple as Tabernacle', *HTR* 56, 1963, 329ff.

Rad, G. von, *Deuteronomy*, Old Testament Library, London and Philadelphia 1966

—— *Das Geschichtsbild des chronistischen Werkes*, BWANT IV.3, Stuttgart 1930

—— 'The Levitical Sermon in the Books of Chronicles', in *The Problem of the Hexateuch and Other Essays*, Edinburgh 1966

—— 'Die Nehemia Denkschrift', *ZAW* 76, 1964, 176ff.

—— *Old Testament Theology*, 2 vols, Edinburgh 1962–65

—— *Die Priesterschrift im Hexateuch*, BWANT IV.13, Berlin 1934

—— *Studies in Deuteronomy*, Studies in Biblical Theology 9, London 1953

Rehm, M., 'Das Opfer der Völker nach Mal. 1.11', in *Lex tua Veritas* (Festschrift H. Junker), ed. H. Gross, Trier 1961, 193ff.

Reifenberg, A., *Ancient Jewish Coins*, Jerusalem ²1947

—— 'A Hebrew Shekel of the Fifth Century BC', *PEQ* 75, 1943, 100ff.

Reisner, G., et al., *Harvard Excavations at Samaria*, 2 vols, Cambridge Mass. 1914

Reventlow, H., *Das Heiligkeitsgesetz*, Neukirchen 1961

Richter, G., 'Greeks in Persia', *AJA* 50, 1946, 15ff.

Rignell, L., *Die Nachtgesichte des Sacharja*, Lund 1950

Robinson, T., and F. Horst, *Die zwölf kleinen Propheten*, HBAT, Tübingen ²1954 (Robinson, 'Hosea bis Micha'; Horst, 'Nahum bis Maleachi')

Rost, L., 'Die Bezeichnungen für Land und Volk im Alten Testament', in *Festschrift Otto Procksch*, Leipzig 1934, 125ff. (= *Credo*, 76ff.)

—— *Das kleine Credo und andere Studien zum Alten Testament*, Heidelberg 1965

Rostovtzeff, M., *The Social and Economic History of the Hellenistic World*, 3 vols, Oxford 1941

—— 'La Syrie Romaine', *Revue Historique* 175, 1935, 1ff.

Rowe, A., *A Catalogue of Egyptian Scarabs, Scaraboids, Seals, and Amulets in the Palestine Archaeological Museum*, Cairo 1936

—— *The Topography and History of Beth Shan*, Philadelphia 1930

Rowley, H., 'The Book of Ezekiel in Modern Study', *BJRL* 36, 1953, 146ff.

—— 'The Chronological Order of Ezra and Nehemiah', in *The Servant of the Lord*, London 1952, 131ff.

—— 'Nehemiah's Mission and Its Historical Background', *BJRL* 37, 1955, 528ff.

—— 'The Samaritan Schism in Legend and History', in *Israel's Prophetic Heritage* (Muilenberg Festschrift), ed. B. Anderson and W. Harrelson, New York 1962, 208ff.

—— 'Sanballat and the Samaritan Temple', *BJRL* 38, 1955, 528ff.

Rudolph, W., *Chronikbücher*, HBAT, Tübingen, 1955

—— *Esra und Nehemiah*, HBAT, Tübingen, 1949

—— 'Wann wirkte Joel?', in *Das ferne and nahe Wort* (Rost Festschrift), ed. F. Maas, *ZAW* Beihefte 105, Berlin 1967, 193ff.

Sale, G., tr. *The Koran*, Philadelphia [5]1856

Sanders, J., 'The Scroll of Psalms (11 QPss) from Cave 11', *BASOR* 165, 1962, 11ff.

Schaeder, H., *Esra der Schreiber*, Beiträge zu historischen Theologie 5, Tübingen 1930

Schiemann, R., Sanballats: *A Study of History and Tradition*, Dissertation, Vanderbilt University 1966

Schlatter, A., *Geschichte Israels*, Stuttgart [2]1925

Schlumberger, D., *L'Argent Grec dans l'Empire Achéménide*, Paris 1953

Schmidt, W., *Die Schöpfungsgeschichte der Priesterschrift*, WMANT, Neukirchen 1964

Schürer, E., *Geschichte des jüdischen Volkes*, 4 vols, Leipzig [3-4]1901–11

Segal, M., *Sepher Ben Sira Hashalem*, Jerusalem 1953

Sellers, O., *The Citadel of Beth Zur*, Philadelphia 1953

Sellin, E., 'Noch einmal der Stein des Sacharja', *ZAW* NF 18, 1942–43, 59ff.

—— *Das Zwölfprophetenbuch*, KAT, Leipzig 1929

Syrig, H., 'Antiquités Syriennes', *Syria* 14, 1933, 238ff. and 263ff.

Smith, M., 'The Common Theology of the Ancient Near East', *JBL* 71, 1952, 135ff.

—— 'The Dead Sea Sect in Relation to Ancient Judaism', *NTS* 7, 1961, 347ff.

—— 'II Isaiah and the Persians', *JAOS* 83, 1963, 415ff.

—— 'Zealots and Sicarii', *HTR* 64, 1971, 1ff.

Smith, S., *Babylonian Historical Texts*, London 1924

—— Isaiah, *Chs. XL–LV. Schweich Lectures, 1940*, London 1944

Snaith, N., 'The Date of Ezra's Arrival in Jerusalem', *ZAW* NF 22, 1952, 53ff.

—— 'Nehemiah XII.36', *VT* 17, 1967, 243

Soggin, J., 'Der offiziell geförderte Synkretismus in Israel während des 10. Jhdts', *ZAW* 78, 1966, 179ff.

Sokolowski, F., *Lois sacrées de l'Asie Mineure*, Ecole Française d'Athènes, Travaux et Mémoires IX, Paris 1955

Sourdel, D., *Les Cultes du Hauran*, Paris 1952

Stein, S., 'The Laws on Interest in the Old Testament', *JTS* NS 4, 1953, 161ff.

Stekeles, M., *see* Mazar

Stern, E., 'Eretz-Israel in the Persian Period' (in Hebrew), *Qadmoniot* 2, 1969, 110ff.

Tadmor, H., 'The Campaigns of Sargon II of Assur', *JCS* 12, 1958, 22ff.

—— 'Philistia under Assyrian Rule', *BA* 29, 1966, 86ff.

Tarn, W., *Hellenistic Civilization*, London ³1952

—— 'Persia, from Xerxes to Alexander', *CAH* 6, 1ff.

—— 'The Struggle of Egypt Against Syria and Macedon', *CAH* 7, 699ff.

Tcherikover, V. A., *Hellenistic Civilization and the Jews*, Philadelphia 1959

—— 'Palestine under the Ptolemies', *Mizraim* 4–5, 1937, 9ff.

Thomas, D. Winton, 'The Sixth Century BC: A Creative Epoch in the History of Israel', *JnlSS* 6, 1961, 33ff.

Torrey, C., *Ezra Studies*, Chicago 1910

Trenker, S., *The Greek Novella in the Classical Period*, Cambridge 1958

Treves, M., 'Conjectures Concerning the Date and Authorship of Zechariah IX–XIV', *VT* 13, 1963, 196ff.

—— 'The Date of Joel', *VT* 7, 1957, 149ff.

Tuland, C., 'Hanani-Hananiah', *JBL* 77, 1958, 157

Ungnad, A., 'Die Zahl der von Sanherib deportierten Judäer', *ZAW* NF 18, 1942–43, 199ff.

Urbach, E., 'Halakot Regarding Slavery as a Source for the Social History of the Second Temple and the Talmudic Period' (in Hebrew), *Zion* 25, 1960, 141ff.

Ure, P., *The Origin of Tyranny*, Cambridge 1922

Vaux, R. de, 'Arche d'alliance et tente de reunion', in *A la recontre de Dieu*, Bibliothèque de la Faculté Catholique . . . de Lyon 8, Paris n.d. (c. 1962)

—— 'Les Decrets de Cyrus et de Darius sur la reconstruction du Temple', *RB* 46, 1937, 29ff. (= *Bible et Orient*, Paris 1967, 83ff.)

—— *Ancient Israel*, London and New York 1961

—— 'Le Lieu que Yahvé a choisi pour y établir son nom', in *Das ferne und nahe Wort* (Rost Festschrift), ed. F. Maas, Berlin 1967, 219ff.

—— Review of A. Gunneweg, *Leviten und Priester*, *RB* 73, 1966, 446f.

—— Review of E. Janssen, *Juda in der Exilszeit*, *RB* 65, 1958, 130f.

—— Review of E. Mader, *Mambre*, *RB* 65, 1958, 595

—— Review of M. Pope, *Job*, *RB* 74, 1967, 128

—— Review of H. Vogt, *Studie zur nachexilischen Gemeinde*, *RB* 73, 1966, 602ff.

—— 'Le sens de l'expression "peuple du pays" dans l'Ancient Testament', *RA* 58, 1964, 167ff.

—— 'Les sacrifices des porcs en Palestine et dans l'Ancien Testament', *ZAW* Beihefte 77, 1958, 250ff.

Vesco, J., 'Le Date du livre de Ruth', *RB* 74, 1967, 235ff.

Vink, J., 'The Date and Origin of the Priestly Code in the Old Testament', *Oudtestamentische Studiën* 15, 1968, 1ff.

Vogelstein, H., *Der Kampf zwischen Priestern und Leviten*, Stettin 1889

Vogt, H., *Studie zur nachexilischen Gemeinde in Ezra-Nehemia*, Werl 1966

Volten, A., *Demotische Traumdeutung*, Analecta Aegyptiaca III, Copenhagen 1942

Volz, P., *Jesaia II*, KAT, Leipzig 1932

Waldman, J., 'Philistine Tombs at Tell Fara and Their Aegean Prototypes', *AJA* 70, 1966, 331ff.

Waltke, B., 'Prolegomena to the Samaritan Pentateuch', *HTR* 58, 1965, 463ff.

Wanke, G., *Die Zionstheologie der Korachiten*, *ZAW* Beihefte 97, Berlin 1966

Waterman, L., 'The Camouflaged Purge of Three Messianic Conspirators', *JNES* 13, 1954, 73ff.

Weinberg, S., *Post-Exilic Palestine*, Proceedings of the Israel Academy of Sciences and Humanities, IV.5, Jerusalem 1969

Weinfeld, M., 'Deuteronomy – the Present State of the Inquiry', *JBL* 86, 1967, 249ff.

—— 'Traces of Assyrian Treaty Formulae in Deuteronomy', *Biblica* 46, 1965, 417ff.

—— 'Universalism and Particularism in the Period of the Exile and the Restoration' (in Hebrew), *Tarbiz* 33, 1964, 228ff.

Welch, A., *Post-Exilic Judaism*, Edinburgh 1935

—— *The Work of the Chronicler. Schweich Lectures 1938*, Oxford 1939

Wellhausen, J., *Die kleinen Propheten*, Berlin [3]1898

Wettstein, J., *Novum Testamentum Graecum*, 2 vols., Amsterdam 1751

Wilcken, U., 'Zur Aegyptischen Prophetie', *Hermes* 40, 1905, 544ff.

Will, E., 'Histoire grecque', *RH* 238, 1967, 377ff.

—— *Korinthiaka*, Paris 1955

—— 'Les Tyrannies dans la Grèce antique', *REG* 69, 1956, 439ff.

Wisemann, D., *Chronicles of the Chaldaean Kings*, London 1956

—— *The Vassal-Treaties of Esarhaddon*, London 1958 (= *Iraq* 20, 1958, Part I)

Wolff, H., *Dodekapropheten Joel*, BKAT, Neukirchen 1963

—— *Studien zum Jonabuch*, Biblische Studien 47, Neukirchen 1965

Wolfson, H. *Philo*, 2 vols, Cambridge, Mass. 1947

Worden, T., 'The Literary Influence of the Ugaritic Fertility Myth on the Old Testament', *VT* 3, 1953, 273ff.

Wright, G., 'The First Campaign at Tell Balatah (Shechem)', *BASOR* 144, 1956, 9ff.

—— 'The Levites in Deuteronomy', *VT* 4, 1954, 325ff.

—— *Shechem*, New York 1965

Wright, J., *The Building of the Second Temple*, London 1958

—— *The Date of Ezra's Coming to Jerusalem*, London 1947

Wurthwein, E., *Der 'amm Ha'arez im Alten Testament*, BWANT IV.17, Stuttgart 1936

Yadin, Y., *The Art of Warfare in Biblical Lands*, 2 vols, New York 1963

—— 'Excavations at Hazor (1955–1958)', *The Biblical Archaeologist Reader* 2, New York 1964

Yeivin, S., *Archaeological Activities in Israel (1948–1955)*, Jerusalem 1955

INDEX OF REFERENCES

The numbers printed in bold refer to pages on which some comment is made about the texts.

INDEX OF SUBJECTS

This index cites only the more important references to the terms listed. For references to biblical books, see the Index of References.